Reclaiming Education for Democracy

Reclaiming Education for Democracy subjects the prophets and doctrines of educational neoliberalism to scrutiny in order to provide a rationale and vision for public education beyond the limits of No Child Left Behind. The authors combine a history of recent education policy with an in-depth analysis of the origins of such policy and its impact on professional educators. The public face of these policies is separated from motives rooted in politics, profit, and ideology. Topics treated in detail include high-stakes testing, teacher testing, social studies curriculum, the teaching of reading, scientifically based research in education, etc. The work of polemicists such as Diane Ravitch is placed in the context of the politics they serve.

Reclaiming Education for Democracy also searches for new insights in understanding the neoliberal and managerialist assault on education by examining the psychology of advocates who demonstrate a special animus toward universal public education. The manipulation of public education by No Child Left Behind is a case study in the general approach to public institutions taken by the politicians and theorists in these camps. K–12 education has been subjected to deceptive descriptive analyses, marginalization of its professional leadership, manipulation of its goals, the imposition of illegitimate quality markers, a grab on its resources by corporate profiteers, and a demoralization of its rank and file. This book helps us think beyond this new common sense of education.

Paul Shaker is a career educator who has served as teacher, teacher educator, and dean in five of the United States, in Asia, and in Canada at Simon Fraser University of British Columbia. An alumnus of Ohio State, Shaker has reinterpreted and sought to advance the progressive legacy in public schools and higher education. His work has focused on the applications of depth psychology to education, teacher education curriculum, and policy and politics in contemporary America. Shaker served as a Fulbright Senior Scholar in Kuwait and has been recognized for his writing by AACTE.

Elizabeth E. Heilman, Ph.D. Associate Professor in the Department of Teacher Education at Michigan State University has served in leadership roles in social studies and curriculum studies both nationally and at Purdue and Michigan State University. She is the author or editor of five books and more than 35 book chapters and articles. Her work explores how social and political imaginations are shaped and how various philosophies, research traditions, and educational policies influence democracy, social justice, and critical democratic and global education.

Sociocultural, Political, and Historical Studies in Education
Joel Spring, Editor

For additional information on titles in the *Studies in Sociocultural, Political, and Historical Studies in Education* series visit www.routledge.com

Reclaiming Education for Democracy

Thinking beyond No Child Left Behind

Paul Shaker
and
Elizabeth E. Heilman

Routledge
Taylor & Francis Group

NEW YORK AND LONDON

First published 2008
by Routledge
270 Madison Ave, New York, NY 10016

Simultaneously published in the UK
by Routledge
2 Park Square, Milton Park, Abingdon, Oxon OX14 4RN

Routledge is an imprint of the Taylor & Francis Group, an informa business

© 2008 Taylor & Francis

Typeset in Sabon by
Book Now Ltd, London
Printed and bound in the United States of American on acid-free paper by
Edwards Brothers, Inc.

Library of Congress Cataloging in Publication Data
Shaker, Paul.
Reclaiming Education for Democracy: Thinking beyond No Child Left
Behind/Paul Shaker, Elizabeth E. Heilman.
    p. cm.—(Sociocultural, political, and historical studies in education)
Includes bibliographical references and index.
[etc.]
1. Education—Political aspects—United States. 2. Education and state—United
States. 3. Democracy and education—United States.
4. United States. No Child Left Behind Act of 2001. I. Heilman, Elizabeth E. II.
Title.
LC89.S475 2008
379.73–dc22   2007050912

ISBN10: 0–8058–5841–5 (hbk)
ISBN10: 0–8058–5842–3 (pbk)
ISBN10: 0–203–89451–0 (ebk)

ISBN13: 978–0–8058–5841–9 (hbk)
ISBN13: 978–0–8058–5842–6 (pbk)
ISBN13: 978–0–203–89451–4 (ebk)

For our mentors:
Paul R. Klohr, *The Ohio State University*
and
Jesse Goodman, *Indiana University*

Contents

Foreword

"The sky is falling" is an entry in the Wikipedia. The fable from which the term comes describes how Chicken Little interprets an acorn dropping on her head as evidence that the sky is falling and, in a panic, alerts all the other animals to the impending disaster. One moral of the fable is to distrust what you hear from people in a panic.

The Chicken Little/Sky is falling fable has partly inured us to listening closely to those who sound warnings about impending disasters, perhaps because there seem to be so many Cassandras among us lately. But every once in a while when the sky does seem to be falling, at least metaphorically, we learn that a panicked counsel had actually been talking to the public about the approaching crisis for some time, although few were listening. In her 1962 book *Silent spring*, Rachel Carson warned the world about environmental degradation and the many man-made carcinogens with which humanity now must deal. Although admired by some, Carson was largely ignored until recently, after much damage to all forms of life on this planet has been done.

My concern for this book is based on such history. This book must not be seen as another panicky "Chicken Little" book to be ignored. The authors provide a warning that is of great consequence to America's future, and it provides, as well, ideas for moving us toward a different future. What these authors do is inform us that the democracy within which American public education grew, and to which it has contributed so much, is in danger of a frightening curtailment. It is possible to imagine a future in which the public schools will not be the origin or the reflection of our American democracy. The U.S. city of New Orleans already has started on that path, but this trend is apparent all over the industrialized world and should be resisted. I am with the authors. I too think the sky is falling and that attention must be paid to the issues they raise.

Lawrence Cremin, the Pulitzer Prize-winning historian of education, once noted that, when the historians of the 21st century studied America's great rise to eminence among nations in the 20th century, they would find the roots of that greatness in an invention of the 19th century. Cremin argued that it wasn't the Gatling gun, the telegraph, the telephone, or Fulton's steamboat that made America great. It was the invention of the common school. Horace Mann, perhaps the common schools' major promoter, noted that it was "beyond all other devices of human origin, ... the great equalizer of the conditions of men, the balance-wheel of the social machinery." It was the public schools school that gave Americans some mobility across social classes, providing a modicum of truth to the myth that we were a classless society. It was the public schools that gave Americans the skills to obtain information and develop knowledge, which Jefferson had rightly noted is the first among the necessary conditions for a democracy to function. But what if movements to destroy the public schools exist? What if the information available to the public about its schools and other tax-supported programs for enhancing the public good are distorted by media controlled by corporate interests? And what if the government's educational policies aid and abet these actions? The result may well be a democracy that cannot long survive. The sky may really be falling!

The evidence for the attack on democracy and our public schools is presented clearly throughout this book. The authors show us how scientific knowledge is distorted, how reports that challenge conservative orthodoxy are suppressed, and how investigators are pressured to produce "proper" results. This allows advocacy to replace scientific knowledge, and government policy to morph into unrestrained propaganda. Current policies for the testing of teachers and students are shown to hurt, not improve, our educational system, driving more people out of the public schools and thus undermining their democratic function. The psychology of the most conservative of the political right is examined in a separate chapter. These are often the perpetrators of the attacks on education, among whom are many of those leading a retreat from participatory democracy. They constitute a formidable enemy. The authors make clear, however, that education is a contested terrain, and so the views of those holding neoliberal economic and conservative political ideologies are certainly to be given voice. What is described here, however, are actions by the political right to deny others voice. Instead of debating the kinds of schools Americans want and need, the political right attach their ideology to their political and fiscal power so as to legislate education that is antithetical to democracy.

Sad as is the present state of American education and our democratic institutions, these authors leave us with hope. Thank goodness! The characteristics of good schools for children, teachers, and democracy are described. With effort, such schools can be created, and they can preserve and enhance democratic life. Progressive and democratic ideas will win out, the authors note, if we can get the public's attention. They rightly sense that only a few percentage points, in a few states, separate the political progressives from taking power away from the anti-democratic, anti-public school forces. As always, the first step in getting those few percent more votes is to make the public aware of, and angry, about the movement to deprive them of their public schools and their democratic systems. Thomas Jefferson knew this: "I know of no safe depository of the ultimate powers of the society but the people themselves; and if we think them not enlightened enough to exercise their control with a wholesome discretion, the remedy is not to take it from them but to inform their discretion." I am pleased to recommend this book as a way to inform the public's discretion.

David C. Berliner
Regents' Professor of Education
Tempe, AZ, December 2007

Preface

Writing for educators and those interested in the future of American education, we characterize the struggle over U.S. public schools as a contest between professional authority and political advocacy. By this pairing we mean to illuminate the ongoing debate between, respectively, professional educators, both at the K–12 and the university level, who are trained in theory and practice and bound to a code of ethics, as opposed to those others who assert authority in media and politics, but who have limited experience or preparation in education and whose loyalties are with other institutions and ideologies.

This divide has become more significant since the 1983 report *A nation at risk*, because education has become increasingly employed as a key political issue in national as well as state and local elections. As such, politicians and a class of public relations specialists who serve them have dominated the policy debates around education. As the voices of these advocates have propagated, the influence of legitimate professional educators has waned. Not only have individual educators been shunted aside, but their organizations have also been marginalized in the public forum. During these years it can be argued, for example, that there has not been a single U.S. Secretary of Education who could be termed both a professional educator and a representative of mainstream progressive views on our public schools. Education was a "soft target," in the words of those who wished to capture it as a political wedge issue and a source of government largesse. We claim this evolution is having tragic consequences. The institution, including the profession of education, has not been protected by a unified accrediting body, politically savvy professional organizations, or charismatic national leaders. After two decades of a steady discrediting of established education authority, Congress, in a bipartisan manner, promulgated No Child Left Behind (NCLB). The results have been most unfortunate but not at all surprising.

This book is organized in three general sections. Initially we lay out the political and policy terrain on which we find ourselves, giving our analysis of how the current situation has emerged. We look at psychological explanations as well as more conventional political and economic analyses. The central chapters are in a sense case studies of particular dimensions of the status quo that serve to detail and concretize our initial claims. The topics explored include defining the science of education, teacher testing, the social studies curriculum, and revisioning the history of 20th-century American education. The concluding section looks forward in an effort to go beyond NCLB and its reauthorization to an educational landscape worthy of our emerging nation and global society.

Reclaiming education for democracy reviews this policy and propaganda progression in several ways. One is by looking seriously at the rhetoric and methods of the high stakes testing movement. The dominant, "scientifically based" paradigm of the advocates, as expressed in NCLB, presumes a value structure that is authoritarian and materialist. Education should in this model be a top-down enterprise focused first and foremost on economic goals. These values are fundamental departures from the progressive ideals of participatory democracy and humanism that educators have held dear for more than a century. The methods of *NCLB* are similarly out of tune with best practices as expressed by education research. For example, the legislation dictates applications of testing that are beyond what is scientifically credible or ethically defensible; the corruption of consequential and construct validity by high stakes testing is ignored; the tragic narrowing and trivializing of the curriculum and imposition of "one size fits all" schooling are promoted. Then there is sheer fraud. The billion dollar a year Reading First program has been manipulated for the financial benefit of political friends while bona fide reforms such as Reading Recovery and Success for All are starved of resources. Bureaucrats ride the profitable merry-go-round from public positions to jobs with their former contractees. Politically connected corporations in the school management, tutoring, and textbook and testing industries receive favored treatment over less market-oriented solutions. Accountability does not follow in the wake of their generous contracts. The federal government launches unprecedented interference with the internal governance and substantive messages of the education profession by, for example, lavishly funding a test-only alternative teacher education entity; by creating a National Reading Panel Report whose dubious credibility is further wiped away by putting its dissemination in the hands of (biased) public relations experts; by funding an ill-conceived alternative teacher education accrediting body; by manipulating the ERIC database; and by coercing the National Council for Accreditation of Teacher Education into lowering the profile of social justice in its standards.

Reclaiming education for democracy also goes behind the scenes into the identity politics that motivate the right-wing advocates in their crusade against our public schools. To a large degree their attacks on education have always been a means to other ends. As a key political issue, education has become a vehicle for coded attacks on groups and classes of society that can be demonized as "other" in order to build solidarity among the ranks of the new right. Those most in opposition to NCLB are convenient foils, since they are painted as against accountability and for wasteful government; against religion and for secular humanism; against the American (material) dream and free markets and for socialism and economic leveling; and against high standards and for indulgence. The public schools, imagined since Horace Mann and John Dewey as a unifying force in society, are transformed in this debate into a wedge issue and a means of turning groups and classes against one another. High stakes testing successfully identifies winners and losers in society, primarily through methods that indirectly calibrate the cultural capital with which students arrive at the schoolhouse door. By ignoring these prior conditions and focusing on forms of testing that are highly correlated with status markers such as parental educational and economic level, the advocates continually send a message to the public that urges the "haves" to seek escape from the "have nots" through vouchers, privatization, and flight to enclaves of test achievers. If politically you set out to govern through the loyalty of 51% of the voters at the expense of others, high stakes testing has proven to be a helpful means of solidifying that base.

Reclaiming education for democracy also approaches current controversy in education policy by examining several issues in depth. Among these is the initiative of the federal government to define scientifically based research in education. This stunning and unprecedented invasion of academic authority by government was the leading edge of a movement that gradually invaded "harder" forms of science including, particularly, medical policy and research, as in stem-cell research, birth control, and late-term abortion. Global warming is another notorious example of scientific opinion being suppressed or corrupted by government. Education also surfaces in this debate over defining science through the Intelligent Design controversy. The science curriculum of public schools has very narrowly survived corruption by an onslaught by religious fundamentalists, often encouraged by politicians, including the President of the United States.

Teacher testing is another case in point explored in *Reclaiming education for democracy*. The false certitude of this movement is based on a set of flawed assumptions similar to those at the heart of several of the right's initiatives. As is typical of high stakes testing initiatives, teacher testing has argued for a simplified and superficial definition of that which is being evaluated, and this redefinition feeds back into the system in various deleterious ways. By rewarding the g factor (general intelligence) and other markers of social and economic advantage, the movement is a barrier to diversity of class and ethnicity in the teacher corps. By emphasizing paper-and-pencil methods as opposed to performance measures, teacher testing corrupts the evaluation of what is a performance field, honoring performativity on tests above actual teaching acts. Teacher testing has contributed to the alternative teacher education movement by making the rationale for the test-only certification of the American Board for Certification of Teacher Excellence seem plausible. Politically the movement does no harm to the advocates of the right, since those most negatively affected are not their constituency.

That the social studies curriculum would be a target of the advocates is no surprise. Of all school experiences, these are the ones consciously created to advance democratic values, and, especially through John Dewey's influence, these have become democratic and *progressive* values. George Counts's notion of "building a new social order" through the schools strikes at the heart of conservative and neoliberal ideas about control and economic instrumentalism as hallmarks of public education. The standards and high stakes movements have unsurprisingly led the curriculum away from democratic ideals by reducing the significance of social studies by defining it outside of the Three Rs and the testing universe with the consequence of its place in the school day being reduced. Social studies standards have notoriously focused on a laundry list approach of inert facts (to use Whitehead's phrase) while making little effort to promote critical thinking, active citizenship, and functional literacy in democratic processes such as community organizing and civil disobedience. At the same time the present climate offers many social studies concepts that call out for examination, such as American exceptionalism, preemptive war, the clash of civilizations, and so on.

As an Ur-text for the advocates, we suggest Diane Ravitch's *Left back: A century of failed school reforms* (2000). This revisionist history of progressive education lays out in detailed form the manner in which the 20th-century history of American education can be rewritten to discredit the dramatic achievements of the American educational system. This system, which on so many levels has been unrivalled in its social and economic contributions to the nation, is painted as a wrongheaded and cumbersome institution badly in need of radical reform. Conveniently underplayed are the other factors influencing the development of youth that are, as we know, beyond the influence of schools and teachers. Worse still, however, is the cynical distortion of the values and ideas of John Dewey and progressive educators in general in what appears to be a book that is a paid-for piece of propaganda created and sent out as disinformation in the prosecution of the culture wars. We now know that these culture wars quickly evolve into political contests.

In an effort to look beyond the NCLB years, *Reclaiming education for democracy* offers a vision of values and practices that would characterize a 21st-century progressive school. With so much of the public debate tied to accountability and testing in recent years, there has been a shortage of the type of visionary thinking offered by, for example, the Romantic critics of education during the late sixties and early seventies. Viable alternatives to

NCLB will not have a retro flavor: American and global society have changed too much for that. Tragically the energy that should be going into effectively adapting our schools to today's social order is being squandered on manufactured crises and overly simplified analyses of issues and solutions. There is, however, a body of extant and emerging education literature that gives an indication of what education for democracy can now mean. There is, too, writing and research from related fields such as psychology, philosophy, and sociology that enriches our educational viewpoint. These works suggest a big, inclusive tent that, once erected, creates a renewed, expanded community or social contract with the schools at its heart.

As a part of such an educational vision one must also contemplate the spiritual possibilities that lie before us—that is, the methods of making meaning that will gain preeminence in the coming years and, one hopes, will lead to a more tranquil, equitable, healthy, and sustainable society. As we think beyond No Child Left Behind, we welcome the opportunity to bring today's frustrated quest for meaning to the forefront. This dissatisfaction with American society's embedded material values has many people of faith seeking as an antidote to place religion in the public school curriculum. Others, buying into the myth of consumerism, want the schools to be economic engines producing a 21st-century version of two chickens in every pot. They assert that the lock step of standards and testing will seamlessly link education to productivity. In our diverse society, however, religious hegemony is futile and millennial materialism has failed. Educators can think beyond the limited aspirations of recent years and, as members of the larger society, contribute their expertise to creating a social order such as we have not known before.

Acknowledgements

The authors wish to acknowledge the following persons for their varied assistance in making this book come to completion. Our administrative secretaries, Devi Pabla and Alana Nordstrand, and local editor, Johanne Provencal, were of invaluable help. We are grateful for the diligent work of research assistants Won Pyo Hon, Matthew T. Missias, Lee Shaker, and Carmen L. Z. Gress. We also very much appreciate the consistent guidance of our Routledge editor, Naomi Silverman.

We have found feelings of inspiration for our writing particularly in the works of John Dewey, David Berliner, Joel Spring, Gerald Bracey, Michael Apple, Alex Molnar, Linda McNeil, Angela Valenzuela, Ken Zeichner, and (albeit reactively) Diane Ravitch.

The following colleagues have contributed in highly meaningful ways, including reading and commenting on the text, encouraging the project, and helping it find its way into print: Donna Adair Breault, Robert Bullough, John Champlin, Leigh Chiarelott, Penny Earley, Elaine Garan, Peter Grimmett, Joe Kincheloe, Craig Kridel, Dan Laitsch, Alan Luke, Dan Marshall, Gary Natriello, Sarah Pessin, William Pinar, Gay Su Pinnell, E. Wayne Ross, William Schubert, and Kenneth Waltzer. Finally, we wish to remember our friend and colleague Landon Beyer.

Acknowledgements, continued

Parts of the following chapters have a relationship to previously published material and are used with permission and/or cited herewith:

Chapter 1
Shaker, P., & Heilman, E. E. (2002). Advocacy versus authority: Silencing the education professoriate. *AACTE Policy Perspectives, 3*(1), 1–8.
(Reprinted with permission from the American Association of Colleges for Teacher Education, August 31, 2004.)

Shaker, P., & Heilman, E. E. (2004, July). The new common sense of education: Advocacy research versus academic authority. *Teachers College Record, 106*(7), 1444–1470.
(Reprinted with permission from Blackwell Publishing, January 21, 2008.)

Chapter 3
Shaker, P. (2008). Human development. In S. Mathison & E. W. Ross (Eds.), *Battleground schools, 1* (pp. 326–332). Westport, CN: Greenwood Press. Copyright © (2008) by Sandra Mathison and E. Wayne Ross.
(Reprinted with permission of editors and publisher, April 16, 2008.)

Chapter 4
Shaker, P., & Ruitenberg, C. (2007, July). Scientifically based research: The art of politics and the distortion of science. *International Journal of Research and Method in Education, 30*(2), 207–219.
(Reprinted with permission of co-author C. Ruitenberg and Taylor & Francis, July 6, 2007.)

Heilman, E. (2004). Federal policy on "student achievement," "quality teaching," and "scientific educational research": Necessary precautions. In L. Coia, N. Brooks, M. Birch, E. Heilman, S. Mayer, A. Mountain, P. Pritchard (Eds.), *Democratic response in an era of standardization. Papers*

from the 4th Curriculum & Pedagogy Conference, Decatur, Georgia, October, 2003. Troy, NY: Educator's International Press.
(Parts of this chapter are based on ideas developed in this paper, published in in conference proceedings.)

Chapter 5
Shaker, P. (2001). "Teacher Testing: A symptom." *Teaching Education, 12*(1), 65–80.
(Reprinted with permission from *Teaching Education Journal*, July 30, 2004 — http://www.tandf.co.uk/journals)

Chapter 6
Waltzer, K., & Heilman, E. (2005, July/August). When going right is going wrong: Education for critical democratic patriotism. *Social Studies, 96*(4), 156–162.
(Reprinted with permission of co-author K. Waltzer and editor E. W. Ross.)

Heilman, E. (2003). Education policy United States. In J. Herrick & P. Stuart (Eds.), *The encyclopedia of social welfare history in North America* (pp. 106–109). NY: Sage Publications.
(Parts of this chapter are based on ideas developed in this article and used with permission of Sage April 21, 2008.)

Chapter 7
Shaker, P. (2004). Essay review on "Left back: A century of failed school reforms." *Journal of Curriculum Studies, 36*(4), 495–507.
(Reprinted with permission from Taylor & Francis Ltd. August 18, 2004.)

Chapter 8
Shaker, P. (2005). Growth: The consummate open-ended aspiration. In D. A. Breault & R. Breault (Eds.) *Experiencing Dewey: Insights for today's classroom* (chapter 18, pp. 59–61). Indianapolis, IN: Kappa Delta Pi— International Honor Society in Education.
(Reprinted with permission of editors and publisher, April 9, 2008.)

Shaker, P. (2005). Standards, testing, and teacher quality: Common sense vs. authority in educational reform. In K. Kesson & E. W. Ross (Eds.) *Defending public schools: Teaching and teacher education, 2,* 43–56. New York: Praeger/ Greenwood. Copyright © (2005) by David Gabbard and E. Wayne Ross.
(Reprinted with permission of editors and publisher, April 16, 2008).

Shaker, P., & Grimmett, P. (2004, Summer). Public schools as public good. *Education Canada, 44*(3), 29–31. Copyright © Canadian Education Association. ISSN 0013-1253.
(Reprinted with permission of co-author and publisher, April 8, 2008.)

Introduction

The changing vision of education in our democratic society

> The soul of democracy—the essence of the word itself—is government of, by, and for the people. And the soul of democracy has been dying, drowning in a rising tide of big money contributed by a narrow, unrepresentative elite, that has betrayed the faith of citizens in self-government.
>
> (Moyers, 2001, p. 11)

Public schooling has traditionally had a rationale rooted in the need for a democratic society to prepare future citizens, although the nature and centrality of this role has varied at different points in American history. In this book we explore the current status of schooling as a public and democratic institution. We shall critically examine ways in which recent policy has explicitly or implicitly conceived of democracy, progressive education, research, teacher education, patriotism, citizenship, and literacy. As you are reading there are three important things to keep in mind about how we are taking up this task: (a) in hoping to reclaim "education for democracy" we are working within a particular political and intellectual tradition; (b) we are not trying to represent equally the entire range of opinion; (c) we aim to improve your critical understanding of this subject, through multidisciplinary engagements.

Defining our terms and methods

There is a certain inevitable vagueness in speaking of a tradition of democratic education, even as we highlight the imperative to reclaim such a phenomenon. As Appiah (2005) has observed, "the liberal tradition—like all intellectual traditions—is not so much a body of doctrine as a set of debates. Still, it is widely agreed that there is such a tradition" (p. ix). Though there are many debates about democracy and democratic education, we assert there are also a few generally agreed upon principles. One is that all people are equal. From this point of view, whatever the important elements of human well-being are (and there may be some disagreement about this claim), these elements belong to *all* human beings—for example, nutrition, health, shelter, security, or, more broadly, happiness, autonomy, education, and cultural freedom. The United States of America's Declaration of Independence and Constitution describe such humanity and inclusivity, and the Universal Declaration of Human Rights (1948) expresses this value on a global scale.

Another conception that underlies democratic governments and education is the idea that all people are capable of enough reason, ability, and character to make legitimate and functional institutions, and this inherent human capability justifies government of, by, and for the people. Citizens have the capacity, right, and duty to create and challenge all public policies and they have the capacity, right, and duty to engage in dialogue, resist egocentric thinking, take into account multiple and opposing viewpoints, and, aided by public institutions, to arrive at suitable compromises to create a more just society. Democracy then seems to require education to develop both our personal and our collective democratic capacities and also to develop our understanding of this democracy.

Democratic understanding should always be understood to be in flux, and this flux requires us, on our way to their realization, to constantly wrestle with the meanings of freedom, rights, voice, fairness, representation, and justice. This is what Cochran (1999) calls "weak foundations." As she describes, while one cannot cling to ontological priority in any strong sense, "critical intelligence and its use of moral imagination can create possibilities for consensus around a democratic ethos through its discursive and institutional aspect" (pp. 279–280). This vision is consistent with Dewey's assumption that individuals create and fulfill themselves in constant interaction with communities, and thus identity and meaning are inherently fluid and collective. The "validity" or ethical strength of such deliberation will be entirely determined by the number of people who can recognize themselves, their values, and their situations in the conversation and vision that ensues. As Barber (1996a) explains:

> The very question, "Does democracy have foundations?" is dangerous for democrats of my tendencies, because it mandates a discussion on the turf of epistemology that leans toward an answer in the affirmative, and yields an understanding of democracy hostile to what I believe are its necessary participatory attributes. But if democracy is concerned with a form of knowledge (say, knowledge of political things such as power, or political values such as rights, or political ends such as justice) or constituted by procedures or institutions that rest on knowledge (say constitutions or the principles of majoritarianism), then unless we wish to invite an abject politics of relativism, or arbitrariness, to the question of whether democracy has

foundations we are, perforce, obliged to reply, "Well, yes, democracy must have foundations in truths antecedent to it and not dependent upon it. … [However] it is practical and not speculative, about action rather than about truth. It yields but is not premised upon an epistemology and in this sense is necessarily pragmatic.

(pp. 348–349)

So, while we stress the looseness and pragmatism of thinking about democracy, we still claim it.

In this sense, we are coming from somewhere. We are not aiming for objective neutrality but instead are offering an ethically rooted critical engagement. This is the second point, that we are not trying equally or empirically to represent a range of opinion. Further, we believe that any critique is inherently and appropriately intolerant. As Pearl (2007) has stated quite nicely in thinking about a paradox formulated by Bertrand Russell in 1901,

Any person who claims to be tolerant naturally defines himself in opposition to those who are intolerant. But that makes him intolerant of certain people—which invalidates his claim to be tolerant. The political lesson of Russell's paradox is that there is no such thing as unqualified tolerance. Ultimately, one must be able to expound intolerance of certain groups or ideologies without surrendering the moral high ground normally linked to tolerance and inclusively. One should, in fact, condemn and resist political doctrines … that undermine the basic norms of civilization, or that seek to make pluralism impossible.

Although our tone may at times be heated or confrontational, it is not our purpose to be drawn into an argument that simplifies the issues or that that pits left and right in opposed corners. John Dewey worked long and hard to urge us to think beyond such binary, either/or categories. As he wrote in *Experience and education*, "Mankind likes to think in terms of extreme opposites. It is given to formulating its beliefs in terms of Either-Ors, between which it recognizes no immediate possibilities" (Dewey, 1987, p. 17). Instead we hope to explore, evaluate, compare, and critique the inevitably multiple and complex debates about public education and to offer chapters that engage the issues with various foci and through different theoretical frameworks, and even in different voices. This is facilitated by both our shared and distinctive scholarly interests. While the most of the book is co-imagined and co-authored, Paul wrote chapters 3, 5, and 7, which explore Jung, the politics of testing, and the legacy of progressive education, respectively, while Elizabeth wrote chapters 2 and 6, which are rooted in critical theory, cultural studies, political philosophy, and history.

The context for our concerns

Today, more than ever before, as Bauman (1999) asserts, neoliberalism as an economic, political, and cultural practice has dismantled the bridges that link private to public life. There is "no easy or obvious way to translate private worries into public issues and, conversely, to discern and pinpoint public issues in private troubles."

A democratic education can be understood narrowly as mostly a matter for the curriculum. Gutmann (1987), for example, describes democratic education as a political and educational ideal concerned with how future citizens will be educated, yet democratic education can be defined more broadly by considering the relationship between the private and the public and issues of access and equity in policy. Public and private interests are sometimes confused and conflated. Labaree (1997) makes a helpful distinction in "Public goods, private goods: the American struggle over educational goals," detailing three visions of the purposes of education as democratic equality, social efficiency, and social mobility. Aiming for democratic equality, "education is purely a public good; for social efficiency, it is a public good in service to the private sector; and for social mobility, it is a private good for personal consumption" (p. 43). As Labaree details, the tension between the political idealism of Thomas Jefferson and the economic realism of Alexander Hamilton (Curti, 1935/1959) has posed an essential problem:

> Unfettered economic freedom leads to a highly unequal distribution of wealth and power, which in turn undercuts the possibility for democratic control; but at the same time, restricting such economic freedom in the name of equality infringes on individual liberty, without which democracy can turn into the dictatorship of the majority.
>
> (Labaree, 1997, p. 41)

Grounded in this contradictory social context, education has come to be a place that simultaneously promotes equality and adapts to inequality, an institution with both private and public missions, and an institution in which these public and private goals are contested in both curriculum and policy.

Since at least the beginning of the Reagan era, however, it has become commonplace to claim that progressive values in U.S. politics appear to be on the wane. As part of this shift, the ascendancy of the right has gradually begun to deeply affect popular opinion of the public schools. This key institution, envied and emulated around the world, is by many measures central to the achievements of U.S. society both economically and geopolitically. These evaluatory measures include the tens of millions of immigrants who have been successfully assimilated into the nation. The "Three Rs," to employ that quintessential cliché, have been taught at a level of success so as to lay a foundation for graduate schools and research facilities that are the envy of the world. On the other hand, the prophets of doom regarding progressive schools have for a century seen their criticisms proven false by the rise of repeated generations of graduates to high levels of national achievement. Nonetheless, the cyclical raging of the right continues to reach a ready audience among media, politicians, and the public and to place the education establishment on the defensive. The most recent, post-*Nation at risk*, cycle has reached a new level of impact by its extension into legislation such as No Child Left Behind (NCLB). More than at any time in U.S. history, the culture of schools is being rapidly altered, and the invasive changes put in place by federal authorities override the consensus views of teachers and scholars in the profession. The following chapters explore the how and why of this course of events while searching for remedies. We wonder why a successful and altruistic profession is so vulnerable to attack and whether the general sense of confidence in public education and the education profession can be reestablished in the face of the passionate rhetoric and power politics of the right.

In biological terms, education is one of the few distinctive activities that defines human beings so as to separate them from their other animal cousins. Rooted in oral language, the enterprise is an aspect of culture that antedates history itself. Education is also different in nature from the instinct and conditioning that characterize animal learning. In human hands, the deliberate conveyance of culture from one person to others quickly exceeds the boundaries of pure imitation and encourages improvisation and personalization by the learner. This openness to the reconstruction of experience is definitional to education. Slavish replication can be called teaching or training but does not merit the title of education. From this urge of one person to bring along another into the special knowledge of the family, the clan, and the tribe has come a series of institutions and practices that we call education. Characterized by a respect for the intelligence and creativity of the learner, education, by definition, is a drawing forth as well as a putting forward of learning.

As with many of the practices of contemporary civilization, education has been refined, intensified, and specialized in so many ways that we generally lose sight of its origins and broader purposes. For example, in contemporary U.S. politics, the economic purposes of schooling dominate the discussion of schooling, often to the exclusion of other legitimate educational purposes. The public schools are seen as socializing, sorting, and training the workforce (Spring, 1997). Due to this limiting analysis, the public education debate has become increasingly sterile and, more importantly, has led to policies that force K–12 public education into such a narrowly defined role. These recent policies specifically have to do with accountability and have reached their apotheosis in the form of national high-stakes testing as mandated by No Child Left Behind. Unsurprisingly, this narrow vision has had bipartisan appeal. Neither major political party has maintained a broad, humanistic view of the mission of the public schools. Testing and economic goal-setting have driven the discussion of education policy since the 1980s and have achieved "common sense" status.

What is ahead: the organization of this book

In this introduction, and in the chapters that follow, our goals are several, but they can be summarized by our wish to analyze, to deconstruct, the moment in which we find ourselves in contemporary U.S. education and to understand how we have arrived here, what the characteristics of our historic moment are, and how we may reinvent the status quo as a more humane future. That urge to reinvent is, as suggested above, the essence of education and the foe of the "learned forgetfulness and complacency" (Willinsky, 1998, p. 263) that inhabits mere teaching. Also we recognize that the transformative or reconstructive aspect of education is profoundly democratic and at the center of John Dewey's definition of our endeavor.

This book is organized into three sections. This introduction, and the first three chapters forming Part I, Mechanisms and motivations of education policy, provide a broad perspective on the traditional purposes of education, and a similar perspective on the new mechanisms and motivations of current education policy. The second section of four chapters, Distortions of the advocates, examines particular cases in which partisan advocacy and pro-market stances distort education issues. It includes discussions of how educational research, teacher testing, social studies education, and the history of education have each been inappropriately defined.

The final section, Visions for change, offers hopeful visions on democratic teaching, schools, and curriculum, and practical advice on how teachers, administrators, and citizens can envision their renewed control of public education.

Balance, conflict and utopia

Education at its best conveys a "sense of utopian possibility" (Giroux, 2004, p. 72) and, for this reason, educators look for a vision of what their work may yield. The fundamental insight of Dewey—his metaphor of growth—identifies the entire enterprise of education with just such an open-ended attitude of hopeful movement toward an unspecified goal. This attitude of combined hope and uncertainty sits poorly with many in society. In some ways, the duality defines the crossroads at which we find ourselves today in educational policy—whether to direct schools and teachers in a defined, linear fashion through standards and standardized testing or whether to trust professional educators to bring students along in the facts of the disciplines while inspiring them to engage critically and personally in those studies. Our societal interest may be to train a generation who can conform to a standardized definition of competence or it may lie in the ancient ideals of liberal education. These ideals are associated more with possibility than production. Another parallel analysis is to contrast the backward looking imperative of faith, which we see as an attempt to address the future by following the strictures of the past. This is posed in opposition to a guiding principle of hope, ill-defined but unfettered by past practice and characterized by an emphasis on the emergent world.

In chapter 8, both Dewey's metaphor of growth and Alfred North Whitehead's Ages of Learning are explored in the context of schooling. This latter theory is mentioned here to counteract the idea that our narrative may slide into the either/or dichotomizing of which Dewey warned us. Education that has as its vision creative possibility still requires the rote and drill of Whitehead's Stage of Precision. There is clearly a place for teaching the fundamentals of the disciplines. The current policy debate in the United States, however, postulates standards and standardized testing as culminating goals, not as tools in pursuit of higher aims. If one doubts this, one need only read a sample of state curriculum standards or look over the tests and testing methods used to measure success against them. Some may argue that higher, integrative aspirations are implicit in the education system and that the standards movement is a parallel and necessary discipline. This argument seems disingenuous, however, for those of us who talk to teachers and school administrators and observe the manner in which accountability measures are "sucking the oxygen" out of the school day and curricular organization. This distortion of educational policy also takes place in media coverage on schools and general public discourse on schooling. The stakes placed on standardized testing are disproportionate to the significance of the learning they can measure. Testing and transformation are not either/or goals of schooling, but they are ones that must be kept in balance, in rightful relation to one another, if a worthy vision of education is to prevail.

To some the image of "balance" may seem passive in light of the current conditions prevailing in the U.S. education debate. For this reason, after Spring (2002), we might substitute for balance the idea of "conflict." Even in utopia, the natural condition for making education policy may be one of conflict, and we may be well advised as educators to embrace this dimension of the democratic process. The desire to see that the standing of education be assured in society due solely to the rightness of its cause is unrealistic. So is the notion that any interest group, however noble its rhetoric, can be assured of a place at the political table or a piece of the economic pie. Over the past two decades, education as a profession has been identified by the practitioners of realpolitik and aggressive interest groups as a soft target, a defenseless institution. Some of these advocates are motivated by righteousness, some by greed, while some honestly disagree with the education establishment and have a message worth hearing. The rights of minorities and the disabled first emerged from vocal partisans outside the establishment. The education debate has continued and gained momentum in part because of the ambivalence of professional educators themselves about joining in the conflict of politics and mobilizing organized efforts to press their point of view. In chapters 1 and 9 we seek to outline the structure of this problem and create strategies of response.

The limits of the free market

A central assumption of the political right, and one that drives much of the conflict over education policy, is the notion that schools are another government function that should be privatized. If one wishes to see a conspiracy underlying NCLB, it is that a statistically impossible standard for public education has been set in the legislation by the multiple criteria that determine adequate annual yearly progress. Each ethnic and other designated subgroup in a school must progress at a given, significant rate or, over a short period of time, the school is designated "failing" and sanctions apply. The odds for failure far outstrip those for success, even in schools that by other criteria are admirable. Ranking schools inherently creates as many losers (bottom half) as winners (top half). This invasive statistical grid is established on a foundation of varied and inconsistent instruments determined by each state. These tests generally are little connected to the curriculum standards and textbooks in use in the respective states. The tests have little teacher input in their construction. The constitution of subgroups varies by state. Accommodations for the disabled and non-English speakers have been grudging. Pseudoscience in the form of this testing scheme is seen as taking priority over the interests of individual children. As we know now, all this has precipitated massive teaching to the test and fraud, particularly in Rod Paige's Houston Independent School District. Of course, NCLB is not science by any means; it is a brute form of politics. Significantly, these statistical anomalies and abuses demonstrate the absence among this legislation's designers of fair and competent psychometricians and statisticians, much less the representatives of other subdisciplines of education. The strong, negative reaction of even "red" states such as Utah and Nebraska to the implementation of the original NCLB continues to illustrate in a nonpartisan way the act's shortcomings—not only in pedagogic terms, but in logic, fairness, and practicality. As these state officials document, the underfunding of NCLB ultimately reveals the insincerity of the administration that propounded it. It is all stick and no carrot if you are a public school educator. It is a game you are fated to lose.

Scientific integrity and the welfare of students aside, discrediting public education is a priority of certain market fundamentalists in society who generalize that few if any functions belong in the state's portfolio, and education is certainly not among them. Vouchers, home schooling, corporate management of schools, and direct funding of private schools with tax dollars are all pet projects of the right. The anti-tax, anti-big government movements are linked together by their faith in markets with the followers of Milton Friedman and other such economist-prophets who have won extensive credibility in the post-Reagan years. The extremism and radical nature of their position do not typically attach to their public profile. Paul Krugman (2004, p. 232), writing shortly after 9/11 in his *New York Times* column, identified "a government agency that, by the usual criteria, should be a prime target for downsizing—maybe even abolition." This agency was the New York Fire Department, and Krugman went on to demonstrate that this same set of principles should apply to the incipient Transportation Security Administration. Krugman was ridiculing Republican leaders in Congress who, in this case, did not prevail. His point of view is exceptional today, however, in U.S. media—he is pigeonholed as a darling of the left and its poster boy on the *Times* op-ed page. Generally, the right opposes nearly every role of government, public education among them. Their principle is that the market economy can provide each service better, with rare exceptions such as, perhaps, combat troops in the military.

As many political observers point out, the market fundamentalists do welcome government involvement when it paves the way through subsidies, sweetheart contracts, and trade policy for increased profits for their corporate interests. Leaving hypocrisy aside for the moment, however, let us consider what has been lost in this debate. If democracy is meaningful at all to members of society, it is so in proportion to the sense of community it engenders. Government, even sovereignty, in a republican democracy such as the United States is none other than a manifestation of the people, collectively. The public schools are one of many informed creations of modern democracies that are established out of a sense of enlightened self-interest. There is an aspect of self-destructiveness as well as cruelty in a society that loses its commitment to institutions that provide for the public good. Among these are a number of natural monopolies and other services that are justifiably considered as appropriate activities of government. Generally there are no bright lines in this process, and states make a variety of choices regarding utilities, transit, and so on. The fundamentalist notion that government is by definition a less qualified player is not supported in fact. This is particularly true of education.

The schools are a special institution, and although there typically are alternatives to the public schools and in some nations there is a strong sectarian influence in the public schools, the idea that the citizenry, in the form of its government, could contract out public education, leaving it to corporate leadership and free market competition, is an abrogation of the community's responsibility and its self-interest. This is especially true in multicultural democracies that are challenged to instill a common political culture in immigrants from many lands. Our purpose here is not to argue for the schools as a public good as much as to point out that in the debate over the control of education the concept of the public good seems absent. The common sense employed for understanding education has shifted toward its economic value rather than its humanistic or civic value, and, in this process, education is defined as a commodity to be provided in the manner of shoes or hamburgers, in a format that is dictated by market forces. Societal values and aspirations, as well as a universal commitment to the sanctity of the individual, fall out of this design.

Advocacy science and scholarship

As Michael Apple has written, the right has been increasingly successful at creating a new common sense for U.S. society. This emerging worldview includes not only the Friedmanesque notions of market fundamentalism outlined above, but other, radical redefinitions of the conventions of society. In this light, the standards and testing movements are a part of a political concept of science that is fostered by advocacy groups and the politicians aligned with them. Although the battle lines are forming, the scientific community in the form of its associations and academies has been slow to respond to these radical signals from Washington, DC. This slowness is due in part to the apolitical identity many in science share and an assurance that this great engine of modernity long ago established its hegemony over traditional attitudes of faith. Secularity seemed to assure science of freedom to act in its designated realms. Reversals in stem-cell research support, the autonomy of National Science Foundation funding, and the place of Darwinian principles in the epistemology of life science have shaken this assurance. Fraudulence in pharmaceutical research, manipulation of the approval of the "morning after pill," and restrictions on Medicaid-funded conversations between physicians and patients have also brought the apolitical status of scientifically based professions into question. In education, the standards and testing movement, as well as the "reading wars," are manifestations of the struggle over the common sense of science. In chapter 4 we explore the contemporary redefinition of the science of education.

Positive science has not been extended to education in a comprehensive and widely accepted manner. Although there are areas of successful application—such as the use of certain prescription medicines and behavior modification as a means of addressing some special education objectives—teaching remains a highly subjective practice—more like social work or counseling than dentistry or medicine. The "dream" that programmed instruction and reinforcement schedules could lead to a revolution in schooling has met with limited success. This same situation prevails, of course, in a variety of fields of endeavor, including the human service professions, the arts, politics, and social science in general. The powerful methods of the physical and natural sciences as well as engineering and technology have proven only marginally translatable outside those realms. This is no surprise to philosophers of science, but apparently their voices are largely absent from the halls of government or media. When applied with skill and restraint, scientific methods have been a useful albeit limited tool. When allowed to dominate fields characterized by human subjectivity, the promise of positive science disappoints or even misleads.

The phenomenon of misdirected science is familiar to educators in the post-World War II era as one attempt after another has been brought forward to automate and regularize life in classrooms. The quiet failures of these projects have not prevented some researchers in and outside education from continuing their attempt to scientize schooling. Classrooms are extremely complex environments with near infinite variability of behavior that is rooted in the mischievous and recursive qualities of human subjectivity and will. The long quest to make education scientific has, unsurprisingly, counteracted these conditions by defining its goals as simple and partial ones. So intelligence is defined as what intelligence tests measure; teacher tests specifically do not claim predictive or consequential validity at fore-telling teacher success; and, for all its ubiquity, SAT at best predicts achievement for the first year of university with no better accuracy than high school grades. In itself, there is nothing inappropriate about defining limited goals and creating methods to achieve them. What we have experienced recently, however, are less benign manipulations of science as it applies to education.

On the one hand, we see the transformation of science from an objective search for testable hypotheses into a propaganda tool. The government-inspired mania for "scientifically based research" has been corrupt from the outset, since it violated a precept of science by arbitrarily limiting the modes of inquiry that could be brought to bear in the research enterprise. Of course, dictating a gold standard for research that is associated only with randomized field studies has had the backdraft effect of redefining what problems researchers can examine. In reading, this tends to mean that discrete elements of the reading act can be isolated and studied, but the more complex overall objective of creating sophisticated, inquiring, and lifelong readers cannot. Some evidence suggests that an overemphasis on early skill development correlates with less success among longer term, more critical criteria. This is extensively discussed in the work of reading experts and summarized in chapter 1.

More insidiously, however, this dumbing down of the goals of the curriculum has been extended to the entire enterprise of public education by introducing objective standardized testing as the one true standard for school success. School quality increasingly is defined in terms of what achievement tests measure. Additionally, as we have discussed above, success achieved at a standard by a great majority of a school's population still is not enough—there must be continuous upward movement in test scores by each subgroup in each school. Perhaps by coincidence, the government sees as the basic tools for educational development those products sold by testing companies and textbook publishers. Reducing class size, increasing teacher compensation, heightening the investment in teacher professional development or job conditions are written off. The Education Department invests over $20 million in a program (American Board for Certification of Teacher Excellence) to create "highly qualified teachers" through a test-only preparation scheme. To call all this a manifestation of science illustrates the Orwellian world we have entered. Hardball politicians, using the tools of media manipulation, have co-opted the language of science in order to seize and maintain power and steer economic resources in the direction of their sponsoring individuals and corporations, while solidifying their political base. We explore the impact of such policies on teacher testing in chapter 5.

This skillful type of propagandizing is not new, but it can be very effective. James Hillman speaks of the manner in which the financial industry since the 18th century has co-opted the language of faith to legitimize its own agenda. The vocabulary that has been transformed is extensive: security, bond, fidelity, interest, trust, and so on. Today, we argue that the right-wing advocates of privatizing the schools and terminating the egalitarian aspirations of public education call their enterprise "No Child Left Behind," a corrupted slogan of liberal child activist Marian Wright Edelman. The right alleges that liberal, humanist educators are guilty of the "soft bigotry of low expectations," while at the same time they establish punitive high-stakes testing and other policies that push lower class students out of school and redirect the curriculum of those who remain to one of less relevance and effectiveness. Improvements to the social safety net and equitable investment in schools that serve areas in poverty—the type of policies economist Richard Rothstein (2004) enumerates—are excluded from the policy agenda. A mania for tax cutting to "starve the beast" assures that there are no resources to address these foundational social issues.

The recent rewriting of the history of education has its most formal manifestation in Diane Ravitch's *Left back* (2000), in which the heroes and accomplishments of progressive education are discredited by any means necessary, including a creative and, we think, invidious definition of the movement and its aspirations. We investigate this long case study, undertaken by a leading advocate, in chapter 7. Similarly, chapter 6 examines the social studies wars and explores the values underpinning opposing points of view. The Fordham Foundation speaks for the right in this study.

Professional authority

There is a "through the looking glass" quality to the recent political initiatives in states such as Kansas, Ohio, and Georgia to infuse the science education curriculum with explanations of the origins of life that compete with Darwinian evolution. The science establishment is nonplussed by this bold invasion of their realm and even further surprised by the perseverance and limited success of the movement. Creationism has morphed into Intelligent Design and along the way gained legitimacy among some school boards and legislators. Scientists have occupied a higher standing in U.S. public opinion than educators, but today they find themselves successfully challenged in institutional places they assumed were theirs to control. This attack on scientific authority occurs at the same time that scientifically inspired medical achievements are more than ever at the center of citizen concerns. Many in U.S. society seem unable to make the connection between the historic independence of the science establishment, including science education, and its ability to contribute to human well-being. In the case of suspending funding for stem-cell research, we see a related but more rational phenomenon. In this instance, certain of the faithful are willing to forego medical advance on a matter of principle—the sanctity of unborn life even at the embryonic level of expression.

We may disapprove of the imposition of sectarian views on everyone's medical care, but objections to stem-cell research are rational and proceed from a subjective but humane value. Intervention into the science curriculum, on the other hand, is a much less defensible posture and signals something other than advocacy of a moral principle. Fundamentalists are offended by the centrality of a non-biblically literalist explanation for life in the science classroom, placing them to the right of the Roman Catholic Church on this issue. They see this curriculum as a political target that is not protected by the boundaries of professional authority. It is significant that the proponents of Intelligent Design do not argue for some place in the school curriculum. They are determined to have a certain place, namely in the science curriculum, since they seek the same legitimacy for their "theory" as those of mainstream science.

We explore the Creationist quest in these pages because it is analogous in some ways to the competition for control of public schools in general. The common themes we are examining are the struggle between advocates of the right in the form of institutions, individuals, and funding sources with the established authority of society as it is manifested in disciplines, professions, and persons of achievement. Education, in comparison with science, is a soft target for the right. Educators are stereotyped as being economic and intellectual weaklings who are in a profession of last resort. Scientists, on the other hand, are princes of the social order, respected for their brainpower, their connections to technical and medical miracles, and their guru-like presence in the media. The traction the right has made against even this powerful establishment demonstrates the parlous position of professional education.

By and large it is unsurprising that persons in the street take professions and institutions for granted. The governance structures of professions are very much in the background of modern society, at least with respect to media and political conversation. Other than discipline regarding teachers, little appears in the news about the workings of professional boards and associations. This low profile contrasts with the centrality of professional services in society, the increasing complexity of professional knowledge, and the importance of self-regulation in terms of ethics. Loosely bound, unregulated "professions," such as those associated with the academic disciplines, are almost ineffable in the manner in which they advance the norms and agenda of their fields. No wonder the general public is oblivious to much of this machination.

This invisibility belies the significance of the professions as building blocks of society. Similar to common law, these institutions and their conventions are as significant as more explicit organizations and regulations. There is a vital place for professions in the social contract. The expansion of reflective, ethical social capital into the everyday work of countless individuals is of great benefit to the public. The professions are expected to be ahead of the law in ethical awareness and policing of their ranks. We need only reflect on the functioning of occupations before and after professionalization, or those that are outside any professional structure and code of ethics, to appreciate this pervasive, quiet infrastructure.

The new common sense of education that is explored in these pages is a deprofessionalized one in which teachers lose their autonomy to lock step curricula and externally imposed evaluation by standardized testing. In the advocates' view, specialized teacher education and state licensure are to be the object of deregulation. Scholarship in education and graduate professional development for teachers are superfluous. There is little need for faculties of education. Some states, led by Florida, are looking at two-year community college preparation of teachers. This initiative is a remarkable decredentialing of a profession which has no parallel in other countries or U.S. precedents. A similar case has been made in a government-sponsored report chaired by Arthur Levine (2005), the then-outgoing president of Teachers College, focusing on a de-emphasis of doctoral study by school administrators. The advocates might claim in this and other ways that they are heralding a new tomorrow in which other societies will join. They can claim, as market fundamentalists do, that they are accommodating the emerging global society and information revolution by their policies and that the established authorities of the field are mired in self-interest and traditionalism.

Magical thinking and thinking

As we think authors should, we are looking for more powerful ways to understand issues in education and move ahead in a progressive manner.

Toward this end, our descriptions of the political landscape of education travel, variously, into the realms of critical theory (chapter 2) and of depth psychology (chapter 3). The former will be familiar to readers and is populated with well-known and admired scholars in education. The latter continues to be a marginalized study, even after a century of looming presence in Western thought. Gradually, this rejection of the psychology of the unconscious is breaking down as neuroscience, social psychology, and philosophy find ways to bridge contemporary notions of science and visionary work such as that of Freud, Jung, and their successors. Authors participating in this convergence include Sharon Begley, in *Train your mind, change your brain* (2007), Timothy Wilson, in *Strangers to ourselves* (2004), and Nicholas Humphrey, in *Seeing red* (2006).

We intend for the spirit of this book to reflect such pathfinding attitudes, because the times call for more effective analyses of the challenges we face in education. Today, U.S. policy and politics are volatile and capable of fundamental shifts in direction. The struggle for control over the schooling of young Americans is very much in play and characterized by a lack of overarching principles and common ground. A number of radical designs for change, such as home schooling networks, vouchers, and invasive federal authority over schools, are in place and growing in influence. Old principles are at risk—for example, the school as a check on the exclusivity of parental influence; as an extension and builder of the community; as a public good and creator of equity; as a zone of protection from base influences; and as a laboratory of democracy for parents and children.

Responses to these challenges must account for the emerging communication forces that surround us in contemporary society. Media and marketing have shifted the ground of public policy formation (Gore, 2007). These fields deliberately employ techniques that are marginally understood and accepted in the academic world, but that continue to prove powerful in the narrowly pragmatic world of winning political campaigns, attracting voters and viewers, and shaping public opinion. We think educators should attend to these strategies and methods. Our battles for professional autonomy and the survival of public schools are being fought out on such terms. At a minimum, we need to have insight into the nature of the forces aligned against us and our vision of education. For these insights we must look to emerging, as well as established, disciplinary knowledge.

Part I

Mechanisms and motivations of education policy

Chapter 1

Political advocacy versus academic authority

Defining educational inquiry and defending public education

Public intellectuals are obliged to practice self-restraint and attend to external criticism so that they do not adopt positions of assumed certainty in a simplified universe. This disposition reflects a delicate and important social contract, particularly within the professoriate. With these purposes in mind during the past century, educators have built an establishment of organizations, institutions, and publications that, for all their limitations, have effectively propagated, as both necessary and appropriate, professional practices such as self-restraint and attention to criticism. An air of transparency and concern for the public good has been sustained, as well as distance from conflicts of interest through the possibility of open debate, honestly brokered, and a process of inquiry that is not tainted by intervening agendas or censorship.

These dispositions and core values are challenged by the voices of the right. Student welfare, these voices would seem to say, is best served in a context framed by certain ideological assumptions. These advocates have such confidence in their assumptions that they appear willing to manipulate scholarly and popular media to advance their policies. The new advocacy academicians interpose values such as a preference for privatization and "free market" control, hostility to unionization, a romantic attachment to an idealized golden age of education and society, and a propensity for controlling and punitive strategies in relating to youth. In this environment the education policy debate is rapidly assuming a polarized form. The two parties to the discussion—the established education professionals and the new advocates—proceed from different sets of assumptions, target different audiences, employ different media, and measure success in different ways.

There are many disturbing messages found within the dialogue of the advocacy academicians. One troubling example is the manner in which their discrediting of public education serves to draw attention away from the social and economic problems of society. Despite the claims of the advocates in mainstream media, public education is not failing. Berliner and Biddle

(1995) have carefully documented the falseness of the claim of failure, beginning with the publication of *The manufactured crisis: Myths, fraud, and the attack on America's public schools*. David Berliner updated and expanded his analysis of the effects of poverty on education in a powerful invited presidential address at the American Educational Research Association annual meeting in 2005; it became a featured article in *Teachers College Record* (Berliner, 2005) and the inspiration for a book, *Collateral damage* (Nichols & Berliner, 2007). Richard Rothstein, in his weekly column in *The New York Times* and his other writing, and Gerald Bracey in his monthly department, "Research," in *Kappan*, also regularly submit hard evidence to support an objective appraisal of our schools. James Popham offers similar insights in *Educational Leadership*. Yet blaming social and economic troubles on failing schools and low Third International Mathematics and Science Study (TIMSS) scores continues to be an extremely effective strategy by those Bracey calls the "Education Scare Industry" (2001, p. 157) for advocating that public education is failing. Discrediting public education has the added threat (or benefit, if you are a player in privatizing what have been long understood as "public goods") of making the enormous education market vulnerable to corporate interests through the creation of vouchers and for-profit or charter schools and additional, expensive standardized tests and canned curricula.

Destructive politicizing

> Another way people liked to refer to what we were doing is waging a 'battle of ideas.' That battle, at least among serious people, is now over. We have won it. [Midge] Decter went on to identify a new enemy: the American education system.
>
> (Brock, 2002, p. 50)

Intellectuals of the right recognized that with the fall of communism a need emerged for another target to coalesce their rhetoric. During the past 20 years, U.S. public education has been increasingly used to fill this void. Undefended by corporate lobbying interests and identified as a Democratic voting block, educators and their institutions provide a useful object for reproach. Education is an institution about which most Americans care and feel informed, and thus it makes a broadly relevant tool as a target for propaganda. Discrediting public education also serves to draw attention away from many fundamental social and economic problems. "Trade deficits that ballooned 20 years ago," Rothstein (2001) writes, "were caused not by low test scores but by corporate bloat, markets that were more open here than elsewhere and a budget deficit that pushed up interest rates and the dollar's value" (p. A–4). These facts are rarely apparent to the average American, who has been conditioned through reductionist and misleading mass media and social studies textbooks that present failing schools, immigrants, and welfare mothers as the source of societal troubles (Spring, 2002, p. 176).

Add to "education as political opportunity" the economic fact that the K–12 education "market" of $732 billion (U.S. Department of Education, 2002c) is arguably the largest reservoir of public funds insulated from full development by corporate America. To the extent that political and economic motives are operating, the critics of public education are not satisfied with articulate responses by educators, well-meaning reforms, or even demonstrations of "results." While educators may hope and assume that they are engaged in an honest policy debate with public-spirited critics, a more comprehensive view suggests other agendas are at work. Advocates dismiss evidence.

In the 1950s, the launch of *Sputnik* raised fears that U.S. public education was not keeping pace in science and technology with the schools of enemy nation-states. In retrospect it has been others who failed to compete successfully, both economically and technologically, in the race to the moon. Next came the great SAT debate in which it was alleged that declining college entrance examination scores demonstrated a decline in American education. *On further examination* (College Board, 1977), the Sandia study (Carson, Huelskamp, & Woodall, 1993), and, most comprehensively, the writings of Gerald Bracey convincingly argued for the following analysis: "If the standard-setting group is compared with a demographically similar group today, the mathematics scores show no decline and the verbal scores show only a small (22-point) decline" (1997, p. 56). Then, during the 1980s, critique of public education emanating from *A nation at risk* (National Commission on Excellence in Education, 1983) stirred similar emotions by alleging that Japan, among other nations, was about to surpass the United States economically—again due to the failures of public schools. Yet education had very little to do with American loss of global market share in the late 20th century, and it was Japan that went into prolonged recession while the U.S. economy enjoyed what is arguably its decade of greatest prosperity. Oddly enough, public education received no noticeable credit for this economic boom although to a large extent it was a spinoff of academic culture and research.

All this is not to claim that educators and public education are not without flaws and imperfections or that the "old common sense" was without contradictions and denials. One such example of the flawed nature of the public institution of education is found in the ongoing union–board friction that has eroded citizen confidence in our public schools, as has cronyism and mismanagement of resources, particularly in urban centers. As scholars such as Jonathan Kozol and Gary Orfield, among many others, have documented, the quality of public education varies enormously, and far too many children attend schools without adequate funding, good teachers, or a meaningful curriculum. These are not, however, "manufactured" crises: They are actual problems and, therefore, can be deliberately addressed by citizens of good will. In contrast, the *Sputnik*/SAT/*Nation* debates are chimeras—impossible to resolve because they were largely rhetorical from the outset, the product of a variety of media hyperbole and scapegoating. These attacks parallel the negative political advertising that has been so successful for the right in general elections.

The loss of fundamental assumptions—the old common sense

Lost in these events are certain fundamental assumptions—the old common sense—on which the profession of education is thought to have been built. Chief among these is the idea that the interests of the student should be preeminent and put in every instance above those of the practitioner and other concerned parties. As members of a human service profession, educators and educational researchers are trusted to place students above profit, personal aggrandizement, or ideological victory. Students, to paraphrase Dewey, are not a means to an end but the end itself. This contradicts the caveat emptor of the marketplace. A student in our public schools should not have to "beware" of the motives or practices of his or her teachers and administrators. This is another of the dimensions of the "zone of protection" that has characterized our U.S. ideal of education. Would K–12 education that is driven by a free market ethos, motivated by profit, and characterized by winner-take-all competition have the benevolent values we presume denote a school environment for children? From what quarter would come restraint, for example, on the marketing to our students of bad food, expensive merchandise, and irresponsible bank credit?

Teacher unionization and the introduction of strikes by teachers to improve their economic conditions are argued by some as the actual turning point in the public's view of education. Without question, union tactics, and particularly strikes, have damaged the public's view of teachers. Further analysis would typically include, however, that ethical behavior does not preclude earning a living wage and that teachers may well have exhausted the systems provided to them by law and convention for addressing their economic plight. Again the questions arise: Did an actual crisis demand extraordinary response? Or were "manufactured crises" employed as a ruse to independently gain economic or political advantage?

A related concept lost in the current debates about education is that a key purpose of education in a democracy is to foster the creation of a critically thinking citizenry that is able to make informed, democratically derived decisions in response to an ever changing world. Though there continues to be a struggle to live by and reach this ideal, it continues to be widely valued. Yet, in contrast to the would-be tenets of democracy, current federal policy often does not welcome critical thinking and would seem instead to support unquestioned obedience to what are presented as taken-for-granted and inalienable truths. "The right to life, liberty and the pursuit of happiness is not a personal opinion, but an eternal truth." President George W. Bush advocates "clear instruction in right and wrong" (Issues—Education, 2001). Furthermore, education is explicitly articulated not as a right of the citizen, but as a national economic investment. As President Bush (2003) has framed the issue, "In return for a lot of money, the federal government, for the first time, is asking, are we getting the kind of return the American people want for every child?"

Historically, democracies have also been suspicious of and resistant toward the merging of state and business leadership. The concern has been—and, for many parents and educators, continues to be—that the private interests of business leaders and the influence and power that business undeniably yields would, in effect, present a very real threat of an undemocratically administered economy that is not compatible with the interests of the children, the parents, the educators, and the public. In the post-*Nation at risk* era both major political parties have moved away from this principle of separating state and business leadership. In NCLB, the concept of educating students for thoughtful participation in a democracy is muted or lost by an emphasis on standardized test results at the expense of higher-order curricula. Instead, education is unquestionably presented and therefore taken for granted as a means of serving economic interests, which begs the question: Whose interests are these, after all? Consistent with the views on education held by the Clinton administration, the Bush administration's 2002 budget blueprint pointed out that "Our schools are not preparing our students adequately for today's knowledge-based, technologically rich society or to become future scientists and engineers" and allocated $200 million to the National Science Foundation to strengthen mathematics and science education in grades K–12 (Blueprint, 2001). In a speech introducing the Education Act, Bush explained, "We'll focus on teacher training efforts where the need is greatest, in early childhood education, special education, math, science and reading instruction" (Bush, 2002). NCLB legislation explains "America's schools are not producing the science excellence required for global economic leadership and homeland security in the 21st century" (U.S. Department of Education, 2003e). While certainly the economy and security may be concerns of the citizenry, to isolate these as the named priorities for what is taught and learned in our schools creates an imperative to question the implications of leaving civics, social studies, multiculturalism, the arts, and literature conspicuously absent.

Equally cynical and misleading is the notion that the forces of the right are truly "free market" and opposed to government intervention. The separation of markets and government is a fundamental common-sense concept in the United States. Yet economic interests (and, again, this begs the question: Whose interests?) not only direct the curriculum described above; these interests are also used as a central metaphor to diagnose problems with education and to suggest reforms. Former U.S. Secretary of Education Rod Paige (2003) explained, "The great companies confronted the realities of their situation in the marketplace, and they changed their entire system of operating in response. I believe our schools must do the same." At the same time, however, private interests are deeply involved in using governmental authority in education to benefit their bottom lines, as can be evidenced by the de facto monopoly found in textbook approval as practiced in California and Texas, among other states. Associated with this process, and dismissive of the objections of superintendents, is the excessive restriction on the uses of state funding, which prevents (among other things) school administrators from applying funds to areas they identify as priority needs, and instead requires that funds be allocated to the purveyors of certain school goods and services, such as tests and textbooks. Another government policy-sanctioned technique that protects private interests is to obtain no-bid contracts for testing or other large school projects. Corporate interests also seek to transfer some of their costs of doing business to a generous government.

The oversight of weak government is also a friend to corporate interests. One example of this is found in blunders in reporting testing results (New York City experienced this under Superintendent Rudy Crew) or when contractors underperform and officials silently acquiesce in gross failures in services. There is also the boondoggle of "creative" accounting practices that are accepted with a wink by taxing authorities (Henriques, 2002; Schrag, 2001; Steffens & Cookson, 2002). (Edison Schools, Inc., through their booking of teacher salaries as revenue to aggrandize their gross receipts and ameliorate their accrual of more than $300 million in debt, is the most recent education example. These salaries were no more than a pass-through for them. This revelation helped fuel a greater than 95% decline in the value of Edison shares in 2002.) What begins as criticism of government oversight and regulation is spun into the rhetoric of independence from government involvement. Sweetheart contracts, typified by those in Philadelphia, Houston, Atlanta, Richmond, and Orlando, with Community Education Partners (CEP) to run alternative schools for suspended students looks like another tale of for-profit exploitation (Fuentes, 2005). Doubling per pupil costs results in high profits for CEP but not higher levels of student performance. Although other scandals (Enron as the prime example) have elevated to a high art the practices of using government influence to manipulate markets and raid the public till, this sort of corruption and scandal is not new. Recent stories of scandal should serve to sound an alarm that opportunists have drawn aim on public education.

An alternate economic history—sans education bashing

In order to best reject the myth that U.S. education policy has been responsible for loss of global economic market share, the real nature of economic change must be understood. This summary analysis is provided to reveal how little public education had to do with American economics in the 1980s and 1990s and, similarly, how little declining market shares and unequal trade balances with Japan had to do with mathematics scores or phonics skills.

After World War II, the United States was in a position to structure global political, economic, and military development for much of the world. The United States was involved in the war for fewer years than most nations and, further, since World War II was not waged on American soil, it did not have to rebuild infrastructure such as factories and roads. Thus, it is often argued, the United States left the war with a stronger economy and military than other nations. Before Japan and Western Europe recovered from the war, the United States was the primary world producer of many important products such as steel, automobiles, and electronic goods. As such, trade conditions favorable to Americans were supported by both formal and informal postwar trade policies. Marshall Plan aid, for example, required countries to sign free-trade pledges.

In addition to prescribing the development of Europe through the Marshall Plan, the United States became involved, often covertly, in the affairs of numerous newly independent countries. Although after World War II, former European colonies in South America, Africa, and Asia gained independence, most remained economically dependent by having to supply markets, labor, and raw materials to America and other first world countries. An example of covert efforts used by the United States to influence economic policy internationally can be seen in the CIA's work to disrupt labor movements in Europe that were not supportive of U.S. trade policy. More dramatically, the CIA was involved in overthrowing leaders who wanted to pursue independent paths of development in countries such as Iran. Such involvement included efforts to subvert progressive governments—including that of democratically elected Jacob Arbenz in 1954 in Guatemala—to protect American business holdings. As a result of these policies, by the late 1950s the United States dominated the globe both economically and strategically (Prados, 1996).

Many Americans think of the 1950s as the halcyon era in which the standard of living was high, as the decade when even working-class families could afford to buy their own homes (and in many ways these years were prosperous, at least for those Americans who had a public voice). The minimum wage was relatively high in constant dollars, and there were many good industrial jobs. By the late 1960s, however, the U.S. economy began to experience three phenomena: economic competition from newly industrialized countries and from a recovered Europe and Asia; a balance-of-payments deficit caused, in part, by the enormous cost of the Vietnam War; and increasingly powerful working- and middle-class labor. To some extent, America's early success was based on being the only salesman—the first to offer many products on the postwar world market. Decline was inevitable as corporations in other nations offered the same exports and developed their own new products. Yet, because American companies had experienced an easy early dominance, they were slow to make innovations. As many Americans are painfully aware, European and Japanese companies recovered from World War II and made innovations in automobiles, electronics, and steel production that enabled them to gain important global market share (Madison, 1989). Also, Asian and European countries such as Japan and Germany directed little federal spending to the military and relatively more to education and infrastructure, whereas the United States continued to spend heavily on the military rather than areas (such as education, urban infrastructure, and health facilities) that return compounded benefits (Friedman, 1989, pp. 204–205).

In response to the economic shift in the global market, during the 1980s many corporations sought to reduce labor costs by "downsizing" not only at the production level, but also at the managerial level. In the 1980s and 1990s corporate consolidation, or large companies buying up smaller ones, also contributed to middle-class job loss and insecure employment. Another trend was (and continues to be) for employers to replace full-time workers (with benefits, pensions, and other costs) with overseas, temporary, or part-time workers (Ayling, 1997). Finally, and more recently, investments have been made in a wide range of high tech product development, requiring a highly educated workforce. Each of these efforts has ultimately benefited corporations and the GDP but has weakened the security of many workers.

Although the past decade demonstrated resoundingly that American ingenuity, expertise, and corporate restructuring once again could leave economic rivals behind, the critical allegations about public education have not been revisited or retracted by those who made them. Nor has the long overdue praise come to our schools and universities for their contribution to an unprecedented technological revolution and economic boom. Public education is able to gain little political capital from its triumphs while its critics too often simply shift their ground to launch new attacks once the old ones have become conspicuously unfounded or unworthy of sensation in the eyes of the media.

Today, according to the rhetoric of officials such as Eugene Hickok, former Undersecretary of Education, it is educators, particularly urban educators, who are allegedly bigots with excuses and low standards, and it is certain politicians who, heroically, will "leave no child behind" (Hickok, 2002). The criterion for success is to be performance on standardized tests, although such tests in themselves are a narrow and inadequate measure of school success. Dropout rates, now rising for the first time in U.S. history due to high-stakes high school exit exams, are doctored or hidden from view, with Texas being the most dramatic case in point (McNeil, 2000). Educators appear to be on the wrong side of the public's common-sense view of schooling, if we look at the extent to which they find themselves on the defensive in explaining how what they do amounts to more than something that can be measured by a test. Educators also seem unable to convince many of their constituents that children deprived to a significant degree of the basic necessities of life are, as a group, at a serious disadvantage in school. This too should be common sense. Even these simple assertions have gained little purchase in the public imagination. Perhaps this should not come as a surprise, given the relentless repetition of popular media messages that simplistically assert accountability defined as testing, while referring to the destructiveness of poverty and neglect as merely the "excuses of educators." This type of denial of environmental factors may be peculiarly American.

Attacking and manipulating promising reforms

Another insidious and ironic manifestation of attacks on public education is the manner in which some of the most promising innovations of educators are restricted or banned from implementation. Reading Recovery provides a case in point. Originally attacked for its so-called skills orientation during its introduction to America, the program since NCLB became anathema to the U.S. Department of Education and the National Institute of Child Health and Human Development. It was accused of being on the wrong side of the reading wars (i.e., in the whole language camp). What these criticisms fail to acknowledge or perhaps recognize is that a closer and arguably more accurate view is that Reading Recovery transcends these categories. The program provides a pragmatic, early intervention with a thoroughly substantiated track record which documents annually the restoration of tens of thousands of new readers to grade level in the United States and which saves these students from eventual special education placement or testing failure as a result of poor literacy (Askew et al., 2002; National Data Evaluation Center, 2002; Schmitt & Gregory, 2001).

Draft guidance by the U.S. Department of Education threatened to subvert the clear intent of Congressional language in the Elementary and Secondary Education Act (ESEA) by directing Reading First funds away from pullout programs such as Reading Recovery. At the same time, researchers professionally associated with NICHD have become engaged in an Internet letter-writing campaign to discredit Reading Recovery by selectively applying research findings and, ironically, employing qualitative research (a paradigm the National Reading Panel [NRP] abjured) to turn Congress against this reform (Reading Recovery Council of North America, 2002, pp. 64–67). In its 78-page self-defense, the Reading Recovery Council of North America begins, "Although the letter purports to be an academic debate, its motivation appears to be political . . . The Internet letter chooses to ignore all of this easily available information in an attempt to undermine public confidence in Reading Recovery" (p. 1).

NICHD policies—embedded in a single point of view—are steering $6 billion into certain reading approaches over the life of the legislation. This political play has "overshadowed the role of the U.S. Department of Education, as well as those of the International Reading Association and the National Council of Teachers of English, which together represent more than 140,000 scholars and educators" (Manzo, 2004, p. 1). By 2007 the Reading First manipulations became public and redress began for the program.

There are other examples of reform efforts being stunted despite their promise. Specifically, *The New York Times* reports that performance assessment designs and integrated curricula in innovative and prestigious New York metropolitan schools have been displaced by standardized testing in that state's rush to impose conformity in testing and standards (Perez-Pena, 2001). If accountability and results were true mantras in this education reform movement, these superior manifestations of pedagogical evaluation would be promoted rather than undermined. Bilingual education has, in another instance, been used as a wedge issue in California, Arizona, Massachusetts, and other states, with Ron Unz achieving success at mandating English-language learner methodology through the proposition route. In a notorious and subsequently discredited example from Oceanside, California, page 1 of *The New York Times* read like a press release from Unz's offices (Steinberg, 2000, p. A–1). Subsequently, Congress has reinforced Unz's agenda by replacing the Bilingual Education Act with provisions in the new English Language Acquisition Act that omit native language skills, eliminate competitive grants, and allow states to impose teaching methods. The net result is a lessening of the states' accountability and freedom to act.

Another targeted reform is the National Board for Professional Teaching Standards (NBPTS). The National Council on Teacher Quality (2002), in a tour de force of imbalance, maintained an entire segment of its website to promulgate only critical articles about the NBPTS. Also, J. E. Stone's attack on the NBPTS, self-published on the Internet in his Education Consumers Consultants Network, attained widespread publicity without any pretense of credible verification (Stone, 2002). *Education Week* and other media ran with the story as if the study had received normal vetting. The magnitude of the attack led the Education Commission of the States in response to sponsor an investigatory study (Zehr, 2002). One can only speculate as to why important media would feature work emanating from what is essentially an electronic vanity press.

Attacking and manipulating educational research

The politics of the education establishment sometimes shares blame for these disputes, as extremists (seen as "left" or "right" or otherwise) have determined the shape of policy by creating a train wreck of process instead of workable compromises. As Zinn (1999) observes regarding government involvement,

> But is it the aim of government to maintain order, as a referee, between two equally matched fighters? Or is it that government has some special interest in maintaining a certain kind of order, a certain distribution of power and wealth, a distribution in which government officials are not neutral referees but participants?
>
> (p. 97)

Moving beyond passive methods, the federal government is asserting its agenda in increasingly aggressive and unprecedented ways. The *Report of the National Reading Panel* (National Institute of Child Health and Human Development, 1999a) was a very public early warning that federal agencies were taking it upon themselves to promulgate a narrow definition of what counts as science and bona fide research in education. The 2001 ESEA/NCLB supports only "strategies and professional development that are established on scientifically based reading research." NCLB defines "scientifically based" to mean research which "employs systematic, empirical methods" and uses "experimental or quasi-experimental designs in which individuals, entities, programs, or activities are assigned to different conditions and with appropriate controls to evaluate the effects of the condition of interest, with a preference for random-assignment experiments" (U.S. Department of Education, 2002b).

This definition threatens to roll back a generation of work that has broadened the field of research in education and accommodated diverse quantitative and qualitative methodologies. One would think that "bona fide research" would take into account the highest quality studies—which would include research that uses both qualitative and quantitative methods—but this is not what the new federal law requires or accepts. Certainly, some dimensions of successful learning are quantifiable and generalizable across contexts. Yet it is also equally certain that some dimensions of successful learning are complex, personal and local and, as such, cannot be captured or understood by quantitative measurements of experimental or quasi-experimental design. Rather, they require narrative, descriptive, and qualitative studies to permit different and equally important insights, research, and results. One would hope that bona fide research and "good science" would begin with an understanding that no single paradigm of research is capable of presenting a whole truth or offering silver bullets for school improvement (see chapter 4).

Unfortunately, education policy in the United States is currently being driven by a highly limited and intellectually naïve concept of research that fails to acknowledge the importance of and the need for multiple research paradigms and methods. In a continuing example, based on supposed "scientific" studies, English-only instruction is being touted as superior by critics of bilingual education (Crawford, 2002). Buttressed by the government's new interest in defining the "science of education," this view of how ESL (English as a second language) students should be educated has become federal policy, disregarding the research that supports the merit of bilingual education (Wiese & Garcia, 1998; Wiley, 1996). Moving forward to set the stage for further federal narrowing of the definition of educational research, HR 3801 created a revised appointment process for the commissioner of education statistics via the director of a new "Academy of Education Sciences." The director will award the National Assessment of Educational Progress (NAEP) contracts and grants as well. It appears both evident and inescapable that there is a federal imperative for the government to shape and define educational research in a manner that in the past has been seen (and, to many in the field of education, continues to be seen) as wholly insufficient and unacceptable. Even Diane Ravitch demurs, stating, "These are both agencies that are truth-telling agencies—assessment and statistics—and both should be insulated to the maximum extent possible from any political controls" (Olson, 2002, p. 24).

Another variation is research of dubious quality that touts alternatives to public education. For example, Paul E. Peterson's heralded study of vouchers in New York City and their positive effect on African-American boys (Howell & Peterson, 2002) is a prime example of widely acclaimed advocacy research in support of privatization efforts. The research was quietly but resoundingly discredited by peers after its damage was done to the reputation of the public schools. This limited study, though uncorroborated by educators and the research community, was initially treated in media as being definitive. David Myers, lead researcher for Mathematica, states, "It is scary how many prominent thinkers in this nation of 290 million were ready to make new policy from a single study that appears to have gone from meaningful to meaningless based on whether 292 children's test scores are discounted or included" (Winerip, 2003, p. A–27).

Research, funding, sponsorship, and misconduct

There is an understanding in the research community (see Randall, Cooper, & Hite, 1999, among others) that, regardless of the definition and methodological rigor of research, its ethical quality ultimately remains rooted in the value and belief systems of the researchers and individuals who sponsor that research. If individuals wish to manipulate their research, either through overt data falsification or, more subtly, through methodological design, there is little that can be done, other than to rely on peer reviewers to expose the misconduct (Howe, 2002; Reeves, 2002; Viadero, 2002). While the general quality of education research has come under fire recently, it is also important to note that research into scientific misconduct in the "hard" sciences has generated similar problems. For example, Mildred Cho, a senior research scholar at Stanford's Center for Biomedical Ethics, found that corporate-sponsored drug research produced results that corroborated what the sponsor hoped to find 98% of the time. By contrast, independent drug research supported researchers' hypotheses only 79% of the time (Press & Washburn, 2000). Clearly this brand of funded "science" requires the careful scrutiny of the research community, not only in the interest of the particular research taken up in a given inquiry, but also in the interest of legitimacy in research writ large.

In a review of research on scientific integrity, Nicholas Steneck (2000) found that serious ethical lapses might be present in as many as one in 100 cases, although the actual reporting rate is only one in 100,000. While 1% may seem low, these figures include only the most serious offenses (defined as fabrication, falsification, and plagiarism). Misrepresentation of findings, authorship irregularities, duplicate publication, bias and conflict of interest, or misconduct in private research efforts are not included. Additionally, Steneck highlights the importance of peer review, self-correction, and formal instruction in the responsible conduct of research—some or all of which are often missing in the research produced by advocacy institutions (Cookson, Molnar, & Embree, 2001; Howe, 2002).

Adding to concerns about bias in education research are issues related to the market economy tendencies evidenced in research funding and grant competitions. Because the education research funding system is essentially a market system—that is, there are limited resources available to support research, creating a competition among researchers to design projects that have the "best chance" of being funded—the demand for specific types of research could indirectly skew the body of scientific knowledge, creating a bias toward questions important to funders, irrespective of the importance of those questions to researchers or the actual value of those questions (Gowri, 2000; Spring, 1998a). For example, if funding agencies define teacher quality according to the impact of teachers on student achievement from year to year, the body of research on teacher quality may begin to neglect other equally important indicators (such as graduation rates, additional educational attainment, economic participation, self-actualization, success, etc.). Additionally, over time, the question could easily be turned into the answer: The question of how to define teacher quality becomes reduced to answers of student achievement on standardized tests. The question of achievement itself has already been transformed in this way into a limited and definitive answer, as achievement is often narrowly prefigured and famously reduced to what achievement tests are able to measure.

Even more insidious is the impact that funding might have on research design. If researchers think funders are seeking specific results, they may structure their research in the way most likely to uncover the hypothesized results. While this is not always actual misconduct, such manipulation of research design is certainly unethical and should be a concern to the research community, educators, and research consumers. Funded research is "interested" research. It is the responsibility of the university to represent independent, scholarly work that satisfies the standards of peer scrutiny and academic integrity. As an article in the *Multinational Monitor* asserts:

> Universities are unique repositories of information and expertise, and society looks to academia to provide disinterested recommendations for, and critique of, policies, technologies and products. When the autonomy of huge swaths of the university is compromised, and when open debate is displaced by corporate norms of proprietary secrecy, then society loses an important pool of potentially independent, trustworthy experts.
>
> (Corporatized university, 1997)

Academic work should not become another territory or mechanism of corporate America, nor should it serve to legitimate any single partisan ideology, yet these are real dangers for research in a wide range of disciplines, including education. As Virginia Ashby Sharpe (Integrity in Science project director for the Center for Science in the Public Interest based in Washington, DC) explains, "There are conflicts of interest when an academic researcher's primary commitment to the use of sound procedures in the unbiased search for truth is placed in competition with other [financial or personal] interests that might eclipse the primary commitment" (Paone, 2002, p. 48).

Education research may be especially vulnerable to certain types of research biases (such as market skewing and the demand of corrupt research), since education research has been historically underfunded when compared with the "hard" sciences. While education research expenditures in the United States are difficult to estimate, they seem generally to account for from 0.03% (National Education Knowledge Industry Association, 2002) to 0.001% (Shavelson & Towne, 2002) of all education expenditures (or approximately $564 million). There is a stark contrast between investment in education research and the National Science Foundation (2002) estimates of federal research expenditures for defense ($34.5 billion), health and human services ($16.4 billion), NASA ($9.7 billion), the Department of Energy ($7.5 billion), and the National Science Foundation ($2.9 billion).

An alternate reality to support the new common sense

> According to calculations made by the *Washington Post*, [Richard Mellon] Scaife gave more than $200 million to conservative institutions between 1974 and 1992 in an attempt to influence government policy and train personnel.
>
> (Brock, 2002, p. 80)

A parallel world of journals, experts, foundations, and organizations has emerged in education over the past 20 years that is gradually rising in prominence and effectiveness, particularly among media and political audiences. Correspondingly, the original structures that during the last century have organically developed out of the need of educators to meet for debate and discussion, as well as the individuals who have risen to prominence through these entities, are increasingly marginalized. These independent and institutional voices are heard within professional circles but are absent from the public sphere. At meetings of political leaders such as those of the Education Commission of the States, in prominent media such as *The New York Times* op-ed page, and even in official government documents such as the "summary" of The *Report of the National Reading Panel: Teaching children to read* (National Institute of Child Health and Human Development, 1999a), a counter-establishment of authority holds sway. Although the message may be brittle and attack-oriented, evidently it has made good media, attracted politicians, and kept the education establishment on the defensive. Foundation support has been forthcoming and, by the sheer volume and repetition of consistent messages, the right has gone a long way toward redefining the conventional wisdom about public education (Shaker & Heilman, 2002a).

Some specifics of the new common sense of education include the following: Standardized tests are the sine qua non of assessing school quality; our public schools are failed and cynical institutions; teachers are self-interested unionists; education faculty are woolly apologists for the status quo; explanations of school problems—including the impact of poverty on children—are only "excuses"; there is no correlation between school quality and school funding; the punitive imposition of high-stakes tests and centralized standards will "shape up" malingering students and teachers; research in education should exclusively follow certain quantitative models; and voucher advocates are the true sponsors of minority advancement. What is equally disturbing is that those who question this new conventional wisdom in community forums do so today at their own peril. "Conservative modernization has radically reshaped the commonsense of society" (Apple, 2001, p. 194), and it has done so while creating a structure that institutionalizes its messages.

There are numerous examples of these new institutions. Among journals there are *Education Next* and *Texas Education Review*. There are centers, think tanks, and research organizations such as the Cato Institute, Center for Education Reform, Center for Policy Studies, Center for School Change, Heartland Institute, Hudson Institute, Manhattan Institute for Policy Research, Mackinaw Center for Public Policy, Center for Research on Education Outcomes, and Pacific Research Institute. Foundations such as Abell, Heritage, Bradley, and Fordham support or themselves conduct such work. The insinuation of the right wing into the U.S. Department of Education (2002d) is particularly evident on their links page, "Where to Go," explaining, "Many of these government and non-profit groups can provide useful information about education." The department then hotlinks citizens to a list, the vast majority of which are organizations engaged in partisan "research" and policy, such as the Manhattan Institute for Policy Research, the Heritage Foundation, Mathematically Correct, the National Council on Teacher Quality, the Pacific Research Institute, and the Core Knowledge Foundation. Most recently word has come of an impending "de-accession" of much of the research archived in the Department of Education's website and the paring down of the Education Resources Information Center (ERIC). There appears little hope for such unwelcome editorial change to be in any sense representative of the research and practice found across the spectrum of work that is being done in the field of education.

Additionally, in a troubling use of federal monies, the American Board for Certification of Teacher Excellence (ABCTE) launched an alternative to the National Board for Professional Teaching Standards through a $5 million grant from the U.S. Department of Education to the National Council on Teacher Quality and the Education Leaders Council (National Council on Teacher Quality, 2002). The monies were allocated in spite of a negative peer review process. This has been followed by a dramatic infusion of Department of Education support during lean budgetary times, as ABCTE received $35 million in late 2003 just as NCLB funding was being reduced. ABCTE programs now seek also to certify new teachers, primarily through a teacher testing approach (American Association of Colleges for Teacher Education, 2003). We can find warnings of the impact of these organizations in words such as these:

> While it is possible to conduct high quality social science research in private think tanks and research centers, it is necessary that the studies be subjected to an internal review process that has integrity and that they are scrutinized by qualified and disinterested external reviewers . . . The way in which Mackinac Center sponsored research characteristically frames questions is biased and the methodology employed of little social science merit.
>
> (Cookson, Molnar, & Embree, 2001)

Scholars in reading have been asserting that such manipulations and mis-representations have invaded federal agencies and their documents, signaling a new level of success by the modernizers of the right. The National Institute of Child Health and Human Development's *Report of the National Reading Panel: Teaching children to read* (National Institute of Child Health and Human Development, 1999a) and its accompanying summary are cases in point. Writing in *Phi Delta Kappan* and *Language Arts*, Elaine Garan (2001a, 2001b, 2001c, 2001d) launched a series of exposés regarding the composition of the National Reading Panel, its curious definition of research (Cunningham, 2001), its suppression of dissent (Yatvin, 2001), and outright distortions in its summary materials (Yatvin, 2002):

> Widmeyer Communications, the powerful Washington, D.C., public rela-tions firm hired by the government to promote the panel's work . . . had rep-resented McGraw-Hill and the Business Roundtable among its most prominent clients. "They wrote the introduction to the final report," says NRP member Joanne Yatvin. "And they wrote the summary, and prepared the video, and did the press release."
>
> (Metcalf, 2002, p. 21)

This approach allowed further manipulation of the *Report*'s message and the obscuring of minority views. Garan (2001a) cites a list of clear contra-dictions between the 600-page *Reports of the subgroups* (of the NRP) and the 34-page summary. In every case a significant bias is introduced in favor of "systematic phonics instruction" (p. 506). The creation of policy and the manipulation of the policy-making environment by self-interested parties—a phenomenon we have seen rising in the energy and environmental fields—is also increasingly the order of the day in education, particularly at the federal level. In cases such as this, federal agencies are not only assuming ide-ologically charged positions, but are caught up in attempts to control the methods of research and the process of academic debate. Partisan officials employing industry lobbyists to define the study of education and to steer business to serve the interests of textbook and test publishers, among other profit-oriented parties, subsume the laborious quest of educational researchers for standards of inquiry and verification.

Kenneth Howe (2002) sees these phenomena as part of a marketing strat-egy for partisan views that "jettisons" educational research as a source of legitimate information. Instead, advocates, in a manner seemingly unbridled by professional ethics, use research, or bowdlerized research, as a "spruced up form of testimonial" (p. 34). The long-upheld ethics of peer review is com promised early in this approach, since it must either be manipulated by cre-ating a sham process or be bypassed by being discredited as a legitimizing technique. We see both strategies operating among advocates of the right:

The alliances between and among foundations, publications, and think tanks can and do create a network in which there is an evident conflict of interest in how peer review is undertaken for one another's projects. Alternately, the NRP summary example illustrates how bona fide peer review is averted: by working directly with public relations firms who define the popular media debate; by shaping the politics of decision-making; and by leaving most academicians on the fringes to dialogue with one another outside of the public's view. The ink was hardly dry on Howe's challenge when Chester E. Finn, Jr. (2002) responded with "The limits of peer review," which argues that, though "helpful," peer review is corruptible and not a "supreme arbiter of the truth" or "deserv[ing] to be deified as the one true god of education research" (p. 30). His theatrical and dichotomizing style may be more revealing than his message, as he goes on to assert that "Second and third opinions are frequently beneficial. But let's not pretend that there's something neutral, objective, or scientific about them ... key decisions should stay with the cognizant editor, funder or consumer" (p. 34). Yielding decisions to "outsiders," Finn argues, "may compromise [editors' and funders'] own publication's or organization's mission or blur its focus." The Fordham Foundation, he goes on, "sees its research mission as engaging in rather than refereeing arguments about education policy" (ibid.). One has to appreciate Finn's candor, even as confidence in his publications ebbs. Since positive science functions imperfectly in education (as well as medical circles, as he argues) one is justified in setting aside the subterfuge and knowingly using scientific forms to package advocacy. In the same issue of *Education Week*, Douglas B. Reeves (2002), while enumerating the limitations of scientific certainty in educational research, concludes with this more temperate assessment: "Real science involves ambiguity, experimentation, and error. However distasteful that trio may be, it is far superior to political agendas, uninformed prejudice and breathless enthusiasm for the flavor of the month" (p. 33).

Finn reveals another emerging strand in the evolution of the debate over education. The right has fueled so many institutions, publications, and foundations that the debates they have among themselves are beginning to rival the displeasure they have with the education establishment. Finn, for example, not only opposes conventional peer review, specifically as manifested by the American Educational Research Association and *Teachers College Record*, but he similarly disparages the commitment of the new Elementary and Secondary Education Act to scientifically proven and research-based programs. Also, while the education mainstream criticizes the National Reading Panel for the composition of its peer panel, its literature review process, and the consequent narrowness of its definition of science (Cunningham, 2001; Garan, 2001a, 2001b, 2001c; Krashen, 2001), Finn takes the conflict as further evidence that peer review is hopelessly partisan and flawed. So at a time when educators are struggling against political correctness and bias in their review process, the advocates of the right debate whether or not dropping the pretense of science and objectivity is more effective than manipulating these forms. The debate becomes more interesting as it becomes fractured into multiple positions.

Pro-market access to media and legitimization

Despite these concerns, it is the voice of the pro-market advocates that most often makes the news and enters public consciousness. The aligned interests of pro-market advocates and conservative corporate media together have tremendous influence on how education debates are presented and taken up in the public sphere. Citizens and policy-makers are given easy access to partisan, pro-market media information through popular media, while they find little access to the world of peer-reviewed research or the opinions of teacher organizations. During this same two-decade period discussed here—the post-*Nation at risk* era—the trends that have emerged in popular media parallel the recent and steady shift that can be seen in U.S. politics. Consider the following:

- The talk show world on radio and television is dominated by the likes of Robert Novak (Crossfire), the McLaughlin Group, The O'Reilly Factor, Hardball, Rush Limbaugh, and Limbaugh imitators.
- An extensive Christian radio and television system propagates the right–left rhetoric by reaching audiences who share values with Jerry Falwell, Pat Robertson, James Dobson, and other faith-based programs.
- Fox News, created by corporate giants Rupert Murdoch and Roger Ailes, is now a major force in national television newscasting. Murdoch owns a TV network, cable stations, a movie studio, 132 newspapers, and book publishers (including HarperCollins).
- Tele-Communications Inc., owned by Rush Limbaugh admirer John Malone, is the largest cable system in the United States (14 million subscribers) and has interests in 91 U.S. cable content services.

(Herman, 1997)

Major network stations also quote conservative think tanks and regularly report the pro-market party line that public schools are in crisis and drastic changes are needed. Through these media organizations, the educational "research" and policy perspectives of Diane Ravitch, Chester Finn, Lamar Alexander, William Bennett, and David Kearn are featured prominently, and their names, views, and faces are made familiar to Americans.

The new commonplace of blaming and shaming

When viewed up close, across a dinner table or from the rostrum of a local civic group, the message of the new common sense of education comes through in a more passionate, less polished manner than when emanating from the op-ed page of *The Wall Street Journal* or in an editorial from *USA Today*. In meetings and conversations among influential citizens in our towns and cities, and as reported in letters to the editor and on the local television news stations, there is a recurrent, intemperate, exaggerated critique of our public schools with the strongest sports metaphors and warfare analogies intended to make the condemnation of the schools stick. Any hint of balance or reflection is abjured in the rush of argument, and it appears that a threshold of restraint has been crossed while respect for the motives and competence of our human service professionals—in this case teachers—is disdained. Mayor Alan Autry in May 2002, for example, in testimony before the California Assembly, characterized the 80,000-student public school system in Fresno, California, as "the worst of the worst" (Maxwell, 2002, p. A–1). Like many others given airtime in the public eye, the mayor could find nothing of merit in the district, ignoring those schools that are ranked in the state's top ten in their categories and the district's many other achievements. True to the current conventional jargon, poverty, hunger, transience, homelessness, and a preponderance of non-English speakers are "excuses," not reasons, for low test scores in cities such as Fresno. The schools have not yet been blamed for the city's nationally ranked air pollution and related childhood asthma rates, but perhaps a connection can yet be found.

The characteristic, rational response of educators to this type of criticism has made little headway. Reasoned, moderate voices countering data with data and accusation with analysis seem to fall short in shaping the debate on education nationally and locally. The penchant for trashing public education and shaming teachers that has become commonplace is more than simply a feature of the current public policy debate. First, there are economic incentives to consider: There are profits to be made from the penetration of previously off-limits education markets such as school management, particularly if the government favors certain interests when the business contracts are parceled out. Second, there are political incentives to consider: There is the need of certain politicians to find an issue through which they can opportunistically advance their careers and conveniently redirect attention from other, intractable problems. In the eyes of many individual citizens, however—persons who gain no economic or political advantage from undermining public education—there is growing sympathy for these overtures from those with economic and political interests in education. Why?

One reason for the acceptance of this callous view of public education is that it has in many quarters, through repetition, become increasingly uncontroversial and familiar—similar to the way in which complaints about gray days in the Great Lakes or the smog in Los Angeles have become commonplace and, as such, no longer worthy of question or discussion. To stand against Main Street's disparagement of schools and teachers is to run the risk of being seen as disruptive to the implicit fellowship of the group. To raise questions or launch into discussion would mean derailing the small talk that is meant as a friendly, bonding expression, not to be taken too seriously.

Another possible interpretation of public acceptance of and participation in the blaming and shaming of public education is that the divisiveness that separates one group from another (in this case, teachers and non-teachers) serves to reinforce the values that are perceived as at risk. Teachers and other educators are therefore marginalized as inefficient, unambitious, economically impaired, with overly sympathetic attitudes toward the "lower" classes and, as such, lacking accountability in what they do. All this is why, the theory goes, profits, discipline, consequences, sanctions, and competition are at once undervalued and heralded as the remedies for what are announced as the failures of public education. These characterizations could be translated to many other human service fields, but none are as pervasive, as familiar, and as (supposedly) non-technical as the public schools. Furthermore, the schools have few organized, powerful defenders who rise up when they are attacked (unlike the American Medical Association and the insurance and pharmaceutical industries in the health field).

Transcending the boundaries of the current debate

Educators embody a set of professional values and ethics that present an alternative to those found on the political stage, in the market economy, and in the mainstream media messages of contemporary American society. A central message of education is that there are intellectual, moral, and aesthetic dimensions to life that coexist with material aspirations.

Education is in this sense subversive of the values of the marketplace. This is not to say that educators need be or often are socialists, extreme environmentalists, or those who have taken a vow of poverty. On the contrary, educators also have families and homes, budgets and dreams. Although it is a tenet of democratic theory that an open society requires an authentic, diverse, independent exchange of ideas for public debate, lifestyle choice, and policy-making, the voices of dissent often are heard as a threat to conventional views, rather than as evidence of a healthy democracy. Since the public media spaces of the United States are so largely taken up with the din of marketing, sales, consumerism, and advertising in general, the alternative voice of educators does take on the character of difference and dissent and, in that sense, does present a challenge to the status quo. Though the media do, in theory, present a public space for discussion that is representative of the diverse views of the public, the advertising-dependent model of mainstream media increasingly raises questions of both political and market censorship in the daily newspapers and nightly news. Programming and journalism, according to the mainstream media business model, is what fills the spaces in between the advertising and generally should support, not dilute, those messages that are paid for (incidentally, by the private interests of the corporate and political elite). In other democratic societies, public television is generously supported by the government and represents a major segment of broadcast programming. As a result, non-corporate ideas and alternative visions are readily available. In America, some theatrical films and premium cable programming address the interests and meet the market demand of viewers for alternatives to the dominant and mainstream media perspectives with such fare as *The Insider, Erin Brockovich, JFK, Traffic, The Constant Gardener*, all critical of corporate and political corruption and, as such, criticized by the corporate and political powers that be. While an occasional blockbuster and independent film and publishing houses do bring some diversity to the media spectrum, unfortunately, the dominant, mainstream media do not present an intellectually, morally, or aesthetically rich or diverse world and do not represent or reflect the identities, interests, and inquiries of the public. As well, mainstream media sources often attack, trivialize, and misrepresent the educators, activists, and artists whose professional ethics and practices provide such a vision of diversity and democracy.

Pressure to conform to society's dominant values has a much longer history than the recent movement toward diversity, which is still emergent and controversial. Education at its best is an agent of change and renewal, so it is perhaps unsurprising that, in the drumbeat of criticism of education, alarmist motivations can be heard. The alarm sounded is similar to that which ostracizes those who practice new religions or no religion, those who dress differently or otherwise ornament themselves unconventionally. Liberties such as these, the liberties of religious pluralism and cultural, artistic, or individual expression, are liberties intrinsic to the professional ethics and practices of educators. Yet, although educators are capable of defining their profession and explaining themselves in an articulate fashion that responds to a climate of criticism, truly effective ways and means of presenting their message have not yet been put into practice. The current reserved and reasoned response seems inadequate and, of course, defensive. There is a need for symbolic action by coalitions of educators, as well as rational discourse. There is a need for analysis that transcends the boundaries of the current debate and helps restore education to a position of civic and moral leadership in our society.

To accomplish this, a critical analysis of the motives, methods, and rhetoric of federal education policy is imperative, as these policies do not represent the best recommendations of educational research or theory, or the values of many states, teachers, parents, or students. Many respected educators and researchers have critiqued these policies and have pointed to a vast body of educational research that offers better ways to promote learning and more suitable rationales for research and for education in a democratic society (Apple, 2001; Darling-Hammond, 2001; Drew, 2000; Kohn, 2002; Shaker & Heilman, 2002a; Spring, 2002). Yet, in spite of the widespread critique by teachers, researchers, and theorists, the above-described policies have been enacted and will have a vast influence on education.

Ultimately, these new common-sense polices need to be understood as ideologically and politically constructed entities, rather than policies that have emerged out of educational research on best practices or the support of communities. The discourse is what Carlson (1993) describes as "hegemonic policy discourse—that represents the worldview and interests of the dominant political coalition" (p. 149). This coalition is powerful, as are the ideologies upon which it is based. The wide, often symbolic appeal of an American cultural and ideological environment of modernist, authoritative, and pro-market concepts reinforces the success of "common-sense" standards, accountability, discipline, and a market economy in education. The rhetoric of the new policy is further reinforced by the ways in which it makes reference to democratic equity through high quality education. These last concepts are rightfully popular, but have been co-opted and misused. For recent federal policy to be successfully challenged, the ideological content and methods of achieving power *and* the soundness of the actual policies need to be examined. As educational researchers, we have often focused on the latter at the expense of the former. Much of the literature critiquing federal policy relates to its specific content, exploring educational claims on their own terms and the effects of policy implementation. Policies are most often examined piece by piece instead of being understood as a set of ideological assumptions, or as political strategy. Given the scarcity of critical attention to how these policies have come about and subsequently achieved national implementation, this chapter has sought to raise critical questions about their axiological and ideological foundations and the broader cultural, political, and economic contexts that have contributed to the creation and acceptance of the current policy. Educators should find a deep passion for this debate.

Chapter 2

Policy as propaganda
A critical examination of NCLB

This chapter will examine recent federal education policy, specifically NCLB, to analyze its ideological positioning and the ways that its language and symbols are co-opted from other domains and used in turn. NCLB needs to be understood not just as a set of institutional changes but more deeply as an attempt to redirect the public's view on the nature and purpose of the public schools. Based on this idea, this chapter contends that, beyond its practical soundness and appropriateness, the ideological rhetoric underlying the Act needs further attention.

The very title "No Child Left Behind" is an appropriation of Marion Wright Edelman's slogan "Leave no child behind," used for her work with the Children's Defense Fund. Commenting on NCLB, and the fact that most urban schools are making no progress in reducing the achievement gap between white and minority students, Edelman said in January of 2006:

> Our children have been hijacked and shackled by bad policy and bad poli-
> tics ... This nation has squandered away four years and billions of dollars
> in education funding. Our children have been tested to death, forced to
> regurgitate and at the end of the day they haven't learned to do basic read-
> ing and math or much less learned to think. It's a national shame.
>
> (Levister, 2006)

Yet, most Americans seem to have a better opinion of the policies, in part because of Wright's slogan. While opinion polls suggest most people actually know few specifics of NCLB, many broad slogans and buzz words in the law have wide support. A poll conducted in January 2004 for the National Education Association (NEA) by one Republican firm and one Democratic firm showed that "Most Americans fully support the goals of the law—high standards, accountability for all, and the belief that no child should be left behind regardless of their background or abilities" (National Education Association, 2004). According to this NEA poll, 37% of respondents said the law was a positive one, while only 21% said it was negative. Yet, the largest segment, 42%, said either they didn't know about NCLB or that it was too soon to judge. The combination of lack of knowledge about the legislation and a general sense that things such as accountability and making sure nobody is left behind are good ideals in effect constitutes a rhetorical coup for the right. The public is just beginning to awaken to the disturbing details of the law.

When parents and educators are lulled by rhetoric and a confusing maze of seemingly positive accountability requirements, their capacity for resistance and protest is significantly diminished. It is important to trace the co-optation of concepts, words, and social myths, since opinion-poll support for policies like these is often not true support but occurs largely because citizens respond to the language, to the surface-level symbols and myths employed. Also, most people have multiple interests and concerns. One purpose of rhetoric (particularly in a political arena) is to craft and mobilize an effective majority out of disparate and idiosyncratic forces and interests that operate within groups, regions, and individuals and their networks. As Downey (1999) explains, "one of the basic properties of political symbols is that their meaning is not interpretable objectively from the nature or content of the symbol itself" (p. 252). Furthermore, "through symbols, movements can appeal to diverse groups, interests, and individuals for different and even incompatible reasons. It is not homogeneity of motivations, but commonality of affective sentiment that unites them" (Elder & Cobb 1983, p. 116). NCLB invokes multiple familiar myths, each with its own emotional appeal. These include democratic equity, individual economic success, national economic dominance, an appreciation for science and modernity, and the need to respect authority. The persuasive language and symbols of NCLB include concepts and terms such as fairness, equity, scientific, freedom, quality, qualified, excellence, security, standards, accountability, achievement, proficiency and values.

A fundamental political myth that mobilizes its activists and supporters forms the core of an ideological message. The term "political myth" in this context does not refer merely to specific historical myths exploited in order to legitimate policies. Rather, it denotes the irrational mainspring of all ideologies irrespective of their surface rationality or apparent "common sense." As Namier (1955) observed, "what matters most are the underlying emotions" (p. 4). The ideological and philosophical foundations or "spirit" of NCLB invokes multiple familiar myths, each with its own emotional appeal. These include children's rights, democratic equity, economic and global hegemony, modernism, and authoritarianism.

First: What is NCLB?

> To ensure that all children have a *fair, equal* and *significant opportunity* to obtain a high-quality education and reach, at a minimum, *proficiency* on challenging State [*sic*] academic achievement standards and state academic *assessments*.
>
> (Section 1001)

On January 8, 2002, President George W. Bush signed into law the reenactment of the Elementary and Secondary Education Act (ESEA), which funds 10 federal programs, the largest of which is Title I. The purposes of this federal policy and the state policies it generates are to create a comprehensive system of standards, testing, and accountability and then, based on the results, give federal money as rewards or impose sanctions through withdrawal of federal funds, pressure for privatization, and public school choice. The four supposedly guiding principles of this legislation are accountability, parental and student choice, flexibility, and scientifically based research (Corwin, 2003). All students in grades 3 through 8 are to be tested in reading and math, with testing in science added in 2005. All students must demonstrate "proficiency" in 12 years (by 2013–2014). Not only is student testing now mandatory, but NCLB also requires the results be reported by student subgroups. Subgroups include Special Education, English-Language Learners, Economically Disadvantaged, White, Hispanic, Asian, African-American, and Native-American students.

Schools are required to attain "adequate yearly progress" (AYP) towards proficiency. To make AYP, all public schools must meet both achievement targets and participation requirements. Subgroups of students must meet statewide proficiency targets in reading and math, which are known as annual measurable objectives (AMO), and 95% of all subgroups must take the reading and math test. Subgroups will be considered for AYP if they have more than 30 students at the particular level (i.e., school, district, or state).

If scores are not high enough, let's say for 30 bilingual children, a school can be sanctioned and required to "shift resources and change personnel." It can be closed, merged with another school, or assigned a special management team, including a for-profit company to operate all or part of the school. When a school fails to make AYP two years in a row, they create a school improvement plan and implement "effective programs" and comprehensive school improvement models, and integrate extended services. Parents have the option to enroll their children in another school or in tutoring services. In the third year, the stage of corrective action, staff can be removed, curricula mandated, management authority revoked, and instructional time extended. Should a school linger and fail to make AYP for yet one more year, major restructuring is to occur via reconstitution, state takeover, conversion into a charter, transfer to a private management company, or other, similarly radical measures. To summarize major goals targeted by NCLB:

- All students will reach high standards, at a minimum attaining proficiency or better in reading and mathematics, by 2013–2014.
- Within 12 years, all students must perform at a proficient level under their state standards.
- By 2013–2014, all students will be proficient in reading by the end of the third grade.

- All limited English proficient students will become proficient in English.
- By 2005–2006, all students will be taught by highly qualified teachers.
- All students will be educated in learning environments that are safe, drug free, and conducive to learning.
- All students will graduate from high school.

To help schools and districts meet these goals, the law provides a blend of requirements, resources, and sanctions. The requirements include:

- the responsibility of schools for improving the academic performance of all students; technical assistance and extra resources are offered first and then sanctions imposed for schools, districts and the state for failure to make AYP.
- "verification" of each state's assessment system via required participation (every other year) by selected districts in the National Assessment of Educational Progress (NAEP) test
- aggregate and disaggregate analysis and reporting of student achievement results
- a state definition and timeline for determining whether a school, a district, and the state are making AYP toward the goal of 100% of students meeting state standards by the 2013–2014 school year
- highly qualified aides or paraprofessionals
- the use of "scientifically based" programs and strategies
- the accountability of the district or school if it continually fails to make adequate progress toward the standards,
- the inclusion in each state accountability system of sanctions and rewards.

Corrective sanctions in the final stage include reopening the school as a charter school; replacing the principal and staff; contracting for a private management company of demonstrated effectiveness; and state takeover.

NCLB is fair and democratic

One of the great ironies of NCLB comes from its use of the language of democracy, particularly as it evokes fairness. As the 14th amendment to the Constitution states, "No State shall make or enforce any law which shall abridge the privileges or immunities of citizens of the United States; nor shall any State deprive any person of life, liberty, or property, without due process of law; nor deny to any person within its jurisdiction the equal protection of the laws." This is a core democratic principle and it is related to a core democratic myth that everyone should have an equal chance in a democracy. Much of the language of NCLB makes reference to the democratic principle of equal opportunity in acknowledgement of a diverse society. Consider the following: The purpose of NCLB is to ensure that all children have a fair, equal, and significant opportunity to obtain a high-quality education and reach, at a minimum, proficiency on challenging ... academic achievement standards and academic assessment.

This program provides extra resources to help improve instruction in high-poverty schools and ensure that poor and minority, homeless, migrant, dis-advantaged, Limited English Proficient, and disabled children all have the same opportunity as other children to meet challenging state academic standards.

State assessment systems must produce results disaggregated by gender, major racial and ethnic groups, English proficiency, migrant status, disability, and status as economically advantaged.

In this law, "all children have a fair, equal, and significant opportunity to obtain a high-quality education" in actuality means that all children will have to meet minimum proficiency on state standardized tests or face serious consequences personally, and collectively as a member of their school, if they do not. However, the NCLB law does not support multiculturalism and lacks a commitment to the redistribution of key educational, economic, and cultural resources needed for an equitable society. In the ideology of radical egalitarianism, the true racists are the ones who bring up the idea of difference. This legislation is deeply homogenizing and ultimately favors a sort of color blindness by sloganeering of words such as "equality" in order to obscure the underlying issues such as equity. A policy of equality gives every child the same thing—in this case children get the same test and receive the same consequences for failure to meet standards. A policy of equity gives every child what they need in acknowledgement of widely divergent circumstances. The focus of the legislation is for all children to meet common standards. Aspects of difference are viewed primarily as obstacles to meeting common goals. It denies the value and authenticity of language and cultural differences that are featured in a culturally responsive curriculum and denies aspects of difference that influence performance on standardized tests.

Not left behind? Is it a race?

The idea of being left behind suggests that education is a sort of race or competition, or at least that education is one factor in part of the great competitive race to get a job and get ahead. This alone bears some scrutiny. The legislation doesn't aim to leave no child uneducated or without critical thinking capacity. This suggests an interpretation of education as a functional good in a race rather than an intrinsic good. Views about education have changed considerably in the last several decades along with the increased competition for jobs.

Perhaps paradoxically, an increasingly stratified economy has resulted in more, rather than fewer, adolescents receiving encouragement to go to college. According to data from the National Center for Educational Statistics, the immediate college (two- or four-year) enrollment rate among high school graduates increased between 1972 and 2004 from 49% to 67%. In 1982, 32% of sophomores were encouraged to go to college; by 1992, 66% were (Gray, 1996). At the same time many of these college graduates will not find professional jobs. Indeed, our current economic structure can't sustain many more people competing for high-wage jobs, since this competition tends to depress salaries, not to mention morale. The National Council for Educational Statistics conducted a survey that showed that 69% of high school sophomore girls expected to be employed in the professions by the age of 30. Aware of difficult job markets, counselors and parents are pressuring adolescents to reach the upper ranks. However, in spite of pressure, most of these ambitions will be frustrated as, although the "knowledge economy" is highly touted, the economy will continue to offer more low- and medium-skilled jobs than high-skilled and professional jobs. In the U.S. Bureau of Labor Statistics (2007) report of the fastest growing occupations between 2004 and 2014, six of the 10 professions do not require a four-year degree, and four of these call for no academic degree at all. Many college graduates are employed in these "high job growth" areas such as retail sales waiters, customer service representatives, janitors, and healthcare aides. One third of all graduates of four-year colleges will not find work requiring a college degree. Up to two thirds of those who enroll in college will not complete a degree (Gray, 2004). The experience can leave students demoralized and in debt. Looking forward to working life can be particularly difficult for young women, and concern for gender equity is startlingly absent from NCLB. In 2005, full-time working women earned only 77 cents for each dollar earned by full-time working men. The rhetoric and related policies of not being left behind in a single race both capitalizes on very real economic fears and fails to prepare students for real and diverse needs of both workers and the economy.

Also, the NCLB law denies the profound nature of structural obstacles such as inequitable school funding and the effects of family and community poverty. The myriad ways in which poverty effects educational, psycho-social, and physical development are disregarded. There are provisions for "extra resources to improve instruction," but these are minimal and cannot begin to address effects of poverty and profound inequity. It has been reported that African-American and Latino students have to drill simple skills and facts to increase test scores in order to escape sanctions, while students in affluent schools are enjoying enriched and intellectually rigorous education (Lipman, 2004). One of the consequences of this racial result is differentiated access to the job market. The U.S. Department of Labor reported in 2006 that the jobless rate among black 16- to 24-year-olds was

35.8%, nearly seven times the overall national average. Pushing students to prove high performance without support to compensate social inequities cannot decrease the inequities. It is more likely to widen the gap between the rich majority and poor minority students in terms of their access to curriculum and the job market.

Thus, we may conclude that the race driven by NCLB is not fair; students do not start from the same line. Some students get more support from their families and schools whereas others are struggling not to be left behind. NCLB is more likely to perpetuate this social inequity instead of helping poor and minority students. Also, the promised result for winners seems to be unrealistic; the current economic structure may not provide a substantially greater number of high-wage jobs in the short term. As a result, NCLB may not contribute to making America more equitable and democratic. It is more likely to stratify American society according to race, class, and gender.

"Economic freedom is good" through neoliberalism

Another featured ideology in current federal education policy is hegemonic capitalism, although proponents of the policies would use much more subtle terminology such as "pro-market thinking." Hegemonic capitalism refers to a system in which most aspects of society are privately owned and where production is guided and income is distributed through the operation of markets and with a desire to maximize profits. This system uses economic, political, and cultural power to maintain and increase its reach. The NCLB law highlights "economic leadership" as a core curricular goal.

> A high-quality education system is essential for America's future prosperity. Today's students will, within a few years, participate in our political system and our economy.
>
> (U.S. Department of Education, 2003b)

> We must improve achievement to maintain our economic leadership. While technology advances with lightning speed, stagnant math performance in schools shortchanges our students' future and endangers our prosperity and our nation's security.
>
> (U.S. Department of Education, 2003d)

> America's schools are not producing the science excellence required for global economic leadership and homeland security in the 21st century.
>
> (U.S. Department of Education, 2003e)

In this legislation, the interests of the undemocratically administered economy are understood to be fully compatible with the interests of the state.

Under current federal policy, the idea of educating students for thoughtful participation in a democracy is muted. Instead, education is understood to be a means of serving the economy or vested interests. Thus, the law straightforwardly explains, "The Higher Education Community recognizes that it has a vested interest in working to improve elementary and secondary math and science achievement" (U.S. Department of Education, 2003h).

We are using the term "hegemony" both in its literal sense, in which it means "the domination of one state over its allies" (Wordnet, 1997; http://dictionary.reference.com), and in its sociological sense. The expression of capitalism in the NCLB law is hegemonic because it refers not just to national capitalism but to economic leadership, or dominance, over other countries. Within sociology, hegemony also means "the power exercised by one social group over another" or, more particularly, "the ideological [and] cultural domination of . . . [various social groups by another group] achieved by engineering consensus through controlling the content of cultural forms and major institutions" (Jary & Jary, 1991, p. 271). Also, capitalism is encroaching upon the public institution of education in both content and form. In this law, principles of capitalism are favoured not only for the man-ufacturing sector but for education as well, which has historically been a public enterprise. Increased involvement of private ownership in education is a key feature of new federal policy. In order to improve schools that fail to make adequate progress, the federal government supports a wide range of plans that are generally known as pro-market or pro-privatization. For example, when a school is identified for improvement after it has not made adequate yearly progress for two consecutive school years, "all students are offered public school choice" in year 1. By year 4 the school may reopen as a charter school or contract for a private management company. Pro-market theory assumes that a system based on competition and minimal regulation will result in better quality education at a lower cost. This deregulatory ide-ology also promotes the removal or reduction of teacher certification and accreditation requirements and the removal of collective bargaining agree-ments. Though these measures are often described as offering "freedom" to children and parents, a clear motive of these changes is for the private sector to have access to the $536 billion annual spending on K–12 education. Furthermore, education is articulated not as a right of the citizen, but as a national economic investment. When the federal government invests in edu-cation it wants to see a return. Recall that George W. Bush explained, "in return for a lot of money, the federal government, for the first time, is ask-ing, are we getting the kind of return the American people want for every child?" (Bush, 2003).

In order to make sure the government is getting its return on its invest-ment, schools must be held accountable. Economic logic is not only high-lighted in the curriculum, as described above, but it is also used to diagnose problems with education and suggest reforms. U.S. Secretary of Education Rod Paige explains: "The great companies confronted the realities of their situation in the marketplace, and they changed their entire system of operating in response. I believe our schools must do the same" (U.S. Department of Education, 2003k). The federal government's relationship to states and schools is one of measurement, surveillance, and punishment. The core logic behind accountability reform comes, however, from the economic sector, in which the term refers to getting one's money's worth.

The whole purported appeal of school vouchers, as extolled by Milton Friedman and his many disciples, including John Chubb and Terry Moe, is that they are supposed to bypass government bureaucracies. Parents "empowered" with vouchers will on their own have the incentives to seek out the best schools for their children without any public agencies intervening. Competition will induce schools, like automakers or airlines, to innovate and demonstrate their superiority to attract "customers". With no oversight intruding from on high in the virtuous cauldron of competition, better outcomes will inevitably emerge.

A significant contradiction, however, lies under the myth of reforming schools according to neoliberalism. The Florida ruling held that the voucher scheme there violated a provision in the state constitution that says: "Adequate provision shall be made by law for a uniform, efficient, safe, secure, and high quality system of free public schools." Because private voucher schools are exempt from most of the requirements imposed on public schools, including standardized tests (though parents are obligated to have their kids assessed) and teacher credentialing rules, they aren't "uniform." They can't be, because they aren't accountable to the state or the public.

Clearly, NCLB is the embodiment of contradictions and tensions within the evolving neoliberal models of education. Whereas one of the basic premises of neoliberal market forces is 'small government,' educators and community members across the country are experiencing a relentless assault on their autonomy when it comes to participating in purported democratic decision-making processes. Federally engineered testing and accountability systems, instructional program mandates, and the forced militarization of our public high schools point towards highly regulated and controlled governing systems. At the end of the year, every public school child in grades 3 to 8 will experience standardized testing that was developed with an estimated price-tag of 2.7 to 7 billion dollars (as cited in Metcalf, 2002).

Science leads to modern progress

The free market economic sector is often mythologized as being an inherently rational system in which the fittest or the best survive. In this vision of economic Darwinism, capitalism is part of modern progress. And, in this legislation, the myth of modernity is closely tied to the myth of economic Darwinism. Modernity adopts the ideology of science, progress, order, and rationality that emerged in the Enlightenment. According to modernist ideology, there is a stable, coherent, knowable self who comprehends and orders the world through reason or rationality. The mode of knowing produced by the objective rational self is "science," which can provide universal truths about the world. In this belief system, anything of importance can be known and measured through science. Also, in a world governed by reason, "the true will always be the same as the good and the right" and "the knowledge/truth produced by science will always lead toward progress and perfection" (Klages, 1997). The new federal policies may owe some of their success to wide cultural support for modernist ideas that have become culturally entrenched since the turn of the modern era, an era in which science is seen as saviour of society. Policies focusing on "facts," "science," and "standards" seem obviously good to many citizens.

In contrast, critical theorists and postmodern philosophers suggest that progress is a social construct, which should be questioned. Progress is understood and used in different ways in different contexts toward different ends. Any "benefits" of progress are culturally relative and are distributed with deep and increasing inequality (consider the cost and consequences of "progress" in terms of cultural and personal degradation and vast environmental exploitation). Certainly, science and technology have improved medicine and industrial production, but they have also created nuclear and biological threats and weapons of mass destruction. Examples such as these may seem to make critical theory self-evident, yet deeply modernist logic prevails. Such logic is difficult to reconcile with postmodern intellectual culture in which the meta-narratives of truth, reason, and progress have been called into question and thoroughly deconstructed (Lyotard, 1979/1984; Best & Keller, 1997, 2001).

In the NCLB law, modernity is expressed in two key ways. First, as the above quotes highlighted, curricula for math, literacy, technology, and science are especially supported. More broadly, however, the entire enterprise of education is viewed as a scientific process or, as described earlier, a credentialing process, not as a humanistic endeavor. With a modernist scientific view of education, complex concepts become simple. In particular, the complex concept of good curriculum is reduced to scientific curriculum; and the complex concepts of improving teaching and learning are reduced to improving data on student achievement. For a detailed discussion on this topic, see chapter 5 of this book.

Authoritarianism: An approximation of "fascism"

The increased power of state and national curriculum directives is reinforced by high-stakes testing, which focuses education on the authority of the standards and on the production of uniformity of performance which itself is authoritarian. Such policy positions teachers primarily as implementers of content and pedagogy as defined by the standards. Rather than making their own choices, both teachers and students obey the logic of others' choices and produce good scores. Rather than creating and exploring knowledge, they are transmitting, performing, and producing it as a static good. As Delandshere and Petrosky (2004) have asserted:

> Alignment, consensus, and consistency through bureaucratic and authoritarian control is antithetical to learning, inquiry, and true democratic participation. Legislating a set of predefined standards for which teacher education programs and prospective teachers are accountable in essence defines the learning of teachers in very specific ways ... Standards-based teacher education imposes on teachers and their learning a fixed political will that shapes their capacities, who they become as teachers, and positions them primarily as implementers of content and pedagogy as defined by the standards.
>
> (pp. 6–7)

Thus, another philosophical strand of recent federal education legislation is authoritarianism with elements of fascistization. Fascistization refers to a nation or aspect of government that begins approximation of "fascism" but has not adopted full fascist ideology or government. Though clearly the American federal government does not overtly advocate an authoritarian form of government, or the victimization of a despised group, or seek a revolution, there is increasing evidence of the penetration of authoritarian ideology and strategies. The recently passed "anti-terrorism" Patriot Act is a widely familiar example. The Act gives the government new powers to criminalize dissent and suppress the struggles of the people. It also increases the arbitrary power of the police to spy and keep files on any and every American, ranging from the books they buy to the websites they visit. In federal education policy there are many signs of fascistization as well. These include the creation or exploitation of crises to consolidate internal power, the tendency to contextualize problems within a moral critique of culture and society and vision for rebirth, the erosion of civil liberties, a heightened focus on surveillance, an emphasis on obedience as a core civic virtue, increased militarism, an undermining of the separation of church and state, and increasingly symbiotic connections between government and economic power.

For example, the entire federal education program is based on the diagnosis of a profound crisis in education. Yet, despite the drumbeat of mainstream media, public education is not failing. Berliner and Biddle (1995) have carefully documented the alleged failure, beginning with the publication of *The manufactured crisis: Myths, fraud, and the attack on America's public schools*. (More recently, Nichols and Berliner [2007], in *Collateral Damage*, have continued this narrative by illustrating the costs of the false diagnosis.) Gerald Bracey, in his monthly department, "Research," in *Phi Delta Kappan*, also regularly presents convincing evidence to support an objective appraisal of our schools. Yet, blaming economic troubles on failing schools and low test scores continues to be an extremely effective strategy. As fascist theorist Georges Sorel believed, societies naturally became decadent and disorganized, and this inevitable decay could best be managed by the leadership of idealists who were willing to use oppressive measures to control unruly citizens and solidify power. Both schools in general and children in particular are characterized as in need of discipline:

> If children do not learn proper values and behavior when they are very young, problems can develop. These problems can mushroom with serious consequences as children grow older—dropping out of school, drug use, teenage pregnancy, violent crime—the list goes on.
>
> (U.S. Department of Education, 2003a)

Obeying the rules with a spirit of patriotism

As the introduction to *The character education handbook* explains, "The cornerstone of the *No Child Left Behind Act of 2001* is academic achievement and professional success built upon a foundation of moral strength and civic virtue" (Dotson & Wisont, 2001).

As Secretary of Education Margaret Spellings has said, "We must not simply teach children how to count, we must teach them what counts." Also, as President Bush pointed out in his New Hampshire speech:

> The real problem comes, not when children challenge the rules, but when adults won't defend the rules. And for about three decades, many American schools surrendered this role. Values were "clarified," not taught. Students were given moral puzzles, not moral guidance ... Our goal is to encourage clear instruction in right and wrong.
>
> (Bush, 1999a)

Under a fascist education system the will is both prior and superior to intellect or reason. Similarly, Bush questions critical thinking and supports instead obedience to eternal truths: "The right to life, liberty and the pursuit of happiness is not a personal opinion, but an eternal truth" (Bush, 1999b). Social studies is the only core curriculum area that is not mandated to be tested. The only time it is mentioned in the legislation, it is disparaged. Patriotism is specifically encouraged. "Any local district that discriminates against or denies equal access to patriotic organizations, such as the Boy Scouts of America, is denied funds" (U.S. Department of Education, 2002e). The specific mention of the boy scouts is interesting because some schools have elected not to host the boy scouts since they passed a policy disallowing the participation of homosexuals. There have also been movements to require school children to take the Pledge of Allegiance and for the national motto "in God We Trust" to be posted in classrooms and school buildings.

The U.S. Department of Education has sponsored mass recitations of hundreds of thousands of students declaiming the Pledge of Allegiance "in one voice" (one on October 12, 2001, another on September 17). Secretary of Education, Rod Paige announced:

> Today, I ask students, teachers, parents and other proud Americans across the country to join me in showing our patriotism by reciting the Pledge of Allegiance at a single time and with a unified voice this Friday ... Together, we can send a loud and powerful message that will be heard around the world: America is 'one nation, under God, indivisible, with liberty and justice for all.'
>
> (U.S. Department of Education, 2003i)

A court case arose from a parent seeking to stop his child's school from having students recite the pledge. The judge held the pledge itself to be unconstitutional, not merely the practice of having students recite it, to the fury of Rod Paige, who said the decision "staggers the imagination" (http://www.ed.gov/PressReleases/06-2002/06272002.html).

Often, patriotism, God, hegemony, capitalism, and democratic equity are merged in single statements, as these quotes from President Bush's addresses illustrate:

> We're a nation of patriots. The attacks of September 11th, and the attacks that have followed, were designed to break our spirit. But instead, they've created a new spirit in America. We have a renewed spirit of patriotism. We see it in the countless flags that are flying everywhere in America. We hear it in familiar phrases that move us more deeply than ever before. We all know that this is one nation, under God. And we pray that God will bless America, the land that we all love, regardless of our race, regardless of our religion, regardless of where we live. ... This is a nation that is resolved to win. And win we must, not only for your generation, but for generations to come.
>
> (U.S. Department of Education, 2003j)

> People who don't have hope can find hope, people who wonder about the American Dream will realize the American experience is meant for them. And one way to ensure that is to unleash the armies of compassion that exist

all across the country. As far as I'm concerned, the federal government will be a welcoming agency. We will allow faith-based programs to compete, side-by-side, with secular programs, all aimed at making sure America is the greatest country possible for every single citizen.

(U.S. Department of Education, 2003g)

As Jane Mansbridge (1990a) describes, "adversary democracy" assumes that the interests of the citizens conflict, that there is no common good or public interest. The notion of democracy that we saw above is based on the clear division between "them" and "us." Instead of encouraging open-mindedness toward multiple perspectives and diverse interpretations, it asks us to select a specific side. It assumes that we are in conflict with other views, denying the possibility of tolerance and conversation. As a result, under a narrowly defined concept of democracy, teachers and students are forced to prove their loyalties to America, or, more exactly, to blindly follow the regulated moral rules and standards. In this concept of democracy, critical reflection and active reasoning is almost invisible.

However, there is another notion of democracy which is deeper and more humanistic. Mansbridge (1990a) points out that

A second, older form of democracy, which can be called "unitary," "communal" or "deliberative" democracy[,] assumes common interests among the citizens. This form of democracy derives its legitimation from reasoning. Its procedure is deliberation. In a deliberative democracy, citizens reason together until they come up with a policy that fits their needs.

(p. 22)

This form of democracy, which would be advocated by Dewey, is also supported by a number of modern theorists. According to Mansbridge (1990b),

Many contemporary democratic theorists, most notably Benjamin Barber in *Strong Democracy*, but also Hanna Pitkin and others[,] have stressed transformation of self and polity through communal deliberation. Recent influential "communitarian" theorists, such as Michael Sandel and Charles Taylor, put collective attributes at the core of individual identity, pointing out that the self must always be "situated" and "encumbered," and that many goods, like language[,] are "irreducibly social."

(p. 145)

Dewey believed that education should be a process of living and not a preparation for an imagined future. In "My pedagogic creed," Dewey believes that, in a community oriented school, each student will "act as a member of a unity, to emerge from his original narrowness of action and feeling and to conceive of himself from the standpoint of the welfare of the group to which he belongs" (Dewey, 1929). It seems obvious that the citizenship regulated by recent civic education goes against this idea of active, deliberative democracy.

Discipline and surveillance

In addition, the state advocates new levels of surveillance. Students will be labeled and watched as never before. For example, NCLB explains that "The Federal Education Rights and Privacy Act (FERPA) has been amended to make it easier for public school districts and local law enforcement authorities to share information regarding disciplinary actions and misconduct by students" (American Association of School Administrators, 2003). A "comprehensive incident database makes it easier to manage resources and complete state and Federal incident reports" (National Council for Educational Statistics, 2002). The federal government asserts its legal right not to protect children's rights, but, instead, to protect the rights of teachers and schools to punish and invade. NCLB allows "Teachers, principals, and school board members acting in their official capacity [to] be shielded from federal liability arising out of their efforts to maintain discipline in the classroom, so long as they do not engage in reckless or criminal misconduct." In a 1999 speech entitled "The true goals of education," George W. Bush asserted, "The days of timid pleading and bargaining and legal haggling with disruptive students must be over."

This situation brings to mind Foucault's (1977) Panopticon, the all-seeing eye capable of watching all areas at once, thus ensuring compliance and control. This surveillance takes the form of an all-powerful adult gaze. Students are aware of their records for testing and behavior and are encouraged to participate in self-surveillance. For Foucault, the Panopticon metaphorically represents the ultimate achievement of Western European societies, which have, he argues, moved from exacting physical punishments on the body to producing disciplined subjects through discourse.

This policy encourages teachers not to spare the rod. Of historical note, the word fascism comes from the word 'fasces,' which is a bundle of rods around an axe carried by the magistrates in ancient Rome as a symbol of power and authority. Project Sentry provides $20 million for new state prosecutors and community task forces to combat juvenile gun crime. Having military personnel in the classroom, it is envisioned, will improve discipline, and Bush's "Troops-to-Teachers" program provides $30 million to recruit former military personnel to America's classrooms (http://www.ed.gov/programs/troops/index.html). Also, Section 9528 of the NCLB law "grants the Pentagon access to directories with students' names, addresses, and phone numbers so that they may be more easily contacted and recruited for military service. Prior to this provision, one-third of the nation's high schools refused recruiters' requests for students' names or access to campus because they believed it was inappropriate for educational institutions to promote military service" (Wells, 2002).

Yet, teachers will also be labeled and watched. "Information" and "quality" labeling will be required for all teachers. "Local districts, upon request, will be required to disclose to parents information about the quality of their child's teacher, as defined by the state" (U.S. Department of Education, 2002f). Perhaps a "good" teacher is one who treats all children with suspicion. After all, as *The Nation* recently noted, "Liz Armstrong, a high school biology teacher near Richmond, Virginia, was fired for objecting when administrators entered her classroom without suspicion and searched students for drugs and weapons" (Nichols, 2001). As "in the Tinker case thirty-two years ago, Justice Abe Fortas said public schools cannot be 'enclaves of totalitarianism.' Yet too many schools are that today—as the Armstrong case illustrates" (ibid.).

Also relevant is Secretary of Education Rod Paige's remark in February 2004 that the largest teacher's union, the 2.7 million-member National Education Association, is a "terrorist organization" (King, 2004).

Conclusion

Many respected educators and researchers have critiqued these policies and have pointed to a vast body of educational research which suggests that there are better ways to promote learning and more suitable rationales for research and for education in a democratic society (Apple, 2001; Darling-Hammond, 2001; Drew, 2000; Kohn, 2002; Poetter, 1998; Shaker & Heilman, 2002b). Yet, in spite of the widespread critique of teachers, researchers, and theorists, the above-described policies have been enacted and are exerting a vast influence on education. A critical analysis of federal education policy is imperative, as these policies do not represent the best of recommendations of educational research or theory, or the values of many teachers, parents, and students. They are ideologically and politically constructed policies, rather than policies that have emerged out of educational research on best practices, or the support of communities. The discourse is what Carlson (1993) describes as "hegemonic policy discourse—that represents the worldview and interests of the dominant political coalition" (p. 149). Yet they are powerful.

Furthermore, the ideologies to which they make reference are also powerful. The broader American cultural and ideological environment in which modernist, authoritative, and pro-market concepts have a wide symbolic appeal reinforces the success of standards, accountability, discipline, and a market economy in education. The rhetoric of the new policy is further reinforced by the ways in which it makes reference to democratic equity and to high quality education. Both of these concepts are very popular, but have been co-opted and misused. The anti-democratic elements of privatization are often hard for people to see. It can be difficult for people to notice that high quality education is being defined as meeting minimum performance on state standardized tests. It is certainly difficult for people to understand that this policy rewards high performing schools and punishes the most vulnerable members of society when the very name of the policy has been adapted from the Children's Defense Fund (CDF)—a group that truly fights for justice for children and has proposed the Act to Leave No Child Behind. The CDF points out that *"the president's similarly named education bill fails to give poor children what they need to succeed"* (2003).

In order for policies to be successfully challenged, both the ideological content and the functionality of policies need to explored. Rhetorical strategies and word use need to be closely examined so that the true implications of policy can more readily be revealed. As educational researchers, we have often focused on the latter at the expense of the former. Much of the literature critiquing federal policy relates to its specific content, exploring educational claims on their own terms and the effects of implementation of policy. Policies are most often examined piece by piece instead of being understood as a set of ideological or philosophical assertions, or as curriculum or social theory. Given the scarcity of critical attention to how these policies have reached national implementation, this chapter has sought to raise critical questions about their intellectual and ideological foundations and the broader cultural, political, and economic contexts which have contributed to their acceptance.

Chapter 3

The cultural psychology of the right

> As scientists would be the first to insist, rational *logos* cannot address questions of ultimate meaning that lie beyond the reach of empirical inquiry. Confronted with the genocidal horrors of our century, reason has nothing to say.
>
> (Armstrong, 2001, p. 365)

There is a back and forth quality to the advancement of human societies. A general reflection on history suggests that Dark Ages as well as Renaissance alternate in the spiral flow of civilization. On a smaller, less dramatic scale we see this ebb and flow in the evolution of society from generation to generation. Whether the political system is traditional and autocratic or a variation on the modern and democratic state, in the manner of waves on the beach, progressive ideas lap forward and then pull back, creating a moving line of popular consensus about the basic values and tone of society. In recent U.S. history, this ebb and flow has normally commonly been identified as the shift between the radical years characterized as the 1960s, followed by the Reagan Revolution, of which George W. Bush is a fulfillment. Reaching back another half century, the commercial boom of the 1920s—during which the "business of America was business"—culminated in economic dislocation and a New Deal that was, arguably, the most progressive moment in U.S. history, save perhaps the revolutionary period.

These social and political oscillations generate explanations from the perspective of economics, science and technology, and political theory, and from across the spectrum of other disciplines. A common example of this pattern from the point of view of science is discussion on the role of the birth-control pill in the countercultural revolution of the 1960s. Economists may argue that the sheer size of the baby-boomer generation and their resultant economic clout was the significant factor in fomenting change. Some social scientists say the draft and the Vietnam War were fundamental to the upheaval. More recently the rise of the right in U.S. politics and culture invites similar speculation. Does the Reagan Revolution owe its success to the perfection of public relations and advertising techniques? Have the rise of corporations and their deliberate program of channeling money into politics fostered the movement's success? On the other hand, could it be that we have a demographic standoff between rural and urban America? Or is race the key motivator, and is the struggle between white and non-white America? If we take the right at its word, their central motivation and central narrative is to resist "big government" and to protect individual freedom as well as traditional Christian values in an era of relativity and secularity.

We are familiar with these lines of argument, and all of them have a contribution to make to our understanding of recent history. In this chapter, however, our purpose is to take a less traveled, more subjective path into the motivations of the right and those who oppose them. We shall set out to examine the cultural psychology that has led to the confrontational political climate we now face and attempt an explanation from this tradition. We are aware of the hazards of this approach, given the abuses of "psychohistory" and other applications of depth psychology to social phenomena. Nevertheless some effort in this direction is necessary because the strict boundaries of disciplinary traditions have their limitations and, as such, leave the psychology of experience unexamined. Richard Rorty provides an interesting, albeit disturbing example and insight in one description of the 1960s left:

> One of the good things, which happened in the Sixties, was that the American Left began to realize that its economic determinism had been too simplistic. Sadism was recognized as having deeper roots than economic insecurity. The delicious pleasure to be had from creating a class of putative inferiors and then humiliating individual members of that class was seen as Freud saw it— as something which would be relished even if everybody were rich.

> (1998, p. 76)

Without the psychological or symbolic interpretation of historical events certain questions are left unasked and unanswered. Why is human progress such an unstable movement? Why does violence continue to be a prevalent approach to extinguishing, rather than resolving, political differences? How could all the advances in human knowledge up through the 20th century have allowed the present times to be the most brutal in human history? Why are so many citizens of a democratic state such as the United States anti-government, when the people create those governments? Why are voters on the right restrictive of the civil liberties of others and determined to limit them on narrow, sectarian religious grounds? In a wealthy nation such as the United States, why is there so little sense of community and compassion for the country's own poor?

To respond to such questions by reverting to breakthroughs in technology or new economic forms is to forget the connection between cultural psychology and the socio-political and economic climate in cities and towns, homes and classrooms. Whether for better or for worse, human beings when so motivated are capable of moving the course of history in spite of material factors. Somewhere in our psychology there are resources and motivations that can only be explained in their own terms: the language of symbol and meaning.

The spiral of development

> The psychology of the mature human being is an unfolding, emergent, oscillating spiraling process marked by progressive subordination of older, lower-order behavior systems to newer, higher-order systems as an individual's existential problems change. ... When the human is centralized in one state of existence, he or she has a psychology which is particular to that state.
>
> (Clare Graves, as cited in Wilber, 2000, p. 5)

Despite attempts at popularization such as *Passages* (Sheehy, 1977), and a history that goes back at least as far as the writings of Rousseau, theories of lifespan human development are not a part of general awareness. Thanks to the pressures of childrearing and K–12 education, there is some appreciation of the stages of childhood and adolescence as revealed in the developmentalist work of Piaget, Erikson, Friedenberg, and others. There is a tacit consensus, however, that these ages and stages end in adolescence and are succeeded by the long, seamless path of adulthood. This uninterrupted stage of maturity is broken at most, in the popular mind, by a midlife crisis for which sports cars and face-lifts are accessible remedies (along with divorce). One of the major misconceptions of contemporary common sense is that early in life, upon entering adulthood, one reaches a level of understanding that is beyond the need of fundamental renewal and transformation. Adults, by virtue of their age, not their behavior or ideas, are "mature" and "grown up."

In theories of psychological development such as Jung's, the innate unfolding of the psyche takes form from birth in the ego's emergence and refinement. This process is characterized by the experience of differentiation, that is, by awareness on the part of the individual of the categories with which he or she is identified and those from which he or she is separated. The sorting or differentiating process goes forward from infancy, along with the acquisition of language. The child accepts being, for example, a male, white, Protestant, American, Republican, Texan athlete, and he sets apart from his identity other religions, nationalities, ethnicities, and so on. We can observe the quest for identity during the teenage years and its occasional extremism, for example, in gang participation, violence against the other, and explicit or implicit racism and/or sexism. This either/or quality of thought and experience also invites a simplified worldview of binaries. We understand it is normal for the adolescent to yearn for a black and white matrix through which to categorize and understand the world. We also are familiar with the discomfort young people typically experience from shades of gray in meaning, relativity in thought and value, and open-ended process as opposed to closure. Those who teach undergraduates become quite familiar with the characteristics of this type of personality.

What we are less aware of are the echoes of this worldview in adulthood. Since our tradition is to presume that the personality is mature as people move into their 20s, there is little ongoing commentary on the impact of egotistic, differentiating thought among adults in society. Further aggravating this presumption of maturity and completeness is the attachment the ego has for declaring its wholeness and supremacy in the individual's consciousness by identifying with a set of traits, real or imagined. Here is how such a worldview may appear when translated to contemporary political analysis:

> Put simply, Radcons have offered America a set of ideas—about morality, prosperity, and patriotism—that celebrate "us" and condemn "them." *We* are virtuous; *they* are venal.
>
> *We* are heterosexual, married and clean living. *They* are gay or lesbian, sexually active outside marriage, and in favor of abortion.
>
> *We* are hardworking, white, and middle class. *They* are idle, poor, black, or Latino or Asian immigrants who don't speak English but benefit from our social services.
>
> *We* are Americans. *They* are terrorists. They are also Muslims and Arabs. They are even French and Germans, or anyone else who is not with *us*.
>
> This dangerously oversimplified way of looking at the world offers many Americans who feel angry and frustrated an easy explanation for what's gone wrong in their lives.
>
> (Reich, 2004, p. 43)

As Erikson and others have pointed out, there is a basic mechanism of stage development at play here: at each level of consciousness, we cling to the concepts of that age and resist deconstructing our achievements, even those who are in pursuit of higher-order experience. This conservational mechanism is one of the vital ideas upon which lifespan developmental psychology is based. Were it widely understood, persons could be alert to its consequences and could be better able to resist its attraction.

Following the theories of Jung and Erikson, among others, we can claim that, for those who have reached fulfillment of the ego and its differentiating techniques, this penchant for stasis is doubly strong. This is because the developed ego is by definition the key instrument of will. Will is therefore turned to the purpose of elevating the ego to an unassailable status of centrality in the psychological life of the individual. With this elevation come characteristic problems. As suggested above, the ego-oriented personality looks for black and white analyses and closure in addressing the world. At this stage of development the individual needs categories to set himself or herself apart, thereby giving meaning to ego identification (categories such as "male, white, Protestant ..."). The ego is ultimately solitary and has relations with others only in terms of how these others serve the purposes of the egotistic individual. "To differentiate well means to differentiate as well between differentiation and splitting, between soul and Ego, and so forth" (Kovel, 1999, p. 233). After a point in the path of healthy maturation, the differentiating attitude of the ego becomes counterproductive, splitting the person from further development.

Selfless relationships, broad acceptance of others, tolerance for diversity, and the suspension of judgment in order to sympathetically understand new ideas: all these experiences are difficult or impossible from an egotistic point of view. Add to this dynamic the presumption that adults are mature and need not pursue further refinement of their personality and we have set the stage for reinforcing arrested development. By our tacit acceptance of adults as fully formed and mature by definition, we legitimize this arrestation of development and assure people that, upon reaching adulthood, they are invited to resist further maturation. The actual lifelong journey of growth is denied and concealed, and what would seem the sensible and preferred attitude of humility is replaced with an invitation to arrogance and self-congratulation.

Jung defines the further pathway of maturation as that of self-realization. By this he means the supra-ego emergence of another locus of personhood, the Self. This culminating complex of associations subsumes the ego as a useful tool in manifesting the will, but does not confuse the ego with who the person can ultimately aspire to be. Self-consciousness in this sense is an expression of an integrative impulse, which is the inclination to experience freely phenomena of many kinds, including those that the ego would set aside. The attitude of the Self is therefore to integrate within the individual even those experiences that ostensibly are alien, or "other." This is not an invitation to total relativism; one may still find many behaviors that are morally reprehensible, for example. This attitude does, however, greatly broaden one's acceptance of the world as well as altering the dynamic of experience. The ego looks for reasons to accept or reject a phenomenon, with this differentiation being the purpose of experience. By contrast, the Self looks for ways to integrate meaning from new experience and presumes that there are purposes of cognition beyond identity formation. Through the

Self the individual takes a leap of hope that he or she is secure in his or her identity and can assume a functioning ego as one element of his or her psyche. This dynamic has implications for useful engagement with society: "Although we might initially discover the spirit within ourselves, in quiet introspection, retreat, seclusion or introversion, once spirit is contacted it brings with it an imperative to go outside ourselves and serve others and the world" (Tacey, 2004, p. 147).

Obviously the theory requires a high level of confidence on the part of the individual that he or she will not be lost in oblivion if an attitude of differentiation is suspended. For this reason, the individual's evolution of consciousness as outlined here is neither described nor understood as a trouble-free, automatic process. If individuals generally do not have a concept that such a developmental process is possible, if they have not been exposed to concepts of this type at home or in school or church, the likelihood of their discovering and traveling such a path is negligible. One under-appreciated alternative route to these kinds of understandings is in the various 12 Step programs. Alcoholics Anonymous (and related groups such as Narcotics Anonymous) acknowledge in their literature a central debt to Jung's theory. The step programs are used almost exclusively today by persons in extremes phases of addiction, out of desperation. If one observes the process and theory of following the steps, however, the path of self-realization becomes transparently clear. The step programs introduce lifespan development and the possibilities of higher-order experience. In contemporary society, ironically, only those in crisis tend to employ this well-conceived path to growth and maturation.

Consider some of the 12 Steps in this light, remembering that it is part of the program that one's definition of "God" is not limited to the Christian or theological understanding of the term. From the point of view of analytic psychology, "God" would be the realized Self; a synonym for AA is "a higher power." Notice, too, the humility and subordination of the will that characterizes the following steps:

1. Made a decision to turn our will and our lives over to the care of God as we understood Him.
2. Made a searching and fearless moral inventory of ourselves.
3. Admitted to God, to ourselves, and to another human being the exact nature of our wrongs.
4. Humbly asked Him to remove our shortcomings.
5. Made direct amends to such people wherever possible, except when to do so would injure them or others.
6. Continued to take personal inventory and when we were wrong promptly admitted it.

(Alcoholics Anonymous, 1972)

Alienation and education

The effects of individual development as described here can manifest them-selves in a number of ways. For our purposes, this analysis is being employed to explore the origins and behavior of the political right. In this process we are attempting to understand the single-minded hostility of the right to contemporary education as manifested particularly in the public schools and by the leadership of the education profession, including those in higher education. A number of sources of this antipathy have been identified, for example,

> One: Modernity tends to undermine the taken-for-granted certainties by which people lived through most of history. ... Two: A purely secular view of reality has its principal social location in an elite culture that, not sur-prisingly, is resented by large numbers of people who are not part of it but who feel its influence (most troublingly, as their children are subjected to an education that ignores or even directly attacks their own beliefs and values).
>
> (Berger, 1999, p. 11)

Alienation is a major effect of education that is little explored in contem-porary discussions of the school and university experience. Educated elites, like other identifiable peer groups, interact frequently in their own world of the like-minded, tending to have more in common intellectually and in terms of values with peer professionals around the world than with tradesmen or businesspeople who live next door. A frequent outcome of education is that it loosens family and religious ties and inculcates students into a new and broader world of peers. Few parents enthusiastically or deliberately sign their children up for such a process. On the contrary, avoiding this social-ization is a central motivation of home schooling and private school initia-tives. In public education, on the way to diplomas and degrees that open up economic opportunity, this quiet subversion of tradition goes on. It has not been in the interest of the mainstream education establishment to publicize or meaningfully dialogue about this side effect of schooling.

To a large degree teachers and professors are trapped in this hostile rela-tionship with convention. The mythic sensibility, as manifested in traditional religion, has rarely been reconciled with the analytic view employed by science, social science, and the world of scholarly inquiry. Professors and scientists feel neither qualified nor motivated to attempt the reconciliation. "While educa-tional theorists have been ignoring religion as though the enlightenment pro-ject had succeeded, more and more people have actually returned to religion" (Noddings, 1993, p. xiv). Faculty tend to be specialists in their disciplines, cer-tified by the Doctor of Philosophy degree, although the title is to some extent a misnomer. The range of their study in the philosophy of their respective disciplines is typically far overshadowed by their attention to more narrow disciplinary knowledge. They are not prepared to conduct discussions on the belief systems that form the foundation of what (in an increasingly global and multicultural community) still tend to be Western traditions, and they do not see this kind of persistent self-reflection as part of their role. The challenges of this type of discourse should not be minimized. Great minds have found frustration in attempts to reconcile philosophy and science with religion. In fact the modern era left this fundamental challenge unresolved. The dichotomy is one that defines the dynamic and limitations of modernity while creating profound social consequences. And yet, there are voices speaking of an integrative view: "Modernity is secular, not in the frequent, rather loose sense of the word, where it designates the absence of religion, but rather in the fact that religion occupies a different place, compatible with the sense that all social action takes place in profane time" (Taylor, 2004, p. 194).

Although the right may seem to be the aggressor in the culture wars around education, it can therefore be argued that psychologically and culturally their position is a defensive one. Partisans of the right's political view feel under siege in terms of the legitimacy of their worldview and even their ability to maintain a community of value in their families. There is in this sense a great deal of motivation to act out against the forces of the modern, secular state and its schools. During the past several decades, political operatives have learned to harness this resentment to create voting blocks. The potential of identity politics has been greatly refined in theory and practice and thereby given the means to translate into votes at the ballot box. Additionally, advanced corporate media are mobilized to solidify and propagate the movement. Linked in coalition with Main Street Republicans and market fundamentalists, the cultural or religious fundamentalists find themselves aligned and forming a majority, controlling all major branches of government as the United States moves into the 21st century.

Those who take part in the community of scholars have pursued their own agendas, motivated by some combination of material appetite, competitive intensity, and an authentic love for the pursuit of knowledge. In the process they have left a wake of angry, resentful countrymen who have found their way into communities of mutual understanding. The cultural and religious segment of the population was marginalized and forgotten until the New Right mobilized them and gave them political standing. Now that both power and citizenry are divided, until there is a popular understanding of a new, unifying "social imaginary," we can expect further tearing of society's fabric and damage to public institutions such as schools. There is a burnt earth aspect to these culture wars, making the stakes for reconciliation high. If there is to be domestic tranquility, society must construct a common view that allows peaceful coexistence even when the heartfelt views of religious or cultural tradition (such as the "right to life") are not the law of the land.

Otherwise the power of the ballot box will be used to override policies and ideas that scholars have understood were unassailable: "All the sadism which the academic Left has tried to make unacceptable to its students will come flooding back" (Rorty, 1998, p. 90). Intelligent Design can become the legislated curriculum of life science. Stem-cell research is already impeded. Women's rights and those of the gay community may be rolled back, as through banning the "morning after pill" and defense of marriage legislation, respectively. Vouchers may give full, public funding to sectarian schools, ending the common school. Teaching as a discernible profession, with licensure and formal preparation, may cease to exist.

The right remembers when their "sacred cows" were eviscerated: when states' rights and Jim Crow allowed greater (if invidious) individual autonomy in public spaces and businesses; when wives were clearly subordinated to their husbands (still a popular religious view); when homosexuality was beyond public mention or legal tolerance; when schools were a place of Christian prayer and ceremony; when abortion was illegal and birth control and sex education were widely restricted. Progressive forces have overridden traditional views in numerous ways, setting a precedent for the use of political power to affect folkways in U.S. society.

Charles Taylor describes the contemporary political principle that permits such action in this way:

> You, like the rest of us, are free just in virtue of the fact that we are ruling ourselves in common and not being ruled by some agency that need take no account of us. Your freedom consists in your having a guaranteed voice in the sovereign, that you can be heard and have some part in making the decision. ... The law defines a community of those whose freedom it realizes/defends together. It defines a collective agency, a people, whose acting together by the law preserves their freedom.
>
> (2004, p. 189)

Given that the relative power of right and left are imbalanced at the present moment, and given that this democratic principle still is dominant, educators and other progressives face a stark reality. Effective propagation of liberal, humane ideas is an urgent need. Either the political balance must be shifted by a change in the public's mind, or the pendulum, which has begun its backward journey, will sweep exceedingly far. The unthinkable has happened before and compassion has been swept aside. The sovereignty of the people is a powerful force and an equally powerful tool. Joseph Goebbels masterminded this force in his day:

> There was no point in seeking to convert the intellectuals. For intellectuals would never be converted and would anyway always yield to the stronger, and

this will always be the "man in the street." Arguments must therefore be crude, clear and forcible, and appeal to emotions and instincts, not the intellect. Truth was unimportant and entirely subordinate to tactics and psychology.

(Danner, 2005, p. 73)

An appetite for affirmation

The primacy of symbol and meaning in human affairs is affirmed by the polarizing struggle now dominating U.S. politics. The community of scholars argues for social justice and economic leveling that contradict their narrow class interests. Leaders of the left ask society to increase the taxes of the socio-economic elite in order to advance the interests of working people and to cede a portion of privilege through affirmative action. The more these agendas fail, the further the advance in wealth and status of the privileged few. The right, on the other hand, abjures collective help through unions or activist government. They urge an end to the "death tax," although only approximately 1.5% of the wealthiest citizens are affected by it. They are unified against public health while over 40 million regular citizens are left uninsured. As the left loses, it wins, and as the Right wins, it loses, at least in economic terms. One interpretation of these anomalies is that something is at stake that trumps the significance of material advancement.

On one level, a force superior to that of economic gain is the need for affirmation. Particularly among those who subscribe to the populist right there is an unending appetite for public figures, ministers, journalists, and commentators to assure them that their beliefs and worldview are correct. The burgeoning popularity of right-wing media, fundamentalist preachers, and the books they spawn are evidence of a need for vocal reassurance that is numbingly repetitive and predictable. The more stacked the programming is to avoid actual inquiry or challenge to predictable positions, the more popular it is with its audience. "Fundamentalism seeks certainty, fixed answers, and absolutism" (Tacey, 2004, p. 11). The difference in tone, purpose, and content between Fox News and CNN is illustrative and well known to media observers. Repetition is a virtue. Witty character assassination and ridicule take the place of insight or new synthesis. Historical analysis is manipulated or disdained entirely. Communication is for the purpose of affirmation and the operant technique is association rather than analysis.

The recent triumphs of Bush–Rove politics have demonstrated the communicative power of staying on message, adhering to one's talking points, and doggedly adhering to repetition in the face of all calls for dialogue that involves real give and take. The association of "standards with testing" in education, of "WMD and Saddam Hussein" in making war, of "choice with liberty" in social security, vouchers, and public health, of "discussions of social justice with class warfare" have all taken hold brilliantly at the ballot box.

Repetition and association have easily supplanted meaningful inquiry and debate over public issues. Hand in hand with these techniques is that of labeling, or dismissing, a nuanced position by giving it a name and insisting that such naming ends the need for further discussion. Teachers' discussion of the impact of poverty on success in school is called "making excuses." In British Columbia, although the courts ruled that teachers had the right during parent–teacher interviews to critique government policies that affected school funding, pundits and advocates called teachers' speech "political," as if placing such a label made their speech about the conditions of professional practice illegitimate.

> "We're saying that teachers hold a special trust and that school meetings, school events, school grounds ought not to be places for political discussion when we're really dealing with education matters. We're not attempting to limit freedom of speech," [Hugh Finlayson, chief executive officer of the BC Public School Employers' Association] added. "We're just saying that the parent–teacher interview is not the appropriate forum."
>
> (Hansen, 2005)

Henry Giroux, citing Umberto Eco, calls this phenomenon the rise of Orwellian Newspeak, "the language of 'eternal fascism,' whose purpose is to produce 'an impoverished vocabulary, and an elementary syntax [whose consequence is] to limit the instruments for complex and critical reasoning'" (2004, p. 22).

Through endless repetition of slogans, labels, and pat formulations the right has achieved political dominance in the United States and threatened the basic achievements of progressive politics, including the separation of church and state, the common public school, social security, women's right to choice, the autonomy of scientific inquiry and science education, and the primacy of professionals in their spheres of expertise, whether they be physicians counseling options for women or teachers developing the curriculum of a course in biology.

This appetite for continual affirmation without a corresponding need for bona fide evidence or analysis is understandable in terms of the arguments made above about ego consciousness. If the choice is made to forgo further maturation and development, the ego-centered personality has one dominant need from communication, and that is ongoing reassurance that the current state of perception and conduct is beyond necessary revision. For this reason the constant drumbeat of slogans with which one concurs is vital, whether their content and impact be irrational, specious, or against one's own larger interests. In the absence of extreme want or suffering, humans quickly turn to meaning and symbol ahead of other appetites, and the opportunity to bask in an environment of ego affirmation is welcome indeed. Clever political handlers, the apotheosis of public relations and advertising professionals, have mobilized this psychological hunger into a movement at the ballot box. Reassurance of the populist right comes now not only in church services but from network news and the Oval Office.

One begins to wonder whether Goebbels was correct in his claim that truth was made merely by tactics and psychology, and, yet, governments that follow this prescription seem notably to fail. The former Soviet Union and communism in general come to mind, as well as the Taliban of Afghanistan and the mullahs of Iran. These types of regime are known for their pervasive propaganda and persecution of free speech and the questioning of authority. Truth may be an unattainable ideal, but substituting religious or ideological faith for inquiry and the honest pursuit of knowledge appears to be a parlous course. Long before 9/11, in 1997, Richard Rorty lectured on this theme:

> For after my imagined strongman takes charge, he will quickly make his peace with the international super-rich, just as Hitler made his with the German industrialists. He will invoke the glorious memory of the Gulf War to provoke military adventures that will generate short-term prosperity. He will be a disaster for the country and the world. People will wonder why there was so little resistance to his evitable rise.
>
> (1998, p. 91)

Robert Reich provides follow-up:

> Much of President Bush's financial support came from those who benefited most directly from the $1.7 trillion worth of tax cuts he engineered between 2001 and 2003. They're the people with incomes of over $1 million a year who received the biggest cuts—and who will avoid taxes on their giant estates as the estate tax is phased out.
>
> (Reich, 2004, p. 95)

Forming a coalition on the right

Those who have enthusiastically joined the right for the reasons outlined thus far have been strengthened politically by their alliance with another faction of the new Republican Party—one that bases its allegiance on economic rather than cultural factors. "The rightward turn has been the result of the successful struggle by the right to form a broad-based alliance. This new alliance has been so successful in part because it has been able to win the battle over commonsense" (Apple, 2001, p. 37). Although greed and religious faith may seem to be uneasy allies, partisans of these camps have found common ground and emerged as two of the three pillars of the coalition that has brought what Reich calls the Radcons to majority power in all three branches of the federal government and numerous other state and local offices. The market fundamentalists do share some habits of mind with their religious partners. There is a sloganeering quality to their devotion of "free markets" and privatization. This attachment has similarities to religious faith in that complexity and analysis are marginalized in political discussion, as is a sustained use of evidence. The intonation of magical terms substitutes for argument, and the consequences of policy count for little in determining the future course of events. Perhaps the most glaring example of this phenomenon is the "cut taxes and balance the budget" pledge of Ronald Reagan that was derived from his adoption of the Laffer Curve. Implemented off and on by Republican administrations since 1981, the policy generates impressive deficits with no suggestion of relief. Nonetheless, it continues to be a useful campaign slogan for the right when it should by now have become an embarrassment.

Similarly, the privatizers have failed repeatedly to deliver on their promises to operate schools and other public agencies more efficiently and effectively than has been achieved by government officials. As discussed in chapter 2, Edison Schools has been a financial disaster, losing over 90% of its market value while hemorrhaging hundreds of millions of investor dollars. At best, with more money per capita to spend, Edison's results are sometimes comparable to demographically similar public schools. Testing and textbook companies provide expensive products of dubious support, currency, and quality. For-profit and faith-based tutoring entities, ushered in by NCLB, have accumulated a rocky track record of misfeasance in Chicago and other districts. Outside of education, Enron set the standard for abuse of the public trust with its gangster-like manipulation of California's electricity market. Enron was not alone in this criminal activity, but had alliances with natural gas and pipeline companies. On the other hand, Los Angeles' publicly owned power system delivered consistent, economical service throughout Enron's manufactured crisis. By contrast, in education, Reading Recovery is an example of a true not-for-profit reform program that reinvests its resources in research and development. This international program's achievements and ongoing renewal are the documented results of a well-managed NGO.

Evidence, however, carries no weight in this non-debate. Repetition, association, slogans, labels, and cynical wit are the currency of the politics of the right. Their common use of such techniques suggests how the two factions of the right have come together.

> Friedman might be called a market fundamentalist. To him and his followers, the free market has the same intoxicating quality that religion has to born-again Christians. Facts aren't especially relevant. The perfection of the market has to be accepted as a matter of faith. And like religious fundamentalism,

market fundamentalism offers the promise of redemption to those who adhere to its gospel.

(Reich, 2004, p. 113)

The sibling fundamentalists—market and religious—arguably share a truncated passage to self-realization, and this best explains their beliefs and behavior. While religion is manipulated to justify egotism in the one case, Mammon fills this role for the other. From colonial times there has been a popular acceptance among many that worldly, material success is a sign of God's favor. Although today's idolaters of greed have dropped the language of Calvinism, the redeeming value of material success remains embedded in the American Dream. Wealth is more than material abundance; it is a symbol of consummate fulfillment. Wealth, in this analysis, validates the individual achiever on every plane of evaluation. Greed is made into an ideal and more than justified; it is defined as a noble aspiration. Lost in this reverie is concern for the economic viability of others. The single-minded fanaticism of market fundamentalists is particularly noteworthy for its lack of compassion. The examples are legion: trapping illegal aliens in a nether land of servitude, raiding social security and other pensions, leaving millions uninsured while bleeding money from health care funding, legalizing payday loan usury, starving urban schools while steering resources to affluent suburban districts. And the list goes on. Traders from the discredited and defunct corporation Enron are on tape callously mocking a representative, vulnerable customer, labeled "Grandma Millie," as they financially impair her in California through manipulation of electricity prices.

Another explanation for this unethical alliance on the right is that the preservation of an arrested worldview requires a thought process tailored for its peculiar needs. Whether to rationalize greed or maintain the inflation of the ego, individuals seek out a mechanism that bears the outward trappings of reason but is adaptable to their broader purposes. The propagandizing techniques of the new common sense have proven to be brilliantly effective and a common bond. One way of understanding this success is to see these techniques as manifestations of "magical thinking" as described by Freud, Piaget and others:

Two laws are operative in "magical thinking": the law of similarity and the law of contagion. In other words, the child is understood as perceiving a world in which subjects with similar predicates appear identical and thus can be perfectly interchanged. Proximity is identity, and things or entities once in contact are always associated.

(Robbins, 1999)

For a discussion to engender understanding and communication, it is necessary that those speaking are sympathetically listening to one another's meaning. The right's techniques of communication are not designed to foster mutual accommodation. Instead they serve to reinforce the views of the speaker and wall off influence from those who disagree. On radio, a talk show host can prescreen and then cut off those who disagree, particularly those who do so in an articulate manner. In more open forums, repetition, slogans, labels, and association—the tools of magical thinking—have proven effective. In electronic and print media, simply limiting the amount of time in which an argument can be expressed consigns the discussion to superficiality. Insisting that only quantitative evidence is legitimate is another strategy. The power of these deceptive variations on dialogue is derived from the payoff they deliver to participants. They confirm the "rightness" of one's views, no matter how much or how well they may be disputed. These techniques insulate those who subscribe to them from meaningful challenge by others to their worldview and their autonomy. Magical thinking is a key tool in resisting the path of psychological development. It provides an inner and common language for rationalizing resistance to healthy processes such as Piaget and Erikson, as well as Jung, have outlined. Individuals are assured of their moral and factual "rightness" regardless of evidence or argument to the contrary. The repetition of talking points in sound bites is what passes for public discourse on an issue.

Ultimately advertising and public relations are structured efforts to communicate in non-discursive, pre-rational ways and, most importantly, to affect behavior. Through repetition, association, slogans, labeling, and other mechanisms, modern consumer market values have been made into a way of life. Further they have now become a way of controlling politics. While this approach to political discourse grows, another is lost:

> As the prevailing discourse of neoliberalism seizes the public imagination, there is no vocabulary for progressive social change, democratically inspired visions, or critical notions of social agency to expand the meaning and purpose of democratic public life.
>
> (Giroux, 2004, p. 66)

A matrix of movements

The tensions between right and left, traditional and postmodern, religion and science can be illustrated by plotting these dichotomies on two axes and locating, for heuristic purposes, the worldviews and institutions we have discussed in this chapter. By definition this is an interpretive and subjective strategy, replete with generalizations. It is offered here for its value to stimulate reflection and not with the presumption that such a device can be precise. We acknowledge that each person and movement mentioned can be taken in many incarnations and through various lenses of interpretation.

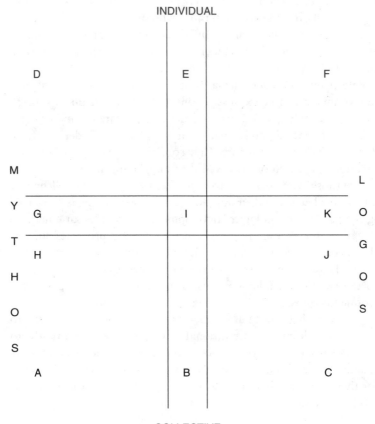

Figure 3.1

With these caveats in place, figure 3.1 is put forward. On the vertical or y-axis we can describe the range of focus from "individual to collective," which is to say the relative emphasis a system of thought or value gives to the interests of the group as opposed to those of the sole actor. Cults, for example, are normally understood to be collective in the extreme with at most a charismatic leader possessing autonomy and authentic choice. The ideal of communes is a more authentic manifestation of the collective as a way of life. (In this setting the leader may be chosen by lot as an expression of complete egalitarianism.) For nature, the paradigmatic collectives are those of the communal insects: bees, ants, termites. These insect communities demonstrate unity of purpose, specialization of roles, and a total subordination of the individual. One is reminded of the beehive as a symbol of industry and community, as in the state seal of Utah. For purposes of this discussion, we are not emphasizing whether the collective is a small community, one as large as a nation, or even the human race in general. Our point is to examine the dynamic of individual versus collective values without entering the separate discussion of the scope of the collective.

On the other hand, philosophies revolving around the "triumph of the will," the Superman (*Übermensch*), and other interpretations of thinkers such as Nietzsche illustrate the individualistic pole of the continuum. Ayn Rand's Objectivism would be another example of an uncompromising elevation of the solitary person and his or her will. Rand's character Howard Roark, the apotheosis in fiction of the independent artist, is a memorable if stylized literary character who embodies an uncompromising, and overwrought, individualism. In nature we think of solitary predators who live much of their lives alone, coming together only to mate. In some cases, such as the praying mantis, the act of mating brings an end to the male's life, as if a trace of dependence took the meaning from the true individual's life. In recent history the "captains of industry" Mellon, Carnegie, Frick, Rockefeller, Ford, Morgan, and their peers, who created triumphant capitalism in the United States between 1880 and 1910, can be seen in this light. They were heroes of industry and business who, during their heyday, dominated government and scorned the laboring masses and others of lesser achievement.

The horizontal or x-axis describes the spectrum from *mythos* to *logos*. *Mythos* is meant to describe the experience of value and meaning for humans as manifested in non-rational realms such as intuition and the arts. The power of *mythos* is undeniable even in modern society. Mass movements, charismatic leaders and celebrities, and popular culture phenomena are all expressions of this human quest for symbols and meaning. As extremely successful examples, George Lucas and J. K. Rowling have met this need through their artistic creations, and they have been rewarded on an Olympian scale. Hero-worship is another pop-culture manifestation of the pursuit of *mythos*. One needs only to look at television programming and other media obsessiveness about celebrity to see this played out to contemporary audiences, who look to these celebrities as models for guidance in how to define themselves in appearance, lifestyle, and spirituality. Both religious and New Age movements address this appetite for meaning. The global Green movement can be seen in this light, as well as variations on traditional religions such as the ecological Christianity of Matthew Fox. Seen in terms of *mythos*, the reference to Joseph Goebbels has a different, more legitimate reading: "Truth was unimportant and entirely subordinate to tactics and psychology" (Danner, 2005, p. 73).

Truth, in the sense of scientific fact and theory and rational analysis, occupies the other end of the x-axis under the rubric of *logos*. Pragmatically, *logos* represents the method for directly influencing physical events, controlling the environment, discovering the logic of nature, and expanding objective knowledge and technology (Armstrong, 2001). Einstein, Hawkings, and other leading physicists would be voices of *logos* in the 20th century, as well as Watson and Crick and those other life scientists who have advanced genetic mapping. Analytic philosophers such as Bertrand Russell and A. J. Ayer have attempted to unify philosophy and *logos* in spite of the doubts of others: "Since logos identifies the word and reality, wisdom begins with the criticism of logos" (Kovel, 1999, p. 230). Modernity and the scientific viewpoint are largely identified as one, and we have become vividly aware of the triumphs as well as the limitations of *logos*.

Many of the clashes described in this book emanate from mutually exclusive worldviews of those at the extremes of the *mythos–logos* continuum. It is a truism to state that science has little to say about meaning and human values, while the mythic viewpoint is notably bankrupt in engineering, computer science, medical research, and related fields. Nevertheless culture wars continue as one "magisterium" threatens the province of the other. Our unsettled time in history is defined in the United States by polarized debates such as whether human life meaningfully begins at conception; whether Intelligent Design should be taught along with evolutionary theory in science classrooms; whether the death penalty is just; and whether human cloning is a sacrilege. The effort to answer scientific questions with myth or to solve spiritual conflicts with logic and fact is a notable and ongoing failure, illustrating the mutual exclusivity of the positions in their purist definitions.

With our matrix established, let us attempt to position some of the significant camps and players who populate the contemporary education and culture wars. For example, the lower left-hand quadrant is the locus for the more otherworldly varieties of religious cults – those, such as Moonies or Hare Krishnas, who reject worldly achievement for their masses and cede their individual will to the collective or to a charismatic leader (A). Other relatively collectivist groups, the Latter Day Saints, Amish, and Scientologists, for example, are more practical in terms of general achievement by the faithful and may be placed well into collectivity, but midway between *mythos* and *logos* (B). One benefit of this worldliness is the ability to raise and hold material resources for the movement.

A cultural category that is collective, while rejecting *mythos* for *logos*, would be the modern manifestations of Marxism–Leninism such as Mao's China and Stalin's Soviet Union (C). Scientific materialism attempted to reject the non-rational and build states based without resort to religion by discovering values and meaning analytically. These movements are also identified with totalitarianism and the pervasive control of culture in its many manifestations. Society is treated as though it were a laboratory experiment designed by a wise scientist who skillfully defines and determines the environment and mechanisms at play.

In the extreme upper left-hand quadrant we can place the monkish ideal, whether Buddhist, Christian, or of other traditions (D). For the monk or hermit, a life of pure individual spirituality is its own justification. The burden of providing food and shelter is on others, who may or may not be fortunate enough to receive a mythic dividend from their philanthropy. Meditation and prayer are justified in their own right without necessary recourse to greater social benefit. Closer to a balance between *mythos* and *logos*, but still quite individualistic, would be members of our international celebrity caste, whether from the arts, athletics, politics, or simply of pure notoriety: personalities who make limited social contributions but whose images are widely recognized (E). They move in the worlds of both myth and material success and may pay some lip service to social responsibility, but ultimately seem above the cares of everyday people. Certainly, we cannot know the soul of another, but here we are trying to identify icons of culture who might lack a significant social conscience, for example: Mick Jagger, Madonna, Michael Jackson, Barry Bonds, Tiger Woods, Princess Diana, Stephanie and Caroline of Monaco, Newt Gingrich, Henry Kissinger, etc. Ayn Rand's Howard Roark represents this value system in literature.

To the right of the matrix, public figures who can be characterized as predominantly immersed in *logos* and absorbed in their own individualism would be those who deal in raw power for their own advantage and do so by the manipulation of material tools such as science, the military, and business (F). The interests of others are not a matter of concern for those who succeed in these terms. This would be the realm of the modern-day robber barons of globalization and corporatism, authoritarian political leaders and dictators, and the heirs of great wealth who use their resources to aggrandize their privileges. Their interest is individual power and they do not extend loyalty to the communities of others, including nation-states. Joel Bakan's *The Corporation* (2004) is a study in the threat created by this point of view. As an illustration, Rupert Murdoch's Fox empire produces what is acknowledged as the sleaziest, soft-core network entertainment while, up the dial, it presents hardline, right-wing commentary on the network's news stations. The international arms trade is another notorious example of amoral profiteering. The Adephi/WorldCom/Health South/Enron scandals all emanate from this value system, as did the Boesky/Milken prosecutions of the 1980s.

Along the *mythos–logos* axis there are also those persons or groups who achieve a general balance between the interest of the individual and that of the collective. Striking this balance, but with a focus on *mythos*, would be religions such as Christian Science, Pentecostals, and democratically grounded, but non-worldly, organizations interested in the study of New Age spirituality, astrology, postmodernism, and the like (G). Mainstream Catholicism and Islam are similarly attached to mythic ideals while sacrificing a conventionally pragmatic view of living in the world. Evidence of this would be their resistance to the practice of birth control, following the idea that pregnancies always involve the active consent of the divine. Since, in teachings such as this, favor is given to the interest of the group over individual conscience, these faiths would be located below the x-axis (H).

At the nexus of the two axes we locate the liberal Protestant denominations and many non-religious persons of good will who attempt to define a center between the poles we have described (I). (The place of religion in Japan, an amalgam of Shinto, Buddhism, and Christianity, which is Nipponized and naturalized, may fit this formulation, but on the collectivist side.) Those who truly benefit from an authentic liberal education at our colleges and universities would also be characteristically found here. At this crossing point is a consideration of the needs of the individual as well as those of the community. Concepts such as "enlightened self-interest" are given meaning. An appropriate posture of humility is adopted in light of each person's original and ongoing debt to society for the collective gift of language and other forms of community nurturance and support. Regarding the x-axis, there is an appreciation of the place of symbol and science, of both the non-rational and the rational. Science and spirituality have a place in one's worldview and are understood to be different, so there is no imperative (moral or scientific) over the same existential turf.

At the *logos* pole of the x-axis are those who make dogma out of science or scientific philosophy (K). Brilliant individuals join the collective march of these fields to lead knowledge forward, striking a balance between the role of the solitary researcher and the community of inquiry that validates and extends inquiry. The triumphs of modern science and technology have invited some to arrogantly proclaim their worldview as absolute and comprehensive. Many see Freud and Marx in this realm, depending on how they are read. The popular significance of this view is beyond question, and this attitude represents one of the mainstreams of conventional modern consciousness: hyper-rational, objective, material, determinist, positivist, reductionist. Extended to social science and education—fields with normative dimensions—this limited worldview has given us the standards and testing movement, behaviorism, and numerous other initiatives that conspicuously lack *mythos*, by whatever name you choose to give it. The human—or should we say humane—aspect is missing.

Where in this schematic do the advocacy forces of the right fit? In their own appraisal, the religious fundamentalists who are so influential in this movement would place themselves near to *mythos* and the Christian God. Their aim is predominantly salvation and they act on the world while believing that its significance is secondary and transitory. Many predict imminent apocalypse. They would see themselves as honoring the free will of the faithful as individuals. According to their own ideology, one would expect to find them nearer to *mythos* than *logos* and more individualistic than collectivist. Here we shall propose an alternate interpretation.

A key distinguishing trait of today's politicized fundamentalists is their emphasis on controlling the political environment and dictating the behavior and educational experience of others as well as their faithful. In this sense, they are closer to the scientific materialists than to the conventionally religious. For example, Pope Benedict XVI may now be raising questions about Darwinian theory, but the Roman Catholic Church shows no interest in urging school boards to introduce Intelligent Design into science classrooms. In the abortion and cloning debates, Catholicism has joined the Christian fundamentalists in strenuously trying to affect government, but this is exceptional on their part. Although increasingly tempted to emulate their fundamentalist peers, the Catholic bishops of the United States have trailed in their initiatives and shown less conviction about shaping the moral and mythical environment for those outside their church. The Catholic Church, for example, does not seem to share with the right an obsession with phonics as the preeminent method of reading instruction or a passion for debunking Darwin. Fundamentalists draw no line between determining the course of their lives and dictating the options of others in fields far distant from the scope of traditional religion. Their methods as well as their goals emphasize the worldly rather than the spiritual. The entry of these Christians into the power relations of society as a political movement has been done in a bare-knuckle fashion, quite antithetical to the traditional understanding of Christ and his way of proselytizing.

Compassion and non-violence, as well as otherworldliness, have been hallmarks of Christianity, but today's Christian right show minimal concern for social justice, while preaching war and preemptive war, and focusing on the reshaping of the contemporary material world. Pat Robertson's advocacy of the assassination of the president of Venezuela in the late summer of 2005 is just one more outburst of hate speech and lawlessness coming from the religious right. For reasons such as these, our placement of the right on this matrix is collectivist and logocentric, similar to the locus of the regimes of Marxism–Leninism (J). Their motives are a collectivist hegemony focused on the control of society according to a series of non-negotiable claims. The meaning of their controlling principles seems less important than their ability to control others. For example, the sanctity of life does not extend to the "collateral damage" of preemptive war or to death row. *Mythos*, rather than being satisfied through symbol and meaning, is displaced by a network of rules controlling behavior and, as much as possible, thoughts and speech as well. Here we are asserting that the fundamentalist right cloaks itself in the imagery of religion, much like totalitarian regimes claim to advocate social justice in their "people's republics." Putting aside very successful propaganda, however, the purposes and methods of the right belie their claims of spiritual enlightenment.

Let us consider the behavior of Muslim fundamentalists who have come to power most notably in Afghanistan and Iran. Their impulse has been to control and their tolerance of respected spiritual points of view (such as Baha'i and Buddhism) has been negligible. The mullahs and Taliban entered into a frenzy of control, continually removing the individual rights of citizens, including freedom of movement and the right to education. This hegemony extended to the destruction of the antiquities at Bamyan, a desecration if ancient Buddhist icons. They have become the new totalitarians, using coercion rather than voluntary conversion to create a new social order. Their motives have been collectivist and controlling and antithetical to the liberation of individual consciousness and the discovery of personal meaning and myth. Given power in the United States, is there any reason to expect that the legions of Christian fundamentalism would pursue a different course? The direction in which society would move is clear: "This dangerous regression is now possible for civilization as a whole, which may be returned to 'the stages of [its] age and youth.' ... Religious fundamentalism is a foreboding sign of our cultural regression" (Tacey, 2004, p. 27).

To return to where we began in this chapter, this aggression can be interpreted as the struggle of ego-centered personalities to create a world that affirms their vision. Passionately attached to their fixed worldview and hungry to live in an environment that allows no challenge or variation, fundamentalists, like the Crusaders of an earlier era, put on holy garb but vie for power and worldly advantage. They make religionism of religion, gutting the essential values of sacred teachings, while co-opting the outward signs and rituals of Christian practice. The necessary subjectivity of religious feeling leaves it open to such gross distortions. Additionally, society's inherent respect for those who claim religious standing gives license to those who use these privileges to deliver anti-democratic messages of hate. Politicized Christian fundamentalism is emerging as the monster child of *logos* in the United States. The success of modern science to call into question all but a material view of life has created a deficit in meaning and symbol in society. Using the tools of modern propaganda, the right is moving to take control of the modern scientific community that they believe has stripped its mythic world away. Even in victory, however, such a crusade cannot find meaning; it can find only power over the material world and the outward manner in which people live.

Part II

Distortions of the advocates

Chapter 4

The myth of scientifically based research

> Love of Truth is one of the strongest motives for replacing what really happens by a streamlined account or, to express it in a less polite manner: Love of Truth is one of the strongest motives for deceiving oneself and others.
>
> (Feyerabend, 1999, p. 158)

This chapter outlines the relationship of the federal government to educational research and explores the origin and implications in educational policy and practice of "scientifically based research." As part of the discussion it also addresses the complex nature of social science research. We assert that it is not possible to be right or find truth; instead we can only hope for research with a good awareness of its necessary limits and compromises. In this interest we describe particular challenges for any research on teaching and learning, and we review ethical challenges endemic to educational research as well as those more specific to our current context. The chapter concludes by discussing resistance to the "scientific research" paradigm and policy and by calling for responses from teachers and researchers.

An historical perspective on the federal government and educational research

In 1983 *A nation at risk* issued a clarion call to Americans by proclaiming: "If an unfriendly foreign power had attempted to impose on America the mediocre educational performance that exists today, we might well have viewed it as an act of war" (National Commission on Excellence in Education, 1983). This declaration caught the public's attention and launched an era of educational reform that continues to find its way into policy boardrooms and school classrooms. In the subsequent decades a steady stream of governmental policies—state and federal—have imposed an agenda on schools and teachers with little regard for the opinions of educators, their organizations, or institutions. Initiatives including teacher testing, high-stakes testing for students, curriculum standards, Goals 2000/America 2000, voucher programs, the privatization of school administration, and so on, are the legacy of this critique. Teachers, school administrators, and professors of education have been cast as opponents of reform and as those resistant to change, regardless of the damage done to our students. In the consultation process for policy formation, educators are typically handpicked, marginalized, or excluded. *A nation at risk*, for example, was drafted by a commission dominated by natural scientists, and, although various public school constituencies were represented, their influence was minimized, while professors and scholars in the field of education were denied membership entirely.

In 1986, another influential report came forward from the Carnegie Task Force on Teaching as a Profession. The pattern of exclusion continued. *A nation prepared: Teachers for the 21st century* was drafted by only 14 commissioners. Just one among them, Mary Futrell, was a practicing teacher, and no professors or scholars in education were included (Carnegie Corporation of New York, 1986). The pattern set by these two influential documents still continues, and narrow cohorts with often questionable expertise are empowered to shape the public debate on educational issues. Numerous individual voices speaking on education are heard in media and government circles, but, upon examination, these forums conspicuously omit the respected mainstream professional authorities that educators would expect to see at the table. Recently this selective approach to policy formation on educational matters has taken a new turn, moving from narrow cohorts making policy to a highly narrow conception of research itself—a conception articulated by public relations specialists.

One prominent example of this shift to a narrow conception of research is the work on the National Reading Panel. Convened by the National Institute of Child Health and Human Development, one of the National Institutes of Health (NIH), it was comprised of 14 persons, only two of whom had significant classroom background in the teaching of reading. One of those members of the panel eventually dissented, strongly opposing the report *Teaching children to read* (Yatvin, 2001). Others on the panel were cognitive scientists with NIH credentials and, in the spirit of NIH's mission, they summarily adopted a medical research model (Garan, 2002). The NRP trumpeted *Teaching children to read*, in the widely distributed *Summary*, as "an evidence-based assessment of the scientific research literature on reading and its implications for reading instruction" (National Institute of Child Health and Human Development, 1999b, p. i). The *Summary* is highly discrepant in comparison to the little seen 600-page *Report* (1999a), due in no small measure to the fact that it was drafted not by the panel, but by Widmeyer Communications, a public relations firm that serves McGraw-Hill (e.g., Open Court), among other corporate clients (Metcalf, 2002, p. 21). While scholars in education have been extensively debating the validity of the NRP's methods and motives and specifically reevaluating its analysis (Camilli, Vargas, & Yureko, 2003), the federal government has moved quickly to institutionalize its approach to educational practice, with little concern for substantive consultation. The 2001 Elementary and Secondary Education Act "No Child Left Behind" (ESEA/NCLB), sponsored by the Bush administration, immediately adopted this "scientific" theme of the National Reading Council (NRC) and introduced across America the notion that education policy should be driven only by "scientifically based research." The pattern is by now familiar to educators, who recognize, in the manner of *A nation at risk*, how quickly propagandistic slogans are transformed into attitudes that in turn dominate discussions of schooling in America.

This process of questionable research turned to slogans and attitudes is not merely a rhetorical exercise. Slogans such as "scientifically based research" turn into policy and curriculum that drive a wide swath of decision-making in schools, overriding practices of local autonomy. For example, the bipartisan ESEA specifically allowed for Title I funding to be used to implement Reading Recovery, which is seen within the communities of reading scholars and classroom teachers as a highly effective early reading intervention that is able to redress the literacy problems of 1st-grade students and bring them to grade level. Since its importation from New Zealand, Reading Recovery has served well over 1 million children in America alone. Shortly after NCLB passed, however, the Department of Education's "draft guidance" for implementing the law unequivocally contradicted the language of the Act to exclude Reading Recovery from Title I eligibility. (Specifically, Congress allowed pullout programs such as Reading Recovery but the draft guidance excluded them.) Congressional hearings demanded by outraged bipartisan supporters of Reading Recovery had the effect of reeducating department officials on the intentions of Congress, and they capitulated at least superficially. Yet, the department's true intentions have continued to prevail with a "wink and a nod," as a number of state officials, given the signal from Washington, have gone on obstructing Reading Recovery despite Congressional calls for fairness.

It is important to recognize that a strong case for Reading Recovery can be made through what NCLB calls "evidence-based assessment of the scientific research literature." An experiment employing a randomly assigned design and published in *Elementary Education* demonstrated extremely strong effects for Reading Recovery (Pinnell, 1989). This research was funded by the MacArthur Foundation and evaluated by external analysts from the University of Chicago. This research also won the Albert Harris Award of the International Reading Association. Further research in support of Reading Recovery was published by *Reading Research Quarterly* (Pinnell *et al.*, 1993). Yet, the NRP declined to look at Reading Recovery research, regardless of its bona fide "scientific" standing, because the panel focused on isolated skills, such as letter-sound instruction, rather than integrated approaches. Reading was viewed only as an assemblage of discrete skills, rather than as a complex, strategic process. With the stage thus set, the Department of Education moved to reverse longstanding precedents and the intentions of Congress to deny funding to this highly effective reform. It should be noted that Reading Recovery is a non-profit organization whose materials are published by numerous houses. There is no corporate advocate, political fundraiser, or Washington lobbyist seeking profits for Reading Recovery. Of course, all this should be irrelevant to the advancement and application of science. But it is not.

Government science?

This sudden interest of NICHD and the Department of Education in imposing a version of science on education is, in itself, worth examining. For decades, the federal government managed to express its influence and foster programs in public education without entering the epistemological battlefield of philosophy of science. In the space of a few months in 2001, this posture was aggressively reversed in a manner that reflected little consideration of the proper role of government in such a debate. The NRP *Report* is an expression that might spontaneously arise from NIH's medical point of view. The emulation of the NRP's approach by the Department of Education is, however, another more controversial matter because this policy threatens to allocate all federal education funding by the manipulation of a particular definition of science. The *Parent's guide* to NCLB states, "The Department of Education is striving to conduct and collect additional research using the same high scientific standards used for reading and to apply the results of that research to math, science, professional development and comprehensive school reform" (U.S. Department of Education, 2002d, p. 19). But did the NRP truly function in accord with high scientific standards? James Cunningham, among others, argues otherwise and claims that the panel did not meet its own criteria in the *Report*, by failing, for example, to cite evidence in support of its approach to determining which studies it selected as meaningful, i.e., "scientific" (2001, p. 328).

Clearly the federal government is making a concentrated effort to dictate the forms of inquiry and practice in the field of education, and it is doing so through a highly selective application of the accumulated body of knowledge that is present today in education. This behavior is reminiscent of two famous historical examples: Pope Urban VIII's forced recanting by Galileo in 1633 of the mathematician's heliocentric assertions and the devolution into political cant of Soviet life science in the 1930s under the regime of Trofim Lysenko. The United States has advanced in science and technology by avoiding such arbitrary or ideological interference by government. With such traditions in mind, educators have broadly questioned Washington's recent activist interventionism and expansion of the scope of government.

> The U.S. Congress, the NICHD, and the Secretary of Education convened the Panel and shaped its goals and operation. Does this mean the National Reading Panel was a bold attempt by powerful political forces to gain control of reading research? That will depend on whether persuasion or enforcement was the goal, and only time will tell.
>
> (Cunningham, 2001, p. 335)

Given NCLB, the goal seems to be enforcement.

Determining the philosophy and method of the human sciences is a problem that has vexed philosophers and social scientists for 200 years. Education as an applied clinical field is among the most difficult of disciplines to define scientifically. Suddenly, under the auspices of the politically charged NICHD, a panel of medically oriented researchers with minimal classroom experience in teaching children to read is able to cut through this cumbersome debate and, at once, solves the problems of how to teach reading and how to define science in education. The scenario might seem absurd if the initiative were not still gaining momentum through NCLB and the media drumbeat around "scientifically based research." Educators have been caught in too many frustrating and wrong-headed battles during the past 20 years not to recognize another forming on the horizon. Once again, the language and research of professional education are casually converted into a political tool and employed against the practicing professionals in the field. The application and design of educational research now stands to be manipulated for partisan purposes in a manner parallel to the way in which standardized tests have been abused for decades. Emerging examples of how the definition of science can lead to abuse are found in the threatened expurgation of certain research from the Department of Education's web archives and the manipulation of state approval for NCLB supplemental educational service providers (although, ironically, under initial Title I draft rules, states could not "demand that providers submit proof that their instructional services are based on 'scientifically-based' research" [Robelen, 2002, p. 26]). The definition of science again proved malleable in the debate over withholding the publication of the National Literacy Panel's English-learners report in the summer of 2005. Grover Whitehurst, Director of the Institute of Education Sciences, reflecting the work of eight anonymous reviewers, claimed "The quality of the research was mismatched with the strength of the assertion" (Zehr, 2005). Unsurprisingly, the suppressed "assertion" countervailed the views of English-only advocates by asserting that bilingual education yielded superior results.

Politics or science?

If one is searching for a motive in all this that goes beyond merely defining the public discourse on education, there are at least two. NRP "results" and NCLB guidance mobilize toward the adoption of expensive, corporately generated curricular programs. The clear message from Washington is to invest in such materials as opposed to other teacher-centered or non-profit options. Secondly, this assault displaces professional educators and their organizations from decision-making roles in public education. Presumably the new cadre of medical researchers and pundits will prove more tractable in future school initiatives. It is worth noting that organizations of educators have been resistant to conservative modernization and have often aligned with its opponents.

Michael Apple's definition of "conservative modernization" is an alternative way in which to view the federal government's new interest in defining the science of education (Apple, 2001, p. 5). Apple sees an alliance operating in post-*Nation at risk* America that has "creatively stitched together different social tendencies and commitments" (ibid., p. 37) and has to a significant degree redefined the common sense of the public with respect to education. Elements of this conversion include viewing the schools as driven by economic rather than civic goals; establishing standardized tests as the sine qua non of school success; supplanting the schools as a public trust with the mechanisms of the free market; employing CEOs and other non-educators as district leaders; and rolling back diversity and bilingual initiatives. In this context, co-opting the term "scientifically based research" can be understood as another public relations (or propaganda) initiative, using words as tools to achieve political ends. Given the lack of academic credibility underpinning the government's foray into philosophy of science and the track record of some politicians in manipulating issues to gain advantage, this analysis bears consideration.

The complex nature of social science research

It is also important, however, to critique not just the politics of "scientifically based research" but the very concept itself and to reassert distinctive nature and inherent complexities of social science and educational research. We inherited from empiricist branches of 19th-century philosophy the idea that humanistic inquiry and, later, social science, as it developed, could follow in the path of natural science and free itself from subjectivity, imprecision, and weak predictive validity. The message of the 20th century may be, however, that this is for at least two reasons a vain pursuit. First, the mainstream of philosophy of science today, and for more than three decades, has accepted that social science will not replicate the methods of natural science and is not likely to achieve the apparent exactitude of those fields. "We need to go beyond the bounds of a science based on verificationism to one which would study the inter-subjective and common meanings embedded in social reality" (Taylor, 1985, p. 52). Second, adhering to the natural science paradigm "has often driven investigators away from a serious concern with the human world into the sterility of purely formal argument and debate" (Rabinow & Sullivan, 1979, p. 5).

At the turn of the 20th century Dilthey (1989) distinguished the cultural and social sciences (*Geisteswissenschaften*) from the natural sciences by noting what each studied and what the appropriate means for knowing about them could be. The natural sciences concern physical phenomena that can be directly studied through observation and measurement. In contrast, the human sciences study people and have been particularly interested in the complexity of how, when, and why people do things in intricate historical and cultural situations. Human sciences are interpretive. As Dilthey offers, "nature we explain; man we understand." Often, attempts to define qualitative research involve both implicit and explicit comparisons to the equally ambiguously used adjective "quantitative." Humanistic research explores complexity and multiplicity of knowledge, and it does not aim for causation, quantification, and control. Though these sorts of debates are often presented as something new, the earliest qualitative versus quantitative debates were evident in the thinking of Vico, who sought to counter the prevailing Cartesianism of his time. Vico's principle of *verum factum* (the true is made) was his refutation of Cartesian subjective certitude, or "scientifically based research," as the ground of real knowledge. Vico points out that even mathematical truths are authored human creations. Social science has "objects such as texts, verbal expressions and actions" which need to be "investigated from the 'inside' through an understanding of their authors' experiences and intentions." As Mallery, Hurwitz, & Duffy (1987) explain:

> Intentional actions are embedded in groups of varying size and are constrained by (re-)created rules and norms—sociocultural traditions. Because of the complexity of these intertwined and mutually-defining webs of relationships, scientific access to them is difficult and "uncertainty principles" abound—whether these involve the difficulties of isolating the object of study from its milieu or changes which communication between the investigator and the subject produces in the subject. The tools of the natural sciences are simply incapable of representing the key concepts in such discussions, namely motivation, belief, and intention, and the complexity of their interactions.
>
> (p. 372)

Reichenbach (1951) has complained that

> it is an unfortunate matter of fact that human beings are inclined to give
> answers even when they do not have the means to find correct answers.
> Scientific explanation demands ample observation and critical thought: the
> higher the generality aspired to, the greater must be the mass of observa-
> tional material, and the more critical the thought.
>
> (p. 8)

However, as David Hume noted, no amount of observation can actually
prove even a "scientific" generalization. Causation reduces to mere regular-
ity, or what he called "constant conjunction." He pointed out that any conviction we have about causal relation comes merely from our subjective
expectations. Hume famously raised radical doubts about the very rationality of the inductive method of science, since the ultimate causes of the phenomena are beyond the reach of human inquiry; however, we do not know
that future instances will resemble our past experience.

Ironically, the trend in the natural sciences is toward recognizing the
limits of research based on binary quantification and thinking instead about
understanding complex systems and ways in which scientists influence
science, and acknowledging the ways in which scientific questions are historically and culturally rooted. There is no absolute reference system against
which things can be measured. Rather human beings are the ultimate cause
and reference system. If such a critique of causality can be made for the hard
sciences then certainly we can abandon it for qualitative work as well. In
education even leaders of positivist research recognized this advance of
theory and accounted for it in the literature since the 1970s (Cronbach,
1975; Guba & Clark, 1975). There has since been a dramatic reconfigura-
tion of educational research that is reflected in journal publications, disser-
tation methodologies, and the composition of research faculties. In support
of this breadth of valuable educational research methodologies, the American
Educational Research Association (AERA), representing more than 20,000
diverse researchers, issued an official statement on scientific research that
served as a strong critique of the federal government's narrow and miscon-
ceived definition.

The complex nature of teaching, learning, and educational research

Under the influence of progressive era scholars John Dewey, W. W. Charters,
and others during the past century, educators have made an ongoing effort to
integrate and apply varieties of modern science to the practice of the education profession. As with all fields in the human sciences, the migration of

education to the status of hard science has often been frustrated. Educators should be cautious of research which envisions the classroom as a "black box" and which treats children's minds and bodies as equivalent and/or identical for the purposes of research. Nonetheless, this is the current federal view. As Valerie Reyna, former deputy of the now dismantled Office of Educational Research and Improvement (OERI), explained:

> The bottom line here is these same rules about what works and how to make inferences about what works, they are exactly the same for educational practice as they would be for medical practice. Same rules, exactly the same logic, whether you are talking about a treatment for cancer or whether you're talking about an intervention to help children learn. . . . When we teach students we really are engaging in a kind of brain surgery.
>
> (U.S. Department of Education, 2003c)

This type of simplicity and reduction is insulting not just to qualitative researchers but also to quantitative educational researchers, who are very careful about their claims. Education is not a medical intervention. Even researchers with the most carefully designed quantitative research projects are cautious in making inferences about what works. Random assignment to experimental and control groups can be desirable, but they are most reliable when they use large numbers of schools (20–25), are appropriate for a limited set of research questions, and can raise ethical questions. Experimental design seeks to remove or generalize personality, context, and the unique local, personal, and cultural aspects of individual teachers and classrooms. Some dimensions of successful learning are complex, personal, and local. What helps or hinders achievement in one place can be very difficult to isolate and even more difficult to replicate. A whole host of local factors can influence a school or classroom randomly assigned to an educational program under study. Also, schools are never "one place" but a series of inherently diverse places and experiences.

Educational research has long been considered a useful tool in helping policy-makers, administrators, and teachers recognize and implement sound policy. As described above, the No Child Left Behind Act, which reauthorized ESEA (the federal government's principle legislative authority for involvement in K–12 public education), specifically requires the use of high quality research in education policy-making. Educators in the United States find themselves working in a climate dominated by calls for high student achievement and increasing demands for accountability. Though these concerns have been around for decades, recent changes in federal and state legislation have placed the force of law and the power of money behind very specific definitions of achievement, teacher quality, school improvement, and strategies to strengthen the core academic subjects using scientifically based research.

In this context, school administrators and teachers have new levels of responsibility for using both school-generated data and scientifically based research to improve student achievement and teacher quality. Yet, their capacity to use educational research appropriately is compromised by the nature of federal law.

The hope for data on student achievement is that the information will identify strengths and weaknesses in student learning, isolate factors that aid and inhibit student learning, and highlight both successful and ineffective approaches to curriculum and teaching. The skillful analysis of data on student achievement is envisioned to reveal clear and systematic strategies for change and improvement. This potential is appealing. Also, policies focusing on "data," "accountability," "scientific research," and "standards" seem transparently good to many citizens accustomed to the U.S. cultural and ideological environment in which modernist, authoritative concepts of progress have a wide, often symbolic, appeal. Yet, even educators and researchers who find the current rhetoric of reform appealing are also finding serious problems with the policies behind the rhetoric. Seemingly straightforward goals, such as improving achievement and quality of teaching, or using educational research in policy, hide a complex reality that requires caution and careful thought.

Improving data or improving learning?

Because many important decisions are made based on student assessments, educators must ensure that both the assessments and the definitions of achievement to which they refer are relevant and reliable. Recently, the federal government has defined student achievement in very limited, narrow, and specific terms. As the No Child Left Behind Act explains:

> The purpose of this title is to ensure that all children have a fair, equal, and significant opportunity to obtain a high-quality education and reach, at a minimum, proficiency on challenging State academic achievement standards and state academic assessments. This purpose can be accomplished by—(1) ensuring that high-quality academic assessments, accountability systems, teacher preparation and training, curriculum, and instructional materials are aligned with challenging State academic standards so that students, teachers, parents, and administrators can measure progress against common expectations for student academic achievement.
>
> (Office of Superintendent of Public Instruction, n.d.)

In the NCLB legislation, "a high-quality education" and "proficiency on challenging State academic achievement standards and state academic assessments" are strongly related, suggesting that what is most important about high-quality education and teaching can be captured and translated into easily measured standards.

In response to this legislation, and in order to change instruction and improve test scores, countless school administrators are currently advancing their skills at analyzing, interpreting, and applying standardized test data on student achievement. It is a mistake, however, to blithely consider this approach as an indication of improved teaching and learning. A growing body of research, highlighted below, suggests that, though schools and entire states can improve student achievement data as measured by standardized tests, such increases often indicate no more than greater test preparation and the exclusion of certain students from testing. Even worse, teaching to a standardized test can easily diminish a teacher's skills and reduce student understanding.

Current federal policy was based, in part, on the reported success of the Texas Assessment of Academic Skills (TAAS). Texas could document rising pass rates and "substantial gains on some of the NAEP tests, specifically in fourth and eighth grade math," yet "other important indicators of educational success, namely high school progression and graduation rates[,] at best rose slightly in the 1990s, and then only in the past few years" (Carnoy, Loeb, & Smith, 2001). In a study published by the Harvard Civil Rights Project, Professors Linda McNeil of Rice University and Angela Valenzuela of the University of Texas, Austin, discovered that Texas teachers were teaching to the test and reducing the instruction that develops higher-order skills, particularly for low-income students. They observed: "Behind the rhetoric of the test scores are a growing set of classroom practices in which test-prep activities are usurping a substantive curriculum" (McNeil & Valenzuela, 2001). In a much wider study, Amrein and Berliner examined ACT, SAT, NAEP and advanced placement test data from 18 states and found that "there is no compelling evidence from a set of states with high-stakes testing policies that those policies result in transfer to the broader domains of knowledge and skill for which high-stakes test scores must be indicators" (Amrein & Berliner, 2002). All of this evidence suggests that high-stakes tests in use today are not valid indicators of genuine learning in secondary schools.

As Eliot Eisner (1967) explained,

> What is most educationally valuable is the development of that mode of curiosity, inventiveness, and insight that is capable of being described only in metaphoric terms. Indeed, the image of the educated man that has been held in the highest esteem for the longest period of time in western civilization is one which is not amenable to standard measurement.

Such qualities, however, can be assessed. Teachers can productively use a wide range of assessments that can reflect things such as curiosity, inventiveness, and insight — but these typically require that teachers are able to follow a specific student's complex and individual thinking and thus are not suitable for inexpensive, standardized testing. The National Center for Fair & Open Testing (2003) points out that state academic assessments typically "reward the ability to quickly answer superficial questions that do not require real thought. They do not measure the ability to think or create in any field. Their use encourages a narrowed curriculum, outdated methods of instruction, and harmful practices such as retention in grade and tracking." Advocates for standardized tests clearly don't address the suitability of various curricular goals for measurement by standardized performance instruments. For example, standardized tests can readily measure the performance of a mathematics problem but not the extent to which its logic is understood. Standardized tests can measure a student's recognition of standard spelling, but not the capacity to write thoughtfully and artfully. Nonetheless, the power of standardized tests in current policy suggests that they measure something very important and comprehensive. As Peter Afflerbach cautions, "Should one examine the inferential path from assessment task, setting, and outcome to the generation of theories of an individual student's development and achievement, one might quickly determine what a tenuous enterprise this is" (Afflerbach, 2002).

Focusing on standardized tests of achievement limits what educators can learn from assessment and, by extension, what they teach as a consequence of assessment. Achievement is a specific performance and is an inherently comparative concept. It narrows and distorts the wide scope of a student's learning when we focus on a specific performance, which in turn is compared to a standard performance and is translated into a result that sorts and ranks students. Teachers understand that a great deal of powerful learning does not produce a standard, predictable product, and this is even more the case in diverse classrooms. Multiple formal and informal assessments that reveal the complexity of individual student thinking and learning are more valuable than evaluation that merely compares students on narrow points of learning. Teachers need access to the complexity of individual student thinking and learning in order to bring each student to the next level of achievement. Most teachers and administrators are very familiar with the complexity of thinking and learning and the need for multiple and varied assessments. However, it will be a challenge for professional educators to continue to value this complexity when external evaluation and reward and punishment systems do not acknowledge it.

Improving data or improving teaching and teachers?

The complexity of good teaching is in similar danger of being reduced to a narrow and simplified standard. In NCLB, the "quality" of new teachers is conflated with their qualifications. As an Education Department press release explains, "The new teacher quality provisions under No Child Left Behind require educators in core academic areas to be licensed by the state, hold a bachelor's degree, and demonstrate competence in their subject area" (U.S. Department of Education, 2002a). Once teachers are actually teaching it is assumed that their "quality" is easily measured and correlated with test scores. In this view, the "best" teachers have the "best" measurable student outcomes according to standardized tests, and attention to standardized outcomes is taken as one of the most important factors in helping teachers become better. These assumptions disregard the profound complexity of teaching and learning. Both the quality of teaching and the quality of teaching outcomes are filtered through the complex layers of circumstance, intention, and activity that comprise teaching. Quality teaching involves a vast array of skills and dispositions and countless decisions that affect students each day and each hour, producing a corresponding array of differing results. If other conditions are favorable, quality teaching may not in some cases be necessary for good outcomes to occur. Some students perform well in spite of teachers. Circumstances and demographics make it easier for some teachers to produce good outcomes. Consider also, if a 1st-grade teacher has a class in which three quarters of the students can already read, is it fair to judge her on the same test results as a teacher who has a class of non-readers?

As educational researchers know, some children typically achieve high scores in reading because those children read a great deal at home and live in a language-rich environment in which standard English is spoken. Such students typically score reasonably well even if teachers provide very poor teaching and curriculum. Yet, it is common for these teachers and schools to take credit for good scores and, by inference, for providing a quality education. The opposite often happens, too. Through the deep commitment and inspired teaching of their faculty, many struggling learners have developed intellectually and achieved academically. If, however, students, or the cohort of demographically similar students, miss one too many standardized test questions, their teachers and school may be labeled as failing. Arbitrary cut-off points for "adequate yearly progress" do not consider the contexts of teachers' work and the nature of students' prior experiences and, therefore, cannot measure school and teacher quality. As the National Education Association (2002) explains, "Any resultant differences between two groups of different children may be attributable to myriad factors only one of which is instructional effectiveness."

Just as a single set of test scores should not be considered separately from their source in the complex contexts of teaching and assessment, teacher assessment should not be considered in isolation. There is a great deal of enthusiasm about the potential of portfolios and work sampling as teacher assessment tools that acknowledge complexity. As Cohen describes, "recognizing that good teaching is a complex art, proponents of teacher performance assessment are looking for strategies that can capture what teachers do in the classroom, as well as their knowledge and judgment as professionals" (Cohen, 1995). Portfolios, however, do not necessarily address the problems presented by heterogeneous teachers and teaching situations. Ultimately, portfolios measure a teacher's ability to create a good portfolio. It is certainly possible to imagine an excellent teacher with a poor portfolio and a poor teacher with an excellent portfolio.

Another approach aimed at resolving the problem of the complexity of assessing quality teaching is the use of multiple evaluations. As Guillaume and Yopp (1995) explain, "because teaching is a complex contextually-bound activity, it is best captured by assessment forms that provide multiple sources of data and that capture the richness of the teaching act." What is needed, however, is not only multiple sources of assessment, but also a heightened awareness of the nature of complexity in teaching that allows for seeming failures and weaknesses (or successes) to be seen in the true light of their complexity, no matter which kinds of assessment have been used. Without this sensitivity, inappropriate evaluations threaten to obscure the complex nature of good teaching and make personal and collective improvement in teaching less attainable. Instead of embracing a single model, administrators and evaluators alike must continue to seek a range of theoretical perspectives and related practical processes which allow for appropriate evaluation of teaching. Once again, the current federal policy climate makes this more challenging than ever, as administrators are being pressured to conflate teacher quality and standardized test scores.

In spite of the precautions outlined above, administrators are being required to respond to evaluations of school quality that rely heavily on state academic assessment through standardized tests. Also, any district currently wishing to qualify for federal government funding must implement "scientifically based" reading instruction. When scope for improvement in other curricular areas is noted, administrators are also being asked to use education programs for classroom instruction and professional development that are derived from "scientifically based" research. "Supporting teachers means giving them the very best tools—the best research-based lessons and materials and the best training—to ensure that no child is left behind" (U.S. Department of Education, 2003f). This assumes that schools aren't as good as they can be because of a lack of "research-based lessons and materials." In this assumption, teachers, administrators, and school culture are not significant variables—a questionable assumption that harkens back to teacher-proof curriculum. More realistically, school contexts, teachers, students, and the curriculum are all important, in different ways and in different places.

Complex ethical challenges for educational research

According to the new law, reading and other scientifically supported curricula are to be aligned with and directly related to state academic content standards. NCLB defines "scientifically based" to mean research which "employs systematic, empirical methods" and uses "experimental or quasi-experimental designs in which individuals, entities, programs, or activities are assigned to different conditions and with appropriate controls to evaluate the effects of the condition of interest, with a preference for random-assignment experiments" (U.S. Department of Education, 2003c). Yet, this definition limits what educators can learn from research. A scientifically based research design alone does not guarantee good results, since researchers still must choose the appropriate study design from among the wide array of choices and analyze and report data in a high quality manner. This does not always happen. "The fact that an approach or a subject is scientific, according to some abstract criterion[,] is ... no guarantee that it will succeed. Each case must be judged separately, especially today, when the inflation of the sciences has added some rather doubtful activities to what used to be a sober enterprise" (Feyerabend, 1999, p. 158). Contemporary science is not a single method or a monaural guide to problem solving: "It is, rather, a delicate interweaving of subjectivity, responsibility, and expectation" (Pessin, 2002).

It is more ethically defensible to use the highest quality studies—including studies that use both qualitative and quantitative methods—but this is not what the NCLB law requires. Naturally, some dimensions of successful learning are generalizable across contexts while others are complex, personal, and local. There is a place for experimental or quasi-experimental designs, but narrative, descriptive, and qualitative studies provide different, also valuable, information. Different research foci and different research paradigms each produce varying data and insights. No single paradigm of research is capable of presenting a whole truth or offering silver bullets for school improvement.

Furthermore, no paradigm of research is complete or value-neutral in terms of its methods and results or its topic of study, and, certainly, its use in policy. In the future, there is likely to be a great deal more research available on mathematics education than on social studies education because, in federal policy, math is connected to scientific progress, economic leadership, prosperity, and national security. As new federal legislation states, "We must improve achievement to maintain our economic leadership. While technology advances with lightning speed, stagnant math performance in schools shortchanges our students' future and endangers our prosperity and our nation's security" (U.S. Department of Education, 2003d). NCLB does not mandate testing or improvement in civics or social studies and barely mentions it, in spite of the fact that the NAEP indicates that nearly six in ten of the nation's high school seniors lack even a basic knowledge of American history. If a community of teachers wishes to improve social studies, there is clearly an imperative to do so, but money for programs and research—scientific or otherwise—will be harder to find.

This concern about bias in education research is related to the market nature of research funding and grant competition. Because the education research funding system is essentially a market system—that is, there are a limited number of resources available to support research, creating a competition among researchers to design projects that have the "best" chance of being funded—the demand for specific types of research could indirectly skew the body of scientific knowledge, creating a bias toward questions important to funders, irrespective of the actual value of those questions (Gowri, 2000; Spring, 1998b). For example, if teacher quality is defined by funders as the impact of teachers on student achievement from year to year, the body of research on teacher quality may begin to skew away from other equally important indicators (such as graduation rates, additional educational attainment, economic participation, self-actualization, success, etc.). Additionally, over time the question might become the answer, resulting in the definition of teacher quality becoming student achievement on standardized tests. Achievement itself is now often narrowly prefigured, since student achievement is typically defined as only what achievement tests measure.

Education research may be especially vulnerable to these types of research bias (that is, the market skewing and the demand for narrowly defined research), since it has been historically underfunded when compared with the "hard" sciences.

This highlights that nearly every educational researcher works in a context of somewhat questionable ethics and mixed values. It is not possible to be right or find truth; instead we can only hope for research with a good awareness of its necessary limits and compromises. Consider how research questions are posed in the first place. The types of research that are funded are often driven by economic and political contexts and by ideological interests. In reviewing results, researchers are likely to consider the following questions. Does it show what my funding agency wanted? Will it help my career? Is it publishable? Is it innovative?

Formal instruction in the responsible conduct of research and rigorous peer review can help mitigate the influence of this power on research. When research is produced by "experts" working outside their field and is disseminated without peer review, power abuses are more likely to occur. In recent articles in *Education Week*, former Assistant Secretary for Research and Improvement at the U.S. Department of Education, Chester Finn (who now heads up the market-oriented Fordham Foundation), has attacked the "tattered raiments" that the peer-review emperor wears, noting that, "by selecting the peers, you're preordaining the outcome of the review" (2002, p. 34), and, when questioned, justifying that, at Fordham, "We're engaged in an argument . . . not refereeing an argument" (Viadero, 2002). Kenneth Howe, director of the Education and the Public Interest Center, later defended the concept of peer review and criticized Finn and "those who market their partisan preferences under the guise of informing public deliberation" through research (2002, p. 35).

Policies justified by research funded, conducted, and published by advocates (typically working in think tanks rather than universities) who bypass traditionally accepted research norms are even more likely to be "interested" rather than disinterested and scientific. A growing counter-establishment of pseudo-academic educational institutions, including journals, centers, think tanks, organizations, and foundations, offer this type of educational research in which conflicts of interest are ignored or concealed, peer review is limited, and open debate over ideas short-circuited. Such "think tank" research plays an active role in educational policy. In fact, the U.S. Department of Education's NCLB site offers links to numerous conservative non-academic think tanks, including the Core Knowledge Network (E. D. Hirsch), the Fordham Foundation (listed as Education Excellence Network), the Heritage Foundation, the Education Consumers Clearinghouse, and the Manhattan Institute, all with research methods that have been questioned by mainstream academics.

Academia should not become another arm of the federal government or of corporate America, nor serve as the legitimator of any single partisan ideology, yet this is a real danger for research in a wide range of disciplines, including education. Ideally the university should represent independent, unbiased, scholarly views.

Accepting state and federally mandated definitions of student achievement and usable research and curriculum can compromise educators' professionalism, and, thus, there are increasing examples of resistance to such practices. In Denver, school principal Lynn Staminate resigned to protest a state legislated ranking of schools from "A" to "F" (based on comparisons of state academic assessments), since she believed this simplistic plan disregarded social and economic factors that contribute to test performance. On a larger scale, former Vermont Governor Howard Dean, who called NCLB legislation "a terribly flawed bill," wanted to refuse federal dollars. He was concerned that 30% of Vermont public schools would be considered "failing" under NCLB even though the schools were performing well by national standards. "It's going to give us a huge incentive to dumb down the standards" (Toppo, 2002), he said. Ultimately, Vermont, like Utah, accepted NCLB. Since federal money comprises about 10% of state educational budgets, neither politicians nor educators think they are in a fiscal position to refuse the mandate. Administrators and teachers face difficult choices as it becomes clear that federal funds are only for programs justified by highly narrow and perhaps compromised definitions of student achievement, teacher quality, and educational research. It will be a challenge for professional educators to continue to value and use curriculum, assessment, and educational research according to their independent professional judgment when a great deal of money is available for some programs and not others—making the consequences of non-conformity costly.

This debate is another challenge to principals, teachers, and other educators whose collective professional judgment it overrides, although, as Howard Gardner has written, best practice is often "finely honed by groups of teachers who have worked together for many years—trying out mini-experiments, reflecting on the results, critiquing one another, co-teaching, visiting other schools to observe, and the like" (2002, p. 72). These are precisely the types of research not called for by the NRP/NCLB. In the face of such non-consultative interference, some effective responses by educators are necessary.

Educational leaders need to challenge the notion of government manipulation of science, the marginalization of the education profession from policy-making in its own field, the dubious quality of the NRP's *Report* and *Summary*, and departures of the Department of Education from the intent of NCLB. As has frequently occurred in recent history, the debate around this educational issue is forfeit if the larger context is left unquestioned. The abuse of standardized testing is a case in point: once it was established by media and political decree that such tests were a comprehensive measure of life in schools, the public debate focused exclusively on numerical results and turned away from valid foundational discussions. Few in policy-making roles understand the psychometrics of the data they cite, but that basic deficiency seems not to matter. The NRP's emphasis on verificationism to the exclusion of applied research and practitioner wisdom is an example of the sterility predicted above, as is the Bush administration's use of the label "science" to marginalize Reading Recovery. The imposition of a narrow version of the medical model of research on an applied human service profession such as education is both reductive and reactionary. The quality of our schools will be gravely damaged if we practice such reductionism in order to gain the appearance of exactitude. Public education is more than a "formal argument and debate."

Educators need to understand the nature of the struggle in which they find themselves. Unlike a good classroom, America's public forum is not dominated by the pursuit of knowledge. It is in the nature of our media and politicians to vie for attention and quick public relations victories. The education establishment continues to be a "soft target" for attack rhetoric. It is lumbering, diffuse, and largely undefended by corporate entities and political action committees. The response of educators should be at the grass roots, by asserting their professional knowledge in conversation, media, and public forums, and through their organizations and institutions to national audiences. This is not a fair fight; it is not what it seems on the surface, and the stakes are high. Education is a public trust that, at society's peril, is being treated as an object of careless partisan attack.

Chapter 5

The "science" of teacher testing

> I know this orbit of mine cannot be swept by a carpenter's compass ...
> (Whitman, *Song of Myself*)

Teacher testing as it is currently construed is a symptom of what is wrong with U.S. public education policy. The fervor for ever higher stakes associated with teacher testing illustrates how deeply entrenched a wrong-headed approach can become. With the inception of Title II of the Higher Education Act (Public Law 105–244), the federal government has begun a process of employing such tests not only for entry to the classroom by individuals, but also for determining which institutions of higher education will have the right to prepare candidates for licensure. (This latter goal would be achieved by restricting the access of colleges and universities to federal education funding, such as student loans.) The No Child Left Behind Act in its definition and requirement of "highly qualified teachers" has extended the central function of testing in licensure. The evolution of standardized testing in American society has been documented extensively, most notably in *None of the above* (Owen, 1985) and more recently in *The big test* (Lemann, 1999). While they emerged from legitimate origins and egalitarian motives, the uses of these tests drifted into increasingly dangerous political waters. In the United States, punitive and unscientific methods of evaluation are reaching their apotheosis in the current practice of high-stakes K–12 student and teacher testing, with consequences that affect the foundations of public education.

Origins

Edward Lee Thorndike is famously quoted as having claimed that everything of value exists in some quantity and can be measured (Johnson, 1936). This attitude has, until recently, proven to be perfectly in tune with the spirit of our scientific and technological times. The revolutionary impact of science and technology in engineering, medicine, agriculture, and manufacturing in the past 200 years has led many in Western society to conclude that the methods of positive, empirical science are transferable and lend control to other fields of endeavor such as human service professions, psychology, politics, and economics. Faith in standardized testing emerges from this expansive generalization about methods of inquiry. At a time when science itself has become more diverse at its frontiers (e.g., the uncertainty principle, chaos theory), political opinion and public policy can frequently be found clinging to discredited theories from the past or making flawed generalizations across disciplinary lines.

To put it another way, there is nothing postmodern about teacher testing. This endeavor is rooted in invalid generalizations of method from one discipline to another, and it is anchored in one era of research when research itself has moved into another. It promises reductive certitude in a complex human service profession. Evidently a hunger for simple answers has overwhelmed good judgment in the application of such an approach to teacher evaluation. On the other hand, authorities in educational research have over the past 20 years recognized that a range of methods is needed to effectively evaluate educational matters. One notable result has been the new eminence of qualitative research; a second is the performance assessment movement. *Although promising, scholarly evaluation movements have emerged in force within educational research, policy-makers have shown little interest in keeping up with the cutting edge of inquiry in the field of education.*

Tribes

Generally we expect those with credentials and expertise to govern a field of endeavor or, at a minimum, to be intimately involved in policy-making in that field. Otherwise, as history has famously illustrated, the consequences prove disastrous: consider Stalin's central bureaucratic control of the arts, social sciences, and science during the 1930s. Ideology reigned over open inquiry. In a parallel example, only during the 1990s did the pope redress the Vatican's interventions into astronomy, which culminated in the forced recantations of Galileo. As decades and centuries pass, such abuses in the name of ideology become so transparent as to become comical. The devastating and destructive consequences of past abuses in their times is largely forgotten.

In the United States the top policy-makers for education are rarely educators or students of education. Instead, they tend to be political operatives, such as Secretaries of Education Richard Riley and Margaret Spellings or the governors of the states. When they consult on educational matters, they are likely to listen to a combination of "policy experts" (typically trained in variations of political science), business leaders, "hard" scientists, and a very few token, ideologically inclined academicians (e.g.,

Chester Finn, Diane Ravitch, William Bennett, John Silber, Arthur Bestor, Alan Bloom, John Chubb, Terry Moe). Normally absent from these discussions are persons with deep experience in the human service professions, schools, or colleges of education, respected education scholars, and leaders of the stakeholder institutions and organizations in education. Indeed, having expertise or experience in schools, in educational organizations, or in colleges of education appears to disqualify persons from being at or near the levers of power in our field. The ongoing evolution of teacher testing is more easily understood when we consider how little influence educators have in the development of policies that govern our profession and how much disdain our legitimate research is met with in the circles of power (Berliner & Biddle, 1995).

In a contemporary society steeped in respect for expertise, formal preparation, advanced degrees, and peer review, why is the field of education governed through an alternative model of power distribution? Why are educators, numerous and omnipresent as they are in society and by far the largest profession, so disenfranchised with respect to their own field of endeavor? A number of explanations are possible, but let us focus here on one in particular, since it subsumes many of the others in its scope. In the popular mind, the rationale for the exclusion of educators from authority in education may be reflected in the adage "Those who can, do. Those who can't, teach." In a society that is dominated by an ideology and economy of free market competition, the meaning of "those who can, do" brings with it a particular bias against "those who can't" and, instead, teach. *That is, a popular bias exists against those who have forsaken free market competition for a career of tenure, government employment, and 180-day work years. This bias is well entrenched but obscures more fundamental motives.* This type of invidious discrimination is not levied on clergy, social workers, philanthropy professionals, and a host of others who work outside business and industry. Educators for some reason attract a special opprobrium.

A Native-American scholar was asked, after a presentation on the horrors of her people's experience at the hands of the U.S. government, why it was that the persecution of Indians was so relentless and excessive, even after they posed no rational threat to white dominance. She responded that the tribes embodied an alternative ideology, a set of values at variance with those of Western Europe. Their social organization, less individualistic and materialistic, more oriented toward the group and common ownership of property, was perceived as a fundamental threat to the new dominant culture of North America and, as such, was forcefully eradicated, with nearly genocidal consequences.

Is there a parallel with educators and their relation to the majoritarian view of U.S. citizens? Could the seemingly senseless governance structure imposed on education and the perverse restrictions on educator input into decision-making in education be explained in this way? Without doubt, educators are a large "tribe" in the United States, numbering in the millions. There are over 3 million teachers, for example, and approximately 50,000 professors of education, among half a million college and university faculty. The institution of education is monumental in size, occupying 25% of the population on any given day, as students, instructors, administrators, or support staff. Size makes us significant, but our values make us a threat. Educators represent an alternative ideological path in U.S. society. They do not by any means reject materialism, but they entertain competing priorities in their scheme of values.

Educators as a group embody an alternative approach to life in U.S. society. For us values such as "the life of the mind," "aesthetic appreciation," and "human service" prevail as motivational priorities and succeed in calling into question "consumerism," "property," "wealth," and "status." Within families and peer groups those who take this alternative path are often subject to pressure and criticism, accused of escaping reality (as "professional students") or of being failures, since they earn fewer economic rewards. Educators are tolerated in society since there is recognition that public education is necessary. There is also a kind of popular understanding that, ultimately, only the "educator-types" seem willing to stay in teaching and work with youth. These adopted views are tempered, however, by stringent controls on the extent to which educators are permitted to control their own institutions lest this massive educational enterprise (advertently or inadvertently) reconceptualize society: namely, to one that more closely reflects the dispositions of the teachers themselves. There is a culture war at the heart of the teacher test debate and its roots run deep into U.S. culture.

Validity and culture

Another old saw of psychometrics goes like this: "What is intelligence? Intelligence is what intelligence tests measure." Through a century of evolution in the testing field, this tautology may be more accepted today than ever before. The types of timed, objective, standardized tests that have been spun from psychology's initial forays into IQ have demonstrated a strong positive correlation to one another and to the mysterious "G factor" we have come to identify as intelligence. The consensus definition of intelligence has come to be defined as the ability to manipulate mathematical and verbal symbols in the decontextualized setting of multiple choice questions. This technique has been generalized to perform gatekeeper functions for selective colleges, scholarship programs, entry to professions and jobs, and a range of other highly significant opportunities in our society. Because this method has resonated with the dominant worldview of powerful U.S. elites, few challenges to it have prevailed and a comprehensive debate over its assumptions has not occurred.

The work of Howard Gardner in multiple intelligences (1993), Daniel Goleman in emotional intelligence (1995), and Robert Sternberg in practical intelligence (2000) are several clear examples among many of how the cutting edge of psychology is not sufficiently taken into account, either by the government policy-makers who dictate the direction of education, or by the popular media that affirm an outdated understanding of human ability. This type of resistance to new directions in the field is yet another cost and consequence of governance in a profession by those who have little or no experience *of* that profession. While researchers such as Gardner and Sternberg have established that intelligence can be explained in a rich, multivariate fashion that better explains the diversified paths through which individuals succeed, in at least 44 states (American Federation of Teachers, 2000), those who aspire to teach continue to be faced with archaic, linear examinations. As an illustration of how another school of thought in psychology interprets this narrowing of evaluation, one can apply Myers–Briggs Type Indicator data. These reaffirm the apparent unfairness of teacher tests through their positive correlation of high achievement on such tests with the "intuitive" preference and corresponding negative correlation of performance on these instruments with the "sensing" preference. The sensing preference is dominant among those who teach elementary school (Myers & McCaulley, 1998).

In the United States, when members of minority groups complain that timed, objective tests discriminate against them, their concerns are regarded by many as unfounded whining and requests for special treatment. The courts typically hold that an adverse impact is acceptable if close examination of the test content supports the assertion that the information tested is essential for teachers (McDowell, 2000). In this way, basic skills tests have been afforded a legitimacy that professional practices and even subject matter content tests have not. More interesting, however, is ongoing research that suggests there is a deeper, more defensible case for the minority resistance to these tests. Here is how the *New York Times* reports the story:

> But the habits of thought—the strategies people adopted in processing information and making sense of the world around them—were, Western scholars assumed, the same for everyone, exemplified by, among other things, a devotion to logical reasoning, a penchant for categorization and an urge to understand situations and events in linear terms of cause and effect. In a series of studies comparing European Americans to East Asians, Dr. Richard Nisbett and his colleagues have found that people who grow up in different cultures do not just think about different things; they think differently. ... Easterners, the researchers find, appear to think more "holistically," paying greater attention to context and relationship, relying more on

experience-based knowledge than abstract logic and showing more tolerance for contradiction. Westerners are more "analytic" in their thinking,
tending to detach objects from their context, to avoid contradictions and to
rely more heavily on formal logic.

(Goode, 2000)

The "America First" argument at this point would be that minority cultures need to conform in their cognitive style, just as they need to conform
to English as the lingua franca. This nativist argument is oblivious to a larger
truth about an immigrant society such as that of the United States: Its historic strength has been achieved through integrating new cultures with its
own, not by imposition of a totalitarian conformity to the old, established
ways. Particularly in the field of education of minorities, in which teachers
are translators among cultures, it is self-defeating to create a teaching corps
that is monochromatic in its cultural awareness and understanding. In
addressing higher-order cognition, the U.S. tradition of standardized testing
is increasingly called into question because of the biases of its approach.
These biases are exercised among individuals within the dominant culture
and toward cultural groups in a diverse society (such as the United States).
Even mainstream behavioral science on its cutting edge is questioning the
conventional testing assumptions.

*In the context of teacher examinations, the error of most contemporary
testing approaches is aggravated by the nature of teaching itself, since among
human endeavors none exceed teaching as a complex act.* Not only is the
teacher attempting to instruct in fundamentals while elevating the character
of students, but also, in a diverse society, these goals are addressed in a context of vast cultural and linguistic differences. The entire enterprise is undertaken in a large group setting, which assures that no one strategy can reach
all students optimally. Instructional hours are limited; teachers' time and
energy is stretched in many (including non-academic) directions. Over 20%
of U.S. students are growing up in economic poverty, helping to render a
large number wanting in what Maslow defined years ago as "deficiency
needs" (Maslow, 1998). In a wealthy nation such as the United States there
continue to be many children who arrive at school hungry, ill-clothed or ill-
housed, and/or lacking medical care. A teacher who is able to be effective in
such settings will necessarily demonstrate a wide range of interpersonal and
communication skills, as well as command of subject matter. These skills
may include a sense of theatre and performance; empathy; multicultural
insight; an ability to employ irony, humor, and persuasion; means of demonstrating conviction and a moral stance; an ability to cope with significant
stress; and so on. Outstanding teachers communicate different messages to
different students during the same teaching moment. Through various messages, regarding both content and affect, these teachers communicate in a

range of modalities to each of the students according to that student's needs and abilities. Needless to say, fine teaching is a triumphant expression of intelligence—broadly defined—as much as it is a triumph of character.

The Interstate New Teacher Assessment and Support Consortium (INTASC) has produced one of the latest and best expressions of "model core standards" for licensing teachers. Prototype classroom performance assessments and the INTASC Test of Teaching Knowledge are also being developed. Examining the 10 principles—and their subcategories of knowledge, dispositions, and performances—demonstrates how elusive teaching professional qualities are when one attempts to reduce them to standardized testing. Performance assessment offers much more promise in this regard, but the economic cost and overall fairness challenges even in this approach are not to be underestimated. There follows a sample principle and selected subcategories. Imagine the multiple-choice questions that are valid to establish these abilities, particularly when we leave the subcategory of "knowledge":

> *Principle #5*: The teacher uses an understanding of individual and group motivation and behavior to create a learning environment that encourages positive social interaction, active engagement in learning, and self-motivation.

> *Knowledge*

> The teacher knows how to help people work productively and cooperatively with each other in complex social settings.

> The teacher understands the principles of effective classroom management and can use a range of strategies to promote positive relationships, cooperation, and purposeful learning in the classroom.

> The teacher recognizes factors and situations that are likely to promote or diminish intrinsic motivation, and knows how to help students become self-motivated.

> *Dispositions*

> The teacher takes responsibility for establishing a positive climate in the classroom and participates in maintaining such a climate in the school as whole.

> The teacher understands how participation supports commitment, and is committed to the expression and use of democratic values in the classroom.

> The teacher values the role of students in promoting each other's learning and recognizes the importance of peer relationships in establishing a climate of learning.

> The teacher recognizes the value of intrinsic motivation to students' life-long growth and learning.

The teacher is committed to the continuous development of individual students' abilities and considers how different motivational strategies are likely to encourage this development for each student.

Performances

The teacher creates a smoothly functioning learning community in which students assume responsibility for themselves and one another, participate in decision-making, work collaboratively and independently, and engage in purposeful learning activities.

The teacher engages students in individual and cooperative learning activities that help them develop the motivation to achieve, by, for example, relating lessons to students' personal interests, allowing students to have choices in their learning, and leading students to ask questions and pursue problems that are meaningful to them.

The teacher organizes, allocates, and manages the resources of time, space, activities, and attention to provide active and equitable engagement of students in productive tasks.

The teacher maximizes the amount of class time spent in learning by creating expectations and processes for communication and behavior along with a physical setting conducive to classroom goals.

The teacher helps the group to develop shared values and expectations for student interactions, academic discussions, and individual and group responsibility that create a positive classroom climate of openness, mutual respect, support, and inquiry.

The teacher analyzes the classroom environment and makes decisions and adjustments to enhance social relationships, student motivation and engagement, and productive work.

The teacher organizes, prepares students for, and monitors independent and group work that allows for full and varied participation of all individuals.

> (Interstate New Teacher Assessment and
> Support Consortium, 1995)

In the face of these realities about teaching, along come decision-makers in government and political leaders who respond that all this may be well and true, but what is available and economical today in teacher testing is standardized tests. Therefore, the argument goes, the standardized testing approach is better than not screening at all. The poverty of this analysis is illustrated by a recent *New York Times* columnist's encounter with the New York Liberal Arts and Sciences Test for teacher licensure:

My results made little sense. I got a perfect score, 300, on the science and math section—bizarre, considering that I failed precalculus in high school and never took another science course after tenth-grade chemistry.

Meanwhile, I am mortified to report that my worst score—a 260—was on the essay.

... Although it is not perfect, the exam seems a necessary gatekeeping device for a profession whose purpose, after all, is imparting knowledge.

(Goodnough, 2000)

So strong is the societal dependency on such tests that, even faced with a "bizarre and mortifying" outcome, the reporter affirms the methodology.

But what about the assertion that questionable testing is better than no testing? These tests may not only be irrelevant and simplistic, but they may also have a negative impact on teacher success in classrooms (Flippo & Riccards, 2000). At a minimum, they serve to define the profession and teacher education curriculum in a wholly inadequate manner. In California, for example, the state legislature mandated a reading examination for elementary, and eventually special education, candidates, which is derived from a set of over 140 objectives provided by the state. This test, the Reading Instruction Competency Assessment (RICA), is emblematic of the imposition of politics into the heart of the teacher education curriculum and the university regardless of the counsel of professional educators, their accrediting bodies, or California's own independent Commission for the Credentialing of Teachers. The purpose was to assure mastery of phonics methodology for the teaching of reading, which has of course become a politicized, overwrought initiative of America's rightists. RICA is much more focused and specific than the run of teacher tests, but is a clear example of how these tests are not without consequences in the preparation teachers receive.

In the initial round of testing, over 90% of candidates statewide passed California's RICA. Predictably, this did not result in accolades from government or media. In approximately the same timeframe, national publicity very much attended to the failure of 53% of Massachusetts' candidates in the first administration of that state's new teacher licensure examination (Melnick & Pullin, 2000). What is missing in such testing events is the public and media understanding that passing scores and rates are often determined, not according to any research-based, criterion-referenced standard, but by political whim or a practical decision about how many licensed teachers the state needs to let through its gauntlet. While psychometricians initially express where the cut scores should fall after a responsible and iterative process, those in political authority make the final judgments. When politics intervenes, the standards are not honest and credible; they are floating standards, moving targets posing as scientific. The courts have for decades been involved in sorting out this issue (as in *Groves* v. *Alabama State Board of Education*) and support cut scores based on validation studies that meet current psychometric standards. These studies are themselves evidence, however, of the uncertainty that accompanies definitions of "good teaching" and the pedagogical knowledge such teaching presumes. Validation studies of this type function in their own world of assumptions—and those assumptions are not rooted in a clear connection between the content validity of the tests and the knowledge and, particularly, the performance of successful teachers.

High-stakes K–12 testing is stimulating new research on the reliability of a single test for making monumental decisions about an individual's future. By using the reliability information provided by test publishers, Professor David Rogosa of Stanford University demonstrates the inadequacy of a single testing event and adds weight to legal challenges which are due to follow.

> About half of fourth-grade students held back for scores below the 30th percentile on a typical reading test will actually have "true" scores above that point. On any particular test, nearly 7 percent of students with true scores at the 40th percentile will likely fail, scoring below the 30th percentile.
>
> (Rothstein, 2000)

Another example of confusion around statistics is illustrated by the following anecdote. A legislator was speaking in Pennsylvania congratulating an audience of teacher educators on the pass rate of candidates on the state licensure examination (a clone of the national teacher examination). Were we wise to inform him that the state department of education had made a policy decision to fail a certain percentage of test-takers and that the pass rate reflected nothing more than this internal decision?

Now that institutions are to be ranked and judged by their graduates' rate of test success, other misleading practices are being introduced. For example:

> While Title II requires only that institutions report test scores for their "program completers," the scores for *all* test takers—who may or may not be enrolled in the institution's teacher education program—sometimes find their way into local newspapers. When substantial numbers of these test takers fail to pass the state licensure exam, institutions' pass rates may be portrayed inaccurately, possibly with devastating headlines.
>
> Another concern for education schools is being assigned blame for poor candidate performance on subject matter exams, despite the fact that preparation in content areas generally occurs in other areas of the institution.
>
> (American Association of Colleges for Teacher Education, 2000)

Institutions that serve minority candidates also suffer invidious comparisons in the testing contest on account of the well-established difficulties such candidates have with such tests. This again brings to mind the assertion that a flawed evaluation is better than no evaluation and "does no harm." The initial results of the California RICA had whites passing at a rate of 94.2%; Latinos, 79.8%; Asians, 87.8%; and African Americans, 77.3% (California Commission on Teacher Credentialing, 1999, p. 23). Recent California basic skills results (CBEST) show whites (non-Hispanic) passing at a rate of 81.2%; Mexican Americans, 54.6%; Asian Americans, 68.7%; and African Americans, 42.4% (Schieffer, 2000, p. 2). The results for universities are not reported in the media with adjustments for the ethnic constitution of an institution's student cohort. So it follows that the universities who answer society's call to recruit and prepare minority teachers appear to nearly all who read the data to provide the least effective preparation of teachers. At the same time elite universities and non-diverse private colleges gain credibility in teacher education based on the test-taking gifts and demographic advantages of their less heterogeneous student bodies.

Along the way, policy-makers have given little attention to the predictive validity of standardized instruments, particularly in the field of teacher testing. In a parallel vein, for all of its breadth of adoption, the SAT is known to predict success only marginally during the first year of college, with no better predictive validity than high school grades and rankings (Owen, 1985). NTE and similar teacher tests are presented by agencies such as the Educational Testing Service (ETS) with no claims of correlation to candidate success in classrooms (another instance of no predictive validity). ETS in fact cautions users not to claim predictive correlation between NTE and teacher performance. Test-makers claim that predicting success in classrooms is not their job. It can be argued, however, that validity comes into question not merely for a test, but also for the interpretation of the test scores and any actions based upon them (Messick, 1989). Given the questionable and controversial nature of testing, test-makers limit their task to simply assuring a minimum of professional knowledge among those licensed to teach. As has been argued here, even identifying what this pedagogical knowledge might be is a daunting task and one that has not been convincingly accomplished. The content validity of the tests rests with a "panel of experts" employed to justify a simplified and reductive understanding of the teaching act that is skewed to the disciplinary background of the test writers themselves (often educational psychology). Yet, there seems to be no interest on the part of policy-makers to address these incongruities. The methods and results of standardized tests are kept beyond legitimate scrutiny.

It is no accident that the National Board for Professional Teaching Standards, in an effort to establish credible evaluation, has adopted performance assessment rather than standardized testing as its methodology. The activities of NBPTS have challenged claims that there are no available alternatives to conventional teacher tests. Performance assessment presents such a choice, and accrediting bodies as well as some state licensure authorities are moving in this direction. Whether they can create cost-effective assessments remains to be seen. What may happen is that the assessment "label" will be illegitimately placed on what are, fundamentally, standardized objective teacher tests, so that a false veneer of quality is laid on what remain inadequate methods. Should this occur, the integrity of performance assessment will be corrupted and discredited by misuse, as with many other ideas and approaches in education. (Note the efforts of Reading Recovery to protect its "brand name" through trade marking. We regularly see this exceptional program wrongly cited in justifying lesser, diluted versions of its approach. The consequences are predictable.)

Performance assessment has entered educational evaluation over a period of the past two decades and it has brought with it great promise of fairness and accuracy. It is possible for assessment to accommodate the complexity of the teaching act far better than what is and is not captured by one-dimensional, standardized tests. In the case of the leading example of performance assessment, however, the results are not yet in on how truly useful and valid the NBPTS approach will prove to be. Up to this point, the rubrics (approximately thirty in number) are not all in place for the range of teaching fields that are to be represented. There is the danger that prior expectations and the conventional views of assessors may influence the scoring of these performances; that presuppositions about what good teaching is (the phenomenon is described by Stigler & Hiebert, 1999) may crowd out creative, nonconforming approaches.

> Cultural scripts are learned implicitly, through observation and participation, and not by deliberate study. ...
>
> People within a culture share a mental picture of what teaching is like. We call this mental picture a *script*. ...
>
> It is not hard to see where the scripts come from or why they are widely shared. ... All of us probably could enter a classroom tomorrow and act like a teacher, because we all share this cultural script.
>
> (pp. 86–87)

In any event, even a tyranny of performance conventions would elevate the debate far beyond where it currently rests. Currently there is virtually no debate over the content of tests of professional knowledge of teachers, since U.S. society, subject to the policy and media rhetoric, accepts that the questions are a kind of trivia crossed with shopworn assumptions about behaviorist educational psychology. Open, credible content analysis of teacher examinations does not take place, even in face of the significance they have for our children and our teachers. *This disconnect between the content of the tests and state and the National Council for Accreditation of Teacher Education (NCATE) standards, teacher education curriculum, and independent guidelines (such as INTASC) is testimony to the inadequacy of the continuum from standards-setting to teacher education curriculum to evaluation of teachers and teacher education.*

U.S. pragmatism

The immediate origins of the current mania for teacher testing in the United States can be traced to the alarmist claims of *A nation at risk* (National Commission on Excellence in Education, 1983), in which the alleged failures of U.S. education were likened to attacks by a foreign enemy. This poorly researched and argued document followed a cyclical tradition of criticisms of U.S. education that traces back to at least the post-World War II era. The ongoing prejudice against educators, discussed earlier, provides fertile ground for such periodic outbursts. The reaction to progressive education in the form of the Life Adjustment Curriculum set off one cycle. *Sputnik* set off the next. The countercultural revolution of the 1960s set off yet another. Falling SAT scores had their day, then economic doldrums and the rise of Japan's economy paved the way for *A nation at risk*. Subsequently and over time, however, the United States invited civic education and other life skills back into the curriculum. The nation eventually won the race to the moon uncontested, integrated the 1960s radicals (even to the level of president), reversed the imagined SAT slide (while playing by the slanted, non-psychometrically sound rules of the media debate), and left the Japanese economy far behind. Instead of celebrating the repeated triumphs of the scapegoat, public education, criticism continues unabated. In place of merited praise we witness a powerful privatization/voucher movement, punitive teacher testing (as in Massachusetts), a drop in teachers' real income in the 1990s, and continual vilification of teachers' unions even though they have joined the reform movement. The No Child Left Behind Act was a culmination of these policies.

Among the most damaging of the attacks is a constant criticism that those who teach are inadequate for the challenge at hand. In contrast, how little recognition has been given to the repeated heroism of teachers at Columbine and the other sites of murderous school violence? The foundation of any profession is respect from society for the expertise and ethics of practitioners. Consequently, there are practical and demoralizing effects of the negative media drumbeat. Teacher testing in turn is based on the assumption by policy-makers that unqualified persons have been taking over U.S. classrooms and becoming fixtures, thereby earning unassailable tenure. In order to combat this "takeover," teacher tests are presented as gatekeepers—or means of "cleaning house"—to assure us of the high quality of our teachers. This cause and effect argument is so distanced from reality, however, that it defies any kind of sensible analysis. It is a truism in the United States that, come September, every classroom will have a "teacher" in the front of the room. In tens of thousands of cases, however, such persons will not be properly credentialed, professional teachers. They will be either college graduates who lack professional preparation, or teachers prepared and licensed in fields other than the one to which they are assigned. In California, the state's figures regularly show that 10% of teachers lack licenses of any kind, except "emergency" licenses; and in high demand fields, such as mathematics, approximately 70% lack proper content preparation (http://www.ctc.ca.gov).

Screening out candidates from the lower ranks of test-takers does not bring more and better candidates into our classrooms. Through perseverance these same persons typically find their way into teaching by back-door routes. The rewards of the profession continue to fall short in attracting and, more importantly, holding persons of the stature we all desire. Also it should be noted that unfair criticism, media bias, and a lack of popular respect further discourage strong candidates from entering or staying in the field. In the United States it is not possible to drive up teachers' salaries or improve their working conditions by creating a shortage of qualified professionals. The nation has a long tradition of filling vacant positions with notably unprepared persons. Nonetheless we continue to march down this fruitless path of bashing the profession in the media, throwing unfair screening hurdles before motivated candidates, leaving salaries depressed, and then filling positions with "any warm body." Although NCLB ostensibly takes on the issue of uncertified teachers through its "highly qualified" standard, its impact has mainly been in wrangling with the states over the definitions of "qualified" and channeling millions of dollars into the dubious certification-by-testing scheme of the American Board for Certification of Teacher Excellence.

Whatever became of American pragmatism? When faced with societal challenges, the nation has often succeeded admirably by moving beyond ideology to find policies that worked in terms of their outcomes. Despite cries of socialism, the New Deal was propagated in the 1930s and, at a minimum, sustained national morale in the face of the Great Depression. Social security and Medicare provided safety nets for the elderly by recognizing that millions of people, for whatever reason, would not or could not voluntarily prepare economically for old age. The Supreme Court, followed by Congress, transcended U.S. legal traditions in civil rights, acknowledging that Jim Crow had to be abolished. In another instance, the court reevaluated longstanding tradition and established a woman's right to choice with respect to pregnancy. Pragmatic responses to real social problems have characterized U.S. democracy at its best. Teacher testing, however, as a means of improving education, fits into a contrarian pattern of the United States—one of denying lived realities in favor of spin-doctored "facts."

Historically, denial of this type has failed as a source of public policy. For example, over a decade passed and organized crime boomed before the United States repealed its failed attempt at Prohibition in 1933. Currently we have a recrudescence of that type of failed "reform" in the nation's address of substance abuse. As the rate of incarceration soars, along with associated social and economic costs, movement toward the medicalization of addiction is stalled. The United States is similarly stymied by the problem of poverty and its relation to education. Policy-makers and the media perpetuate the myth that schools alone can overcome all the environmental deficiencies facing a child and educate that child successfully (Rothstein, 2004). Hunger, abuse, and constant transience have no impact on a child's learning in the eyes of pundits, and for teachers to claim otherwise is to "hide behind excuses."

American pragmatism appears irregularly in our public life, yet it is capable of leading us to great social victories. It is a tradition that competes, however, with lesser dispositions fueled and sustained by denial, prejudice, and magical thinking. In the realm of teacher supply and teacher quality, the United States is not learning from the past failures and successes of its own history. It is not difficult to see that by improving the compensation and working conditions for teachers the nation could attract and retain sufficient numbers of the candidates we desire. Mid-career teachers currently earn approximately $25,000 less than comparably prepared persons in other fields. Working conditions in many urban settings are hazardous—psychologically if not somatically. The toughest teaching assignments typically pay the least and are left to the newest teachers, as veterans move up the career ladder within a district, or to another district.

Ultimately there is no shortage of prepared teachers. Hundreds of thousands have taken their credentials and talent and left the profession. Others complete preparation but decline to enter the profession. In competition for teaching talent in the open marketplace of our economy, society does assert itself adequately. *In none of these policy areas do teacher tests make an impact: the tests are simply irrelevant to the great challenges facing public education. They are a distraction and a sideshow that take attention away from the reforms that need to be made.* If our profession were attracting and retaining in sufficient numbers the talent that it should, we would be moving away from testing as some professions have (e.g., architecture), because candidate competition for desirable jobs would play out successfully in the marketplace. The quality issues we have are not rooted in keeping candidates out of the profession, they are in society's failure to attract and retain the candidates we want in the profession.

The shift in women's career choices lends testimony to the most dramatic example of the brain drain in the teaching profession. Before the successes of the women's movement, approximately 5% of law and medical students were female. Thirty years later, the rate of women's participation in these schools hovers around 50%. This change is due in large part to the compensation and working conditions found in public school teaching. The intrinsic attractiveness of teaching as a human endeavor is strong—historically the role of the teacher has been admired, and currently society's ability to attract fine professors gives evidence that this value remains with us. But when the gap in salary and workplace difficulties becomes too great, talent leaves teaching. The outflow of gifted women attests to this and is paralleled in the African-American community, which today provides fewer and fewer teachers. A similar analysis seems to fit both groups: teaching—historically the most accessible of professions to minorities and women—is increasingly bypassed by talented members of those groups as equal opportunity has opened the doors to other professions with better working conditions and competitive salaries. Even the innate attractiveness of the act of teaching cannot capture for the profession the talent our society needs.

Conclusion

In 2000 the American Educational Research Association, together with the American Psychological Association and the National Council on Measurement in Education, published a position statement on *High stakes testing in preK–12 education* that was based on their *Standards for educational and psychological testing* (1999). These guidelines are also quite relevant to high-stakes teacher testing and illustrate how far current practice has drifted from scientific and ethical responsibility. According to these documents, testing programs should have:

- protection against high-stakes decisions based on a single test.
- adequate resources and opportunity to learn.
- validation for each separate intended use.
- full disclosure of likely negative consequences of high-stakes testing programs.
- alignment between the test and the curriculum.
- validity of passing scores and achievement levels.
- opportunities for meaningful remediation for examinees who fail high-stakes tests.
- appropriate attention to language differences among examinees.
- appropriate attention to students with disabilities.
- careful adherence to explicit rules for determining which students are to be tested.
- sufficient reliability for each intended use.
- ongoing evaluation of intended and unintended effects of high-stakes testing.

As teacher tests are currently employed, it can be argued that none of these standards is adequately met, yet all are truly critical to fairness and accuracy in testing. For example, tests are often used as a solitary gatekeeping event, and they are frequently used outside the purposes for which they were validated. Since teaching is so complex and there is little consensus on the knowledge base for the beginning teacher, there is inadequate alignment between the tests, state and national standards, and the curriculum. The validity of passing scores is dubious at best. Further, the unintended effects of this system—the demoralization and banning of certain candidates—have not been sufficiently examined.

In some manner educators need to further the long march toward good practice in teacher testing. Enforcing high standards in the application of the tests is an overdue initiative, as is the propagation of performance assessment. The abuses demonstrated in this field are symptoms of the general misunderstanding and mistreatment educators experience in U.S. society. In order to combat this disposition, teacher testing should be an immediate point of contact that forcefully engages educators and our organizations with the larger political system. What is at stake is our concept of ourselves as professionals, as well as the future character of education. The validation of a teacher will not be found in numbers or ultimately even in words. As the poet suggests, complexity and uncertainty are part of our condition:

> No one could find a single word to attach the free electron. Then they noticed
>
> visible things too avoided their language: a blue Adirondack chair on a warped paintless pier,
>
> ocean on the beach, and the wind, foam of another sea, burning in the treetops, that other shore:
>
> such things fell on their eyes and fell to the bottom of their skulls
>
> and never mixed with the words already lying there ...
>
> (Moritz, 2000, p. 42)

Chapter 6

Contested visions of public schooling for a democratic society

American public schooling has traditionally had a rationale rooted in the need for a democratic society to prepare future citizens. The nature and centrality of this role, however, has varied at different points in American history, although the burden of transmitting a democratic education has consistently fallen on the shoulders of the social studies curriculum. Social studies as a discipline, and in particular through the subject area of history, has been charged with the responsibility of being the arbiter between the curricular desires of policy-makers and an educator-driven pedagogy that develops requisite intellectual proficiency for students to engage in active citizenry. The conditions are often at odds with one another. Ironically through sociocultural debates and enacted policies, preparing the youth of American society for their eventual role as active citizens in a democracy has been a central tenet of schooling, while the ever evolving role of schools in this process is largely dictated by those outside of educational institutions. The consequence of these contradictions, throughout history and today, is that the curriculum itself becomes a locus for the debate, a debate which often has political and ideological ramifications. This chapter begins by providing a context for the history and current status of schooling for democracy and critically explores ways in which the right has recently defined democracy, patriotism, citizenship, and literacy in recent initiatives and in the agendas of major foundations and organizations.

The historical context: public schooling for democracy

In early American schooling, one of the primary goals of education was to develop social ethics and prepare students for participation in democracy as self-governing citizens. With the establishment of the new nation in 1776 and in the years that followed, new curriculum materials such as Noah Webster's standardized American dictionary and the *New England Primer*, the pledge of allegiance, and stories about national heroes entered the curriculum to nurture national identity and pride. More profoundly, many new Americans, such as Thomas Jefferson, believed democracy required educated reason to preserve "a due degree of liberty." Jefferson, writing in 1787 in a letter to James Madison, wrote, "Above all things, I hope the education of the common people will be attended to: conviction that on their good senses we may rely with the most security for the preservation of a due degree of liberty" (Boyd, 1950, vol. 12, p. 442). For 80 years, however, all attempts at government-legislated education, at the state or national level, failed. Americans were uneasy about giving either state or national government too much power, thinking education should be a local concern. In the early 19th century, American schools hence varied widely by size, condition, funding, hours in session, curriculum, and teacher quality. In general, local communities resisted taxing themselves to raise money for schools, so user fees were common. Lack of oversight and consistent funding meant that the quality of schooling was typically poor.

The extension of suffrage after 1828 and the increase in immigration from Ireland and Germany in the 1830s and 1840s created a change in the cultural climate that contributed to interest in a more organized and more democratic system of education. Expanded suffrage heightened fear among elites of the power of the uneducated mob, and immigrant cultures were seen as threatening to, particularly, Protestant culture. In addition, an expanding economy and increased population mobility also heightened the perceived need for schooling, since young adults less frequently lived lives in one community or served long apprenticeships. Thus, when Horace Mann led a common-school movement, states fell in line providing consistent funding, building and curriculum improvements, teacher training, and attendance laws. Massachusetts passed the first compulsory schooling laws in 1848. Horace Mann allowed for the sort of "functional economic worker" preparation argument for education that is common today, but it is clear that to him public and civic values and capacities were considered to be much more important. In his *Fifth annual report* (1842) Mann explains:

> the advocates and eulogists of education have, rarely if ever, descended to so humble a duty as to demonstrate its pecuniary value, both to individuals and to society ... this utilitarian view of education, as it may be called, which regards it as the dispenser of private competence, and the promoter of national wealth, is by no means the first which would address itself to an enlightened and benevolent mind.

(p. 82)

Common schools were to teach a common democratic curriculum of social and political values and were to be attended in common by children from diverse cultural and social class backgrounds. School life and discussion with diverse fellow students was intended to have a democratizing effect on students. Common public schools, Mann argues in his *Twelfth annual report* (1848), would "open a wider area over which the social feelings will expand, and if this education should be universal and complete, it would do more than all things else to obliterate factious distinctions in society." Citizens educated in this manner would be able to think beyond their own class and personal interests, it was posited, and this is a key feature of citizenship. Citizens are to consider what is best for the public interest and not simply for their private and personal interest when voting or deliberating on policy. Such an experience and curriculum would depart from much of 19th-century curriculum, in which geography had been much more prevalent than history and civic education. In the 19th century what might be called social studies (although this is a progressive era concept) focused on American exceptionalism and the development of patriotism. The work of historian George Bancroft (1800–1891), who wrote 10 volumes on the history of the United States from 1834 to 1873, was typical of such curriculum, and its aim was to inspire a sense of destiny and providence. Historians would later criticize what they saw as Bancroft's subjective approach, which that vaulted a "factitious" and "spurious" patriotism over one that was more reasoned and intelligent (Novick, 1988, as cited in Halvorsen, 2006, p. 33).

A different vision of citizenship education came from Horace Mann. Mann's concern about democratic citizenship education is evident in his *Twelfth annual report*, in which he argues, "It may be an easy thing to make a Republic but it is a very laborious thing to make Republicans; and woe to the Republic that rests upon no foundations than ignorance, selfishness, and passion." He felt schools could help counteract the growth of selfishness (arising from a burgeoning capitalist economy) by instilling in their charges a personal dedication to the public good. Mann also notes "that vast and overshadowing private fortunes are among the greatest dangers to which the happiness of the people in a republic can be subjected," and he argued that "surely, nothing but Universal Education can counter-work this tendency to the domination of capital and the servility of labor," acting as "the balance-wheel of the social machinery" (Mann, 1848). Common schools, the "great equalizer of the conditions of men," were envisioned to help alleviate poverty and crime and to reduce ethnic and class tensions. They were favored both by workingmen's parties, which argued that public education provided necessary knowledge for protecting against the rich, as well as by reformers, who viewed education as means of disciplining the poor. Education would forge a common citizenry, to make public minded Americans out of immigrants and capitalists alike.

The actual diversity of common-school children, however, was limited. Richest and poorest children did not attend, and instead were privately tutored or remained unschooled. Black and minority children were systematically segregated in separate schools. Later, in California, this would affect Asian children. The curriculum also did not often accommodate diversity. Moral education was based on the King James Bible and McGuffy readers, and often emphasized patriotism and heroism while referring in racist ways to immigrants. School texts also described the poor as in need of regulation while extolling the moral virtue of the rich. Yet, in places like New York, nearly half of the residents were immigrants, and included large numbers of Irish Catholics. In the tense atmosphere caused by urban rioting and church burnings, Catholics demanded funds for separate Catholic schools, and created an alternative school system when demands were ignored. African Americans also created schools. In the Reconstruction South, freed slaves sought the education that had been denied to them for so long as a means of upward mobility. Yet, at the same time, many Southern whites, who held social and political power, aimed to keep blacks in their servile roles by maintaining a segregated labor force and economy and schools with minimal resources and limited curriculum. In response ex-slaves built schools all over the South, by themselves and with the help of aid societies and abolitionists, laying the foundation for many of the black colleges that exist today.

While public education excluded most minorities, education for Native Americans involved a deliberate process of deculturalization in order, as Carlisle Indian school founder Richard Henry Pratt explained, to "kill the Indian and save the white man." Beginning in 1887, the federal government removed thousands of children from their extended families and tribal nations and placed them in almost 150 boarding schools around the United States. Children were forced to take new names, were forbidden to speak their languages, and had their hair cut and their clothes removed, and their sacred objects were banned. As in other common schools, the curriculum typically focused on patriotic history and Protestant morality. Only in 1928 were most boarding schools replaced by community day schools, which Indian tribes struggle to control to the present day. In Canada the residential schools continued into the 1980s.

In the early 20th century education policy was influenced by dramatic changes in population and by the rise of an industrial political economy. From 1866 to 1870, 98% of European immigrants came from the North and West of Europe. Between 1906 and 1920 this shrank to 22%, with the bulk now coming from the South and East of Europe—Catholics from southern Italy and Slavic lands and East European Jews from Tsarist Russia. Like Irish Catholics before them, these immigrants and their children were disdained and discriminated against, although immigrant children comprised huge numbers in the cities. Work and residence had changed as well. Earlier the majority of Americans were self-employed in agriculture or industry and lived in rural areas, but most people now were employees, with many working in poor conditions under a regime of industrial production and living in urban areas. Workers resisted conditions through socialism and trade unionism, and state and federal governments grew increasingly active, regulating business, industry, labor, and education. During World War I, government heightened its use of schools to help make loyal new Americans from immigrants.

In 1900 only 11% of children attended secondary school; by 1930 more than half were so enrolled, and three intervening decades were marked by fervent debate about the type of education American society required. Progressives believed that a curriculum of memorized classics, math, science, and history should be replaced and schools should consider the nature of the child as well as the needs of society in a modern scientific manner. Educators such as John Dewey believed that democracy requires active collaborative participation by all citizens in social, political, and economic decisions and that curriculum should reflect the interests of both students and society. Alternatively, social efficiency advocates felt that children should be scientifically tested to determine their probable careers and be tracked into segmented curricula. The science of IQ and placement testing was based on a belief in human inequality that correlated closely with class and ethnicity. In these modern, presumably meritocratic, schools, minorities were consistently tracked into vocational education while white middle-class Protestants populated college prep courses. This was considered democratic because students were educated according to their "probable destiny" in life, and society had places for maids as well as managers.

During the Depression, growing popular disillusionment with laissez-faire capitalism and corporate industrialization contributed to a momentary strengthening of critical democratic approaches to education. George Counts believed schools could "build a new social order," and *Social Frontier* detailed this vision. Harold Rugg's widely used social science textbook series, *Man and his changing world*, reflected a vision of democratic citizenship, cross-cultural understanding, greater equality between sexes, and social justice. While progressive education was often inelegantly added into the existing curriculum of tracked, social efficiency schools, the 1930s ended with "a general shift to the left and toward increasing innovation in curriculum planning, toward approaches centered on social problems, and toward curriculum integration" (Evans, 2004, p. 69). The eight-year study powerfully validated progressive innovations (Kridel & Bullough, 2007). In the 1940s, "life-adjustment education" was conceived to meet the needs of most students in "general tracks" and curriculum generally departed widely from Dewey and Counts progressivism, assuming "average" students were not suited to academic rigor.

After World War II, when secondary enrollments approached 90%, education policy again became hotly debated. New leaders denounced progressive education and called for a return to basics, memorization, and facts.

The Russian launch of *Sputnik*, the first man-made satellite, served the critics' point, and the National Defense Education Act of 1958 emphasized education policy not to revitalize democracy but to fortify national defense, shifting attention to strengthening education in math, science, and foreign languages. The "rising cultural aversion toward controversial topics," linked with anticommunist fears, caused "a shift away from a social problems approach"; "the disciplines had a full advantage" (Evans, 2004, p. 119), while the progressive attitude lost its influence. During this period small districts and schools were consolidated into large district high schools with more differentiated curriculum and new advanced courses.

While in the 1960s and 1970s curriculum increasingly included issues-oriented materials reflective of the times, the focus was on the policy issue of equity. In 1954, pushed by a growing civil rights movement and by the legal challenge of the NAACP, the Supreme Court, in *Brown* v. *Board of Education*, declared racial segregation in education to be unconstitutional. This important triumph set the stage for a major new development in American education: the desegregation of Southern schools. Such desegregation was slow and deeply resisted. Sustained work over a decade backed by the expanding resources of the federal government brought an end—eventually—to legally sanctioned Jim Crow in education. Yet in 1964, 10 years after the Supreme Court decision, less than 1% of all black children in the South went to desegregated schools. In 1965 the Elementary and Secondary Education Act allocated 1 billion dollars annually to schools with high concentrations of low-income children. Schools were now pressured to change or lose money. During the 1970s, following legislation and legal action, schools recognized the educational rights of females, the handicapped, and non-English-speaking students.

In the late 1970s public tolerance of change and government commitment to new programs and legislation declined, and by the 1980s schools graduated a greater percentage of students and attended to more aspects of diversity than ever before, and yet the public schools were under increasing attack. The 1983 report *A nation at risk* asserted that the poor performance of public schools was a national security threat and was damaging the nation's capacity to compete economically. The report's methods were problematic, as we have discussed in chapter 2, but ushered in the start of a new era of emphasis on rigorous standards and accountability mechanisms to homogenize and improve curricula, teaching, and learning. This conservative view promoted the revival of history and geography, the return to the basics, and the pursuit of testing excellence. Though minimum competency tests were "dumbing down" curricula, and reducing teacher autonomy and professionalization, the movement has expanded to the present day. As this book describes, in the 1990s and 2000s a turn backward toward increased involvement by private ownership in education is a key feature of policy, which assumes that a system based on competition and minimal regulation rather than expanded public provision will result in better quality education at a lower cost. This perspective also offers the rationale for the choice movement, charter schools, home schooling, and the reduction of teacher certification and accreditation requirements, and attacks collective bargaining agreements.

While the dual intentions of education to prepare functional workers to build the economy and to prepare thoughtful, liberally educated citizens have always existed, and often existed in some tension, recent legislation has greatly strengthened the functional economic purpose of schooling at the expense of liberal, democratic education for citizenship. As chapter 3 detailed, the increased power of state and national curriculum directives reinforced by high-stakes testing focuses education on the curricular authority of the standards and on the production of uniformity and conformity of performance which itself is authoritarian. Teachers become implementers of content and pedagogy as defined by lock-step curricula and standards; students become performers more than thinkers, and the performances that matter are the functional math and reading skills.

The current context: A crisis in civic life amidst economic and political divide

As the above review details, throughout American history democratic public education has been responsive to the demands of the economy and to fluctuating political values and anxieties. Many social commentators and educators believe that an emphasis on active citizenship and democratic participation is particularly important for schools today because of the many challenges facing the nation—from globalization to terrorism, to the loss of industrial jobs, to divisiveness about equity issues. These occur amidst a perceived crisis in democracy. Just as *A nation at risk* focused attention on a crisis in American economic competitiveness, the publication in 1997 of Putnam's *Bowling alone: America's declining social capital* focused attention on a crisis in American civic understanding and participation at a time of increasing change and conflict. A number of studies reveal declining participation by Americans in civil society and government (American Civic Forum, 1994; Bahmueller, 1997). Today the United States is struggling politically with both domestic and global issues in the context of economic, cultural, and political polarization. The national political environment is deeply divisive on a wide range of issues—on abortion, gay marriage, affirmative action, and judicial conservatism; on taxes and national debt; on eroding civil liberties and due process of law; on global trade and American unemployment and labor trends; on what to do about global warming and radical weather disasters such as Hurricane Katrina; on what to do about national health care as well as global endemics from AIDS to avian flu; on the Iraq "quagmire" and the much broader question of the appropriate role for the USA in the post-Cold War, post 9/11 world.

Domestic tensions and polarization are also rooted in economic insecurity and deepening inequality. For most of the 20th century, Americans were becoming a more equal society in terms of income. The gap between rich and poor was shrinking, but since 1973 the national distribution of income and wealth has become increasingly inequitable. The top 20% of American households receive 49.7% of total income, while the lowest 20% of American households receive 3.5%. The top 5% of households alone receive 21.7% of all available income. The distribution of wealth measured by net worth is even more highly skewed. The richest 1% of households (99th–100th percentile) account for nearly a third of all available net worth, while the bottom half of households (0–50th percentile) account for only 2.8% of all available net worth (Kennickell, 2003). The majority of the nation's and the world's people are not benefiting from the neoliberal model of economic growth. For most, living standards have stagnated or declined, while the burdens of work and job insecurity have grown. Sometimes reports on the economy can be confusing. Mass media and presidential State of the Union addresses accurately report that GNP has been steadily growing and many jobs have been created. One often repeated joke among working-class families, however, goes like this: "The president created 200,000 jobs and I have six of them." Many new jobs are part-time, low-wage jobs without benefits.

By all measures inequality is increasing even as wealth is increasing. In 1978, CEOs earned roughly 60 times the pay of the average worker; by 1995, they earned 175 times the pay of the average worker (Mishel, Bernstein, & Schmitt, 1997, p. 7). *Executive excess 2005*, a study published by the Institute for Policy Studies and United for a Fair Economy, reveals that the ratio of average CEO pay (now $11.8 million) to worker pay (now $27,460) then further spiked up, from 301 to 1 in 2003 to 431 to 1 in 2004. As this study observes, "If the minimum wage had risen as fast as CEO pay since 1990, the lowest paid workers in the US would be earning $23.03 an hour today, not $5.15 an hour" (Anderson, Cavanagh, Klinger, & Stanton, 2005). According to Kevin J. Murphy, E. Morgan Stanley Chair in Business Administration at the Marshall School of Business, University of Southern California, the average top executive at a Standard & Poor's 500 company now makes 550 times what the average worker makes (Wheaton, 2008). The U.S. Bureau of the Census reported that, in 2004, 13 million children, or 17.8%, were poor, including 33% of black children and 28% of Latino children. The actual numbers of the poor are much higher, given that a parent with two children must earn less than $15,220 to be considered in poverty and that this is not a living wage. Recent surveys among advanced societies showed the United Kingdom as last in its treatment of children and the USA as next to last among 21 nations. A study conducted by the Catholic Campaign for Human Development (2007) showed that most Americans believe it takes closer to $35,000 annually to adequately house, clothe, and feed a family of four. Yet poor people are much less likely to vote than rich people, and fewer than half of eligible voters typically vote.

As Michael Lind (1995) describes,

> In any other democracy, an enraged citizenry would have rebelled by now against a national elite that weakens unions, slashes wages and benefits, pits workers against low wage foreign and immigrant competition—then informs its victims that the chief source of their economic problems is a lack of "high personal diligence." But for whom could an enraged citizen vote? The American overclass manages to protect itself from popular insurgencies, not only openly through its ownership of the news media but also by financial control of elections and its use of affirmative action patronage. ... We were taught in civics classes that the United States is a "pluralistic" democracy in which Madisonian "factions" balance one another, ensuring that no single minority or economic interest will prevail. We were lied to. Labor does not balance big business; consumer groups do not balance big business; nobody balances big business anymore. Contrary to conservative claims that liberal and left-wing "special interests" dominate Congress, PAC funds come, overwhelmingly, from business. Citizens vote occasionally; dollars vote continually.
>
> (p. 43)

In place of an enraged citizenry we find contemporary Americans are less involved than other generations in civic and political life, voting rates are disappointing, few citizens show up for public hearings, and membership in a range of social action and volunteer groups has waned, although there has just recently been some resurgence. Robert Putnam (1995) reported that attendance at public meetings had fallen by a third since 1973 and volunteering declined by about one sixth from 1974 to 1989; by 2000, voter turnout had declined by nearly a quarter, from a high in the early 1960s. In a counter-trend voting rates have increased, since 60% of eligible voters turned out to vote in the 2004 election—the highest turnout since 1968. Putnam reports that, in America, "social capital," which means "features of social organizations such as networks, norms, and social trust, that facilitate coordination and cooperation for mutual benefit" (1995, p. 374), is in serious decline. As he explains, social capital refers to connections among individuals—social networks and the norms of reciprocity and trustworthiness that arise from them. In that sense social capital is closely related to what some have called "civic virtue." The difference is that "social capital" calls attention to the fact that civic virtue is most powerful when embedded in a sense network of reciprocal social relations. A society of many virtuous but isolated individuals is not necessarily rich in social capital (2000, p. 19). At the same time, participation in clearly "anti-democratic" groups such as armed militia groups, Christian Patriots, and neo-Nazi white supremacist groups is on the rise (Levitas, 2002).

There are thus very real fears as to whether or not democracy can coexist with an economic sphere dominated by concentrated capitalism or with a public sphere of often contentious cultural and religious groups. These tensions are global as well as national and local. Barber observes a paralyzing "politics of fear" following the September 11th attacks and the war on terrorism—we scare ourselves into abandoning our ideals and polarizing our politics. He suggests that fear works on a psychological level to create a vicious cycle of inaction that cripples civic engagement. The citizen is reduced to a passive spectatorship to world events, the only antidote to which, paradoxically, is engagement. Yet everything is simplified; "issues of democracy, civil comity and social justice—let alone nuance, complexity and interdependence simply vanish" (2002, p. 17). Responding or becoming effectively involved seems impossible in a context of both terrorism and complex and entrenched global systems of power that few understand or feel adequate to influence.

Furthermore, critics point out that participating in democracy and understanding politics and economics is limited by media monopolies. Debate in a free marketplace of ideas has been diminished by corporate control of print, radio, and TV media, deeply limiting access to a range of perspectives on issues. Six huge corporations now control the major U.S. media: Rupert Murdoch's News Corporation (FOX, HarperCollins, *New York Post*, *Weekly Standard*, *TV Guide*, DirecTV, and TV stations), General Electric (NBC, CNBC, MSNBC, Telemundo, Bravo, Universal Pictures, and TV stations), Time Warner (AOL, CNN, Warner Bros., *Time*, and its 130-plus magazines), Disney (ABC, Disney Channel, ESPN, 10 TV and radio stations), Viacom (CBS, MTV, Nickelodeon, Paramount Pictures, Simon & Schuster, and U.S. radio stations), and Bertelsmann (Random House and its more than 120 imprints worldwide, and Gruner + Jahr and its more than 110 magazines in 10 countries). This is a big change.

> In 1983, fifty corporations dominated most of every mass medium and the biggest media merger in history was a $340 million deal. ... [I]n 1987, the fifty companies had shrunk to twenty-nine. ... [I]n 1990, the twenty-nine had shrunk to twenty three. ... [I]n 1997, the biggest firms numbered ten and involved the $19 billion Disney–ABC deal, at the time the biggest media merger ever. ... [In 2000] AOL Time Warner's $350 billion merged corporation [was] more than 1,000 times larger [than the biggest deal of 1983]."
>
> (Bagdikian, 2000, pp. xx–xxi)

In addition, as Shecter (1998) observes, media can also become dominated by a privatist, for-profit ethos that goes beyond ownership to pervade the enterprise. Instead of journalism as a public good providing information to citizens, media can instead focus on private profit.

> Media executives speak in the language of war—of bombarding audiences, targeting markets, capturing grosses, killing the competition, and winning, by which they mean making more money than the other guy. Some news organizations even refer to their employees as "the troops." It is hard for media workers, including journalists, to operate outside the ethos of hyper-competitition and ratings mania. As willing or unwilling conscripts in the media war, journalists imbibe its values and become warriors themselves.

The increasing use of Internet and communications technology is also a concern. While some point to new technology as a democratizing force, others see it as alienating (Shaker, 2006). A hopeful view is that, by creating and fostering communities of interest, distant disenfranchised sections of the population will begin to establish new partnerships, which will help to transform political activity. Sian Kevill (2003) of the BBC believes that the Internet "has the potential to create a new dynamic between the powerful few and the powerless many ... through ... new coalitions of interest," allowing people "to exert their aggregated power faster than in previous eras." Martyn Perks (2003) disagrees, arguing, "offering us more choice in how we connect with one another does nothing to redress imbalances of power, especially when social relationships are established in such a touchy-feely way." Wellman (2001) traces a transformation in social organization from traditional group life to an emerging phenomenon that he calls "networked individualism." Enabled by decentralizing communications technology, networked individualism is "characterized by high levels of personal autonomy; multiple, specialized relationships with others based on shared interests; and a lack of overarching control." In this view the Internet promotes individual choice more than group solidarity, and loyalties are easily changed.

The curriculum context: Critical civic education loses to tradition and basics

In response to these trends, the National Council for the Social Studies, critical theorists, multiculturalists, and global educationists are all calling for a return to meaningful democratic education that will enable students to make reasoned decisions for the public good as "citizens of a culturally diverse, democratic society in an interdependent world" (National Council for the Social Studies, 1994). There is widespread agreement that civic education needs to improve. The National Commission on Civic Renewal warns, "In a time that cries out for civic action, we are in danger of becoming a nation of spectators" (1988, p. 6). The American Federation of Teachers' Albert Shanker Institute lamented American students' alarming lack of civic and historical knowledge and called for an invigoration of the field of social studies (Education for Democracy Initiative, 2003). The National Council for the Social Studies (NCSS) defended the fields in an article by Phipps and Adler (2003), arguing that history has not been diminished by NCSS and that social studies was generally well thought out, well taught, and effective in educating young people for life in American democracy.

A very different response has been offered by the White House, members of Congress, and major advocacy foundations and interest groups, who offer policies that either ignore and marginalize social studies or argue against critical citizenship education in favor of the teaching of traditional history to promote democratic values and patriotism. The field of social studies, like most, has long been marked by contestation. As Evans (2004) describes it, the field includes traditional historians, who support history as the core of social studies; mandarins, advocates of social studies as a social science; social efficiency educators, who hope to create a smoothly controlled and more efficient society; social meliorists and Deweyan experimentalists, who want to develop students' reflective thinking and contribute to social improvement; and social reconstructionists, who cast social studies in schools in a leading role in the transformation of American society. As Ross and Marker (2005) have further explained,

> while we have to be careful not to construct the conflict in purely dualistic terms, differences among social studies educators can be described along a continuum with polar purposes of "indoctrination" (e.g., what Barr, Barth, and Shermis (1977) have famously described as "citizenship transmission") and "critical thought" (e.g., what Stanley and Nelson (1994) labeled "informed social criticism").

What is different now is that the federal government, with support from right-wing think tanks, has generally pushed social studies into the margin because they are not tested under NCLB. At the same time, in place of social studies, the federal government has funded a number of initiatives to support "traditional American history." What was once a debate among academics and teachers has moved to a war that has been won through funding and policy. Civic education and all forms of social studies have been weakened in terms of time spent and performance achieved.

The effects of recent policy initiatives on critical, liberal, and civic learning

Although current research includes conflicting evidence, most of it suggests that recent federal policy initiatives have had a negative impact on critical, liberal, and civic learning as well as on equity. Because teachers are spending so much of their time preparing students for the state test, they have less and less time to teach the things that are of interest to their students or are not on the test (Smith, 1991; Berliner & Biddle, 1995; Stecher & Hamilton, 2002; Mathison & Freeman, 2003). Standardized testing is creating standardized curriculum and instruction in schools (Jones & Whitford, 2000). Teachers are making instructional decisions based on what they believe will help their students score well on the test, but high-stakes testing disenfranchises students who are poor or minority (Madaus, 1988). As students are given test preparation-type instruction, their particular learning styles and needs are ignored (Jones & Whitford, 2000). Students who are not being served will not be engaged in their learning. The more these students, the ones the policy is most interested in helping, are ignored and humiliated by these tests, the more likely they are to quit school (Hursh & Martina, 2003). The end result is a widening rather than a narrowing of the achievement gap (McNeil, 2000).

The Council for Basic Education (2004) surveyed 1,000 principals to gain understanding of how the No Child Left Behind Act is influencing instruction time and professional development in key subject areas. They found that schools increasingly marginalize education related to liberal education, critical thinking, democracy, and civic participation. Their study *Academic atrophy: The condition of the liberal arts in America's public schools*, not surprisingly, revealed that schools are spending increased time on reading, math, and science and much less time on social studies, civics, geography, languages, and the arts. While the amount of instructional time devoted to social studies instruction has declined since the implementation of NCLB, the decline is most extreme in low-performing schools, with 30% of elementary school principals and 50% of principals in schools with large minorities reporting a reduction of time spent on social studies instruction. Concerns of curriculum and instruction are related to how standards and the tests, even though they do provide a focus, also narrow the curriculum in negative ways (Madaus, 1988). What is taught is being limited to what is on the test as teachers seek to increase test scores and avoid sanctions (Jones & Whitford, 2000). This limits what students receive as far as curriculum is concerned, including such things as citizenship, which is not tested (Clotfelter & Ladd, 1996).

In addition to reduced instruction in social studies and liberal arts, reading instruction has moved to a paradigm that mandates the least critical approaches. States can only obtain reading funds by committing themselves to professional development based upon and limited to the view of reading instruction embodied in the Reading First Initiative. This initiative has been tarnished by questions regarding the integrity of its processes. New federal definitions of research employed by the federally sponsored National Reading Panel use a narrow operational conception of reading and a highly limited perspective even on operational literacy. The panel found that teaching phonics and word sounds and "giving feedback on oral reading was the "most effective way to teach reading" (National Institute of Child Health and Human Development, 2000). By contrast, from a sociocultural perspective, literacy must be seen as having three interlocking dimensions—the operational, the cultural, and the critical—which bring together language, meaning, and context (Green 1988, 1997a, 1997b).Critical literacy is "learning to read and write as part of the process of becoming conscious of one's experience as historically constructed within specific power relations" (Anderson & Irvine, 82). This is an idea of literacy as a social study rather than a mere functional skill.

As Berlak (2005) explains, there are three identifiable approaches to teaching of reading in U.S. schools.

> 1. *Direct phonics instruction.* By National Reading Panel definition there are two aspects to direct phonics instruction (a) systematic acquisition of a sequence of discrete phonic skills and (b) their application to reading 2. A *Whole language* (also referred to as a literature-*based*, or *constructivist*) approach emphasizes the importance of learning from context, and drawing upon learners' previous experience and their capacity to use visual and textual clues. The assumption is that most children bought up in print rich communities grasp the elements of phonics—the association of spoken language with alphabetic symbols—from their daily life, their active experience with books, and conversations about books with peers and adults. This approach usually employs systematic phonics instruction, but rejects the idea that all children must master a fixed sequence of discrete phonetic skills *before* they are capable of reading 'real' books. And 3. A *Critical literacy* emphasis requires children to go beyond taking meaning from print, to develop the capacity to become critical of experience and the texts they read, and to learn to observe and make critical judgments on both the texts they read and the world around them.

Among teachers and researchers, the meaning of literacy had become increasingly sophisticated, moving from simple decoding to functional literacy—the ability to use reading, writing, and computational skills in everyday life, such as filling out job applications and reading medicine bottles.

> Critical literacy would make clear the connection between knowledge and power. It would present knowledge as a social construction linked to norms and values, and it would demonstrate modes of critique that illuminate how, in some cases, knowledge serves very specific economic, political and social interests. Moreover, critical literacy would function as a theoretical tool to help students and others develop a critical relationship to their own knowledge.
>
> (Aronowitz & Giroux, 1993, p. 132)

With this kind of literacy, students "learn how to read the world and their lives critically and relatedly ... and, most importantly, it points to forms of social action and collective struggle" (ibid.).

Schools have received mandates for phonics instruction and a renewed focus on decoding and the process skills of reading. While this is not an inevitable result, and while teachers are still autonomous actors who can mediate and adapt policy, NCLB and high-stakes testing seem to be limiting thoughtful analysis and discussion. For example, in Chicago, Anagnostopolous (2005) found that teachers in an urban high school were failing to engage in discussions of issues about a novel because these were not covered on the test. She concludes that "efforts to raise standards through testing policies can result in limiting students' opportunities to construct understandings of curricular texts and of the social ideas at their core" (p. 35). In Kentucky, Hillocks (2002) observed that in some schools teachers focused on grammar and mechanics similar to the writing on state assessments rather than creative writing and analytic thinking. As teachers seek to increase test scores, they often find themselves teaching in test format and using test language (Anagnostopolous, 2005; Stecher & Hamilton, 2002; Anagnostopolous, 2003; Smith, 1991).

Federal initiatives in history education

In 2001, Congress approved the Teaching American History (TAH) grant program promoted by Senator Robert Byrd (D-WV). Byrd explained what he meant by the teaching of "traditional" American history:

> An unfortunate trend of blending history with a variety of other subjects to form a hybrid called "social studies" has taken hold in our schools. I am not against social studies, but I want history. If we are going to have social studies, that is OK, but let's have history. Further, the history books provided to our young people, all too frequently, gloss over the finer points of America's past. My amendment provides incentives to help spur a return to the teaching of traditional American history.
>
> (Byrd, 2001)

In 2004–6 the U.S. Department of Education spent just under $120 million to improve teachers' knowledge and understanding of and appreciation for traditional U.S. history through the Teaching American History grant program. The National Endowment for the Humanities (NEH) has been implementing its "We the People" initiative, which was funded in 2002 to further improve history education. It began with an essay contest for high school students and an annual NEH "Heroes in History" lecture. The "We the People" launch also included a White House forum in spring 2003 to explore, in the words of the president, "new policies to improve the teaching of history and civics in elementary and secondary schools, and in our colleges and universities." Only a few of the panelists were historians, and professional and academic associations of historians were invited as spectators rather than as participants. This technique has been used with other groups such as deans of education. In another example, Judd Gregg (R-NH) introduced the Higher Education for Freedom Act in the Senate of the United States (s.1614, September 6, 2005), which gives the secretary of education the authority to award grants to post-secondary programs that teach "traditional American history; the history, nature, and threats to free institutions; and the history of Western Civilization."

Many states are revising standards and debating the role of history to teach citizenship, democracy, and patriotism, and the places of American history and world history. Michigan now requires world geography for all students, while other states are adding civics and expanding traditional history. The national debate over history pits what is being called "traditional history" against "revisionism," or the critical exploration of the past. Revisionist history is blamed for being unpatriotic and relativistic. The Thomas B. Fordham Foundation and the American Council of Trustees and Alumni published reports that capture the main points of this now common argument.

Distorting history and the social studies: The Fordham Foundation

It is our belief that national pride and patriotism are not and should not be the preserve of the American right. In *The lost promise of patriotism*, Jonathan M. Hansen (2003) recalls a group of early 20th-century "cosmopolitan patriots," including John Dewey, Randolph Bourne, Jane Addams, and others, who thought the potential of American civic identity could be realized by rethinking liberalism and its links with acquisitive individualism, laissez-faire economics, Anglo ethnocentrism, and bullying overseas expansion. These "cosmopolitan patriots" instead worried about the illiberal outcomes of a corporate-industrial order, embraced social democracy, fought to bridge the chasm between classes and expand cultural diversity, and opposed the worst excesses of intervention abroad. Such American progressives sought a social solidarity based on democratic social reciprocity and civic deliberation involving all citizens while embracing all newcomers as citizens-in-the-making. They envisioned the schools as a crucible to forge democratic community and to prepare Americans for civic deliberation.

It is a radical leap in time and mindset—and in pessimism—to the contemporary complaint and jeremiad offered in *Where did social studies go wrong?* by James Leming, Lucien Ellington, and Kathleen Porter-Magee (2003). In their concern that the schools must work to deepen understanding of

American history and prepare young Americans for national defense, they worry that "lunatics" now control "the asylum," and the schools are capable of educating only civic "idiots." Jonathan Burack (2003), in his essay "The student, the world, and the global education ideology," perhaps goes furthest, lamenting the influence of an anti-American ideology spread from colleges of education to the schools that is "deeply suspicious of America's institutions, values, and role in the world," opposes American "exceptionalism," and is aimed at "instilling indifference to any patriotic appeal at all."

The role of schools in creating "knowledgeable and patriotic citizens," Finn, Burack, and others assert, is the vision of America put forward by the contemporary right—respectful of (carefully selected) traditions, the market, cultural homogeneity, and righteous interventionism. Students, they say, should study an American history that emphasizes "true heroes of the American story." They should learn about the extraordinary achievements of the American political system. They should be free of exposure to the darker side of American history. They should sidestep irrelevant emphases on multicultural differences. Above all, they should be freed from the alleged globalist influence in social studies curricula, which, in its emphases on multicultural celebration, cultural relativism, and "transnational progressivism," aims at substituting another set of loyalties for those of American patriotic pride.

Our chapter seeks to counter this ideological foolishness, acknowledging some claims in common with the right about contemporary education and about some tendencies in multicultural and global education, but identifying the shoddy character of their critique. Nowhere is it clear that global education has the extensive influence and shapes what goes on in the schools that the right claims. We seek also to differentiate sharply between education for what Burack calls "patriotic pride" and what we call "critical democratic patriotism." It is mistaken to assert that educating students for patriotism disallows critical stances toward American history and policy. American history has been no straight-line story of Whiggish progress toward greater freedom, equality, and improvement but has instead been a more complex story of advance and setback, gains won and lost, accomplishments, and also failures (Foner, 2002, pp. 149–166). Critical approaches to the past can help educate and prepare students to take active part in a deliberative democracy. Seeing the schools through the lens of right-wing "patriotic pride" leads, we think, to a misinterpretation of American experience and the true meaning of patriotism, and misreads the political, moral, pragmatic, and imaginative dimensions of education for democratic citizenship.

A shoddy, inaccurate complaint

The right and progressives potentially share an interest in civic education and may reasonably worry together about low performance scores by students on civics exams. Just 26% of American high school students attained the level of "proficient" on the 1998 National Assessment of Educational Progress civics exam. Just 11% of American students reached that same level on the 2001 assessment of knowledge of American history. Many students reach college without mastery even of a simple scaffolding of American history or an ability to place themselves within the national story. Many are prisoners in a relentless present, lacking ability to distinguish key features of the past, key debates, key turning points in national development, or enduring tensions. Finn and his associates react diplomatically to efforts by professional historians in recent years to rethink and internationalize American history teaching to fit an increasingly global age. By better contextualizing American experience in a global setting, historian Thomas Bender (2002) has written, we may better appreciate the nature of its exceptional qualities. Burack admits no one should quarrel with this soft globalist way of putting it.

Yet Finn, Burack, *et al.* demand the right's kind of civic education, and they want American history to be taught first—America first, not social studies or global education. They believe that schools should transmit core ideas and principles and information about American values and institutions. Their complaint is that, nurtured by "too many education school professors," and consistent with progressive traditions and postmodern beliefs, our schools fail to do this and fail as well to distinguish good and evil, right and wrong, what is American and what is not. The right sneers at the stated goal of the NCSS to help empower students to "make informed and reasoned decisions for the public good as citizens of a culturally diverse democratic society in an interdependent world" (National Council for the Social Studies, n.d.). They want instead study of American values, institutions, and heroes, and narratives that emphasize moral and political action and national pride.

Burack claims that a "global education ideology" drives the spreading interest in world history in the schools. This promotes moral relativism, cynicism, and indifference. Transnational progressives conspire to push the schools to stress postnational global citizenship and minimize national citizenship. This is "citizenship without sovereignty," Burack says, not true citizenship, for citizenship cannot "float freely ... unhinged from ... sovereign national authority" (2003, p. 19). Multiculturalists, on the other hand, push global education approaches that characterize differences among peoples without clear ideas about culture, and either offer exotic travelogues without true purpose (diversity as an end itself) or fail to confront intractable differences that exist between cultures. Emphasis on tolerating and appreciating hence becomes teaching students in the schools to tolerate the intolerable. Globalists willfully deemphasize the West and "great leaders." In contrast, the right proposes teaching about Western civilization, the birth of freedom in ancient Greece, the Enlightenment, and modern democratic revolutions—Western history without colonialism, and without Auschwitz.

In our view, it is erroneous, without evidence, to presume that a global education ideology has taken hold of social studies or globalists determine things in schools, or that such a coherent ideology produces, or even powerfully influences, the results the right fears. This is an empirical question— What do associations promote and education professors advocate, what are state standards, and what do teachers actually do in the schools?—and nowhere do Finn and his fellows report on such concrete investigation of teachers and schools. We think it is also unclear at times to whom Burack and others actually refer, for global education and multicultural thinkers operate from diverse philosophical and disciplinary assumptions and differ sharply among themselves in what is meant by global education or multiculturalism and in the goals they seek. The right conveniently lumps globalists and multiculturalists together, without specifying and stating who they are, imputing hidden agendas and conspiratorial purposes to their varied and often sharply contending positions. Theirs is not a convincing indictment. It is, in fact, a case study of the type of advocacy we seek to identify through this work.

Our own reading of the global education literature actually reveals a variety of purposes and meanings to global education. We note at least *four* kinds of ideas coexisting uneasily. Firstly, sometimes advocates speak about *raising consciousness and awareness, or lifting horizons*, among students, opening up students to the wider world and its problems. Secondly they often also mean *attuning students to difference and instilling a vague and happy multiculturalism*, presumed to help students function better in a world of difference. Here, the right has a point: that advocates of this kind of global multiculturalism often neglect to talk about intractable differences and implacable hatreds that cannot be tolerated. The idea instead is on "seeing the other," and appreciating "multiple truths," not confronting intractable differences (see Mirel, 2003, pp. 53–57).

A third way in which advocates talk about global education is *helping students to know and think critically about the world*, increasing relevant knowledge, capacities, and skills to comprehend an increasingly interconnected world and its complex interrelations and issues. Why hasn't the Middle East modernized? What is the real legacy of colonialism in formerly subordinated parts of the globe? Finally, a fourth way advocates write about global education is about *shaping a cosmopolitan spirit and identity and sense of responsibility for all humanity*. This is a way to encourage students to recognize the modern condition of "multiple belongings" (Cornwell & Stoddard, 2003) and to see and imagine themselves at one and the same time as having memberships in local communities, the nation, and the world of all humans. This goes beyond raising horizons or awareness, encouraging tolerance, or expanding knowledge and capacities for critical thinking; it goes to impacting identities and shaping commitment. The right emphasizes commitment also, but in a less critical, narrower, and less deliberative frame.

Misinterpreting American exceptionalism

Nothing is dearer to the right than the claim that their opponents downplay the idea of American exceptionalism, that America is not merely different from other societies, but *unique*—a new world Israel, a special nation with a special destiny, the first, best, and greatest hope of mankind. This is an old belief and cultural rhetoric with a history of its own. The idea was well developed, historian Jack P. Greene (1993) writes, before Americans imagined and created their independent nation in rebellion against Great Britain. Tocqueville encountered it when he observed in the 1830s that Americans were "not very remote from believing themselves to be a distinct species of mankind," Herman Melville employed the language of national election in *White-jacket* in 1850: "We Americans are the peculiar, chosen people—the Israel of our time; we bear the ark of the liberties of the world. God has predestined ... great things" (Melville, 1850/1970, p. 151). This idea of exceptionalism is akin to a "political religion," a faith myth to be breathed into every American child. History is providential, and America is at history's cutting edge.

America is distinctive, with enduring features that indeed contribute to making its history different and special, including its comparative fluidity, its creedal basis for citizenship, its absence of feudal remnants, its expansive frontier, its remarkable constitution and decentralized state, its recurring waves of immigration, and more, the richness of American experience. But these are not encapsulated in the conservatives' providential view of American uniqueness. Since the 1960s, American scholars and writers have grown wary of broad generalizations about a unitary nation and ethos and about a single providential line of national history. Instead, in the post-civil rights and post-Vietnam era, they have become more aware of the United States as a national community of multiple, competing tendencies, divided and contentious, and of a complex record of national progress and retrogression, inclusion and exclusion. Historians have emphasized change in the polity, society, and culture over time and explored continuing tensions in our civilization—between freedom and unfreedom, civic and ascriptive nationalism, the market and national purposes, and a republic and an empire.

Historians have also become more aware of America as "but one fractional (and internally fractionated) unit in a polyglot world" (Vesey, 1979, p. 458). They have been impressed by American variety and heterogeneity rather than unitariness, and by change and complexity, such that, historian Michael Kammen (1993) has observed, "we have not had a singular mode or pattern of exceptionalism." Still, the normative ideology of American exceptionalism (as opposed to the empirical reality) exists as a strong cultural reality and rhetoric with its own powerful force, and conservatives have revived and instrumentalized the rhetoric for current political purposes. The right has since the 1990s made American exceptionalism a watchword for conservative restoration.

The move to resurrect this rhetoric began with Newt Gingrich's *To renew America* (1995a), and his video TV series "Renewing American Civilization" (1995b), after the Congressional elections of 1994, when the radical Republican described the five pillars of American civilization and argued that "there is an American exceptionalism that can be best understood through history" (Gingrich, 1995b). The argument in Gingrich's *ersatz* "take" on America was that, from the arrival of the English-speaking peoples, the United States had a culture of liberty that developed and flowered during and after the American revolution, and that this nation and culture, rooted in individualism and religious belief, survived until the mid-1960s, when suddenly it went awry; Gingrich thought he and others were starting on the path to bringing it back after 1994. "This course is an argument that we have to reassert and renew American Exceptionalism, that it is a struggle for our generation, that our Gettysburg and our Normandy may be inside us as a people" (ibid.). Gingrich's message was that, in American exceptionalism, conservatives might find a key theme and rhetoric to teach and learn American history and through which to restore for students an older moral order of patriotic beliefs, signs, and symbols.

"Today's millenarian right ... is ... high on the potent drug of American exceptionalism," Todd Gitlin (2002) observed. "Yesterday, America was utterly evil; today, America has the capacity to be exceptionally good (as soon as it is liberated from the forces of evil)." The millenarianism, demonization of opposition, and belief in conspiracy present in Gingrich's analysis runs throughout Finn's report and Burack's essay. Overheated rhetoric about turning the keys of Rome over to the Goths and the Huns, hyped-up talk about good and evil, and the call to arms with the schools as battleground suggest that the kind of American history to be promoted is not the multi-vocal, complex, and multi-perspective history produced by American historians in recent decades but a more purposeful univocal story of a virtuous, selfless, singular nation.

Of course, the question raised is whether recitation of pledges, repetition of American exceptionalism mantras, narrative stories of American heroism, and strident calls for a singular narrative comprise the kind of approach to the American past that truly prepares students to participate in a healthy democracy and interdependent world—whether it prepares them to encounter differences in background and view, in interest, and in membership, identity, and allegiance. Equally important, another question is whether it equips students with the critical thinking skills and skeptical habits of mind necessary to be able to assess, analyze, and use evidence to practice science, and to appraise and evaluate competing arguments and interpretations. These are core building blocks of democratic thought and vital to preparing young Americans to take democratic stands in the world and to understand what national defense is really about. Our American nation has been imagined and reimagined in such competing arguments over the years and is the more vital for this variety of narratives.

Misinterpreting patriotism and what it means to be a citizen

What conservatives understate in discussions of American exceptionalism is that, from the beginning, American civic identity has been potentially (although not always actually) broadly inclusive and critical as well as celebratory and particular. To put it another way, American civic identity has been "a remarkable mixture of cosmopolitanism and parochialism" (Barber, 1996b, p. 31). American patriotism was something different from other national patriotisms, for citizenship here represented loyalty not to an ancient land (*patria*) or descent group but to a critical set of political ideas and ideals. The sacred texts and "tribal" sources from which Americans have derived a sense of national civic identity are the Declaration of Independence, the Constitution and Bill of Rights, the inaugural addresses of selected presidents, Lincoln's Gettysburg Address, and Martin Luther King's "free at last" sermon at the Lincoln Monument. The patriotism of Americans is, in part, oriented toward universal ideals of potentially cosmopolitan reach, the same ideals that Lincoln thought made America the "last best hope" for people everywhere, and the same ideals that inform the poetry of Langston Hughes in "Let America be America again," stating unrealized values in the national soul:

> O, let America be America again—
> The land that never has been yet—
> And yet must be—the land where *every* man is free.
> The land that's mine—the poor man's, Indian's, Negro's, ME—
> Who made America ...

We are a cosmopolitan *patria*, according to the poet Robert Pinsky (1996, 86). We are not a "homeland," writes Michael Walzer (1996, pp. 24–27); we are "an association of citizens." Our oneness is a political oneness, involving membership in a community of creed. At the core is the proposition that all men are created equal, deserving of equal moral respect.

Hence, American patriotism is connected with basically universal and partially cosmopolitan ideals, and can be broad and cosmopolitan, because of the basic creed. The very foundations of our democracy and community are universal, turning our heads outward—to repeat, "all humans are created equal." Jonathan Burack complains that the ideal of global citizenship that informs educators in their efforts at bringing global education or world history into the schools is a chimera, as citizenship requires a national container to have any concreteness or authority (2003, pp. 59ff.). But Burack confuses and conflates status or national citizenship and citizenship as a democratic practice—two different notions of citizenship, and two completely different ideas of being.

The former definition of citizenship comes from T. H. Marshall (1950), who considered citizenship "a status" bestowed on those who are full members of a community and who have equal rights. A different conception of citizenship entails optional duties freely chosen by individuals and introduces an important ethical dimension, highlighting the need for persons to make judgments about policies and actions that affect others and to listen to others across membership in communities of difference. These intellectual and ethical capacities are not natural; students do not come pre-equipped with these, and they require thoughtful and challenging education if they are to be successfully realized. Oldfield (1990) distinguishes these types of citizenship as *status citizenship versus citizenship as a practice*. Status citizenship is geographically specific and exclusive. In contrast, the justification for democratic citizenship as practice refers to human rights and capacities and is broadly inclusive.

Two important conceptions of humanity underlie the possibilities of an expansive democratic citizenship. One is the belief that all people are equal. From this view, whatever the important elements of human well-being are (and there is disagreement about these), such elements belong by right to all human beings. Democratic citizenship posits that, in this ultimate sense, one's loyalty is and should be to all that is human, that is, *to all humans*. Another conception of humanity that underlies the possibilities of democratic citizenship is the idea that all people are capable of enough reason to justify government of, by, and for the people. Governments derive their just powers from the sovereignty of the people, and humans, by nature, are believed to have the capacity to examine the appropriateness of public policies, engage in dialogue, take into account multiple and opposing viewpoints, and, aided by institutions, arrive at compromises. They have the ability to work with others to create a decent society. By contrast, Burack understands the duty and practice of citizenship narrowly, explaining, "Participation as a citizen means above all the right to ratify the decisions of the government regularly through elections and to change leaders when necessary" (2003, p. 59).

Philosophically, it is difficult to argue that the conception of humanity at the root of democratic theory is exclusive to those who hold status citizenship. These are not and cannot be qualities of Americans alone. Others often migrate here and become Americans. Still others do not migrate here but possess these qualities. In our view, the philosophical rationale for national democratic citizenship of human equality, human reason, and faith in democratic dialogue by humans is exactly the same philosophical rationale for a more extended citizenship, which we might view as global citizenship—a set of orientations and practices to those beyond as well as in the national community.

In addition, there are obligations involved in citizenship not necessarily because of shared or common membership in an actual political community, or even obligations based on internationally recognized human rights. Some obligations stem from our actual material connections with others. Things we do and decide actually affect others; their lives affect ours; webs of interconnections and mutuality bind us all, though we may live separately behind distinctive national boundaries. As status citizens in the most powerful nation in the world, where American strategic power and hegemony shape much that goes on, we are, by the nature of those relations, morally implicated in policies and practices shaping others' lives.

Burack worries that transnational progressives endorse a concept of postnational (global) citizenship and seek to shift authority from the national community to an institutional network of international organizations and subnational political actors not bound within any clear democratic, constitutional framework. But this makes no sense. In global areas, citizenship identities are not *shifted*, they are *extended*. The sort of either/or thinking that Burack outlines does not and cannot occur. Cosmopolitanism, as a mode of thought, and claims for global citizenship do not suggest that one does not have a nation or leave one's national belonging or situation out of the picture. It suggests instead that one should have critical distance from the actual *practices* of the nation that can be explored through the universal *ideals* of the nation. Democratic citizenship requires uncertainly toward authority, including the authority of one's own nation.

Global citizenship in this sense is an extension of national citizenship, both pragmatically and philosophically. It also just makes good sense when the global is increasingly implicated in the local and regional, and the local and regional shape the global. While some Americans live more globally than others, with networks that are more transnational and connected, others have interests that cross local, regional, national, and global boundaries. If these are to be pursued appropriately, orientations cannot be purely national. We are the products of multiple belongings and connections, and, in some of our identities and belongings, we are both global and national.

Misinterpreting global and democratic perspectives on tolerance

Burack (2003) caricatures global education in saying that advocates "seek [mainly] to promote respect and sympathetic understanding across cultures."

Critical democratic education doesn't ask for full understanding across all cultural and other differences but for efforts at a fair hearing. It understands that forging understanding across cultural differences is difficult. It also understands that the world is a plural place. Cross-cultural knowing and interaction demand neither complete acceptance nor absence of judgment. Tolerance does not mean multicultural celebration. NCSS advocates providing learners in the schools with opportunities to "investigate, interpret, and analyze multiple historical and contemporary viewpoints with and across cultures related to important events, recurring dilemmas, and persistent issues, while employing *empathy, skepticism, and critical judgments*" (our italics). Burack also was appalled at the emphasis in schools on the "need for students to practice tolerance toward Muslims and Arabs in the wake of 9/11." This was action proudly in keeping with American ideals, we emphasize, not a globalist ideology, and was endorsed by our political leaders.

The attacks of September 11th were carried out by approximately 20 terrorists, mostly Saudi in origin. Neither the Saudi-born terrorists nor al-Qaeda represent a "culture." This well-educated, somewhat Westernized, terrorist subgroup was not even representative of al-Qaeda, filled with illiterate men from Afghanistan and Pakistan, alienated exiles from Egypt, Jordan, Pakistan, and Palestine, and alienated second-generation Muslims raised in European states. It is hard to know to what extent their mobilization in a fundamentalist Islamic political movement that opposes the West and seeks to restore a mythic caliphate can be said to be "a culture." The very question of how to draw boundaries around cultures is an important topic for global education. Some ethical relativists argue we should tolerate all forms of cultural expression since we have no empirical basis for judgment. Tolerance becomes the only non-negotiable principle. Democracy and democratic education, by contrast, sit in the family of moral objectivism in which moral, political, and educational systems rely on an objective belief in a common human nature and common human rights. Burack misses this point. In democratic theory and law, the idea of human rights trumps the idea of tolerance. Violations of human rights are not to be tolerated. Thus, there is no inconsistency or inappropriateness when teachers castigate 9/11 terrorists and also urge tolerance toward Muslims in general.

This mistake is typical of many writings of the right which reflect a misunderstanding of objective principles in democracy. In their rush toward a moral stance, they argue for a fixity that reflects authoritarianism and is not democratic at all. As Secretary of Education Rod Paige (2001) said, "We must not simply teach children how to count, we must teach them what counts." Democracy is a specific kind of moral and political theory that accepts the replacement of immutable truths based on orthodoxy with verifiable and mutable theories discussed and tested among equals. Democracy replaced governance rooted in hierarchy with governance in which reasoning people have rights, and institutionalize the collective processes, to control their own destiny. It is legitimate to the extent that everyone has some capacity to affect outcomes. Democracy is a method of governance that is ultimately legitimated not by its *content* but by its *process and ideals*. What is true and right must always be considered, reconsidered, and contested. This is not moral relativism, because deliberation must occur regarding freedom, rights, voice, fairness, representation, and justice. Democratic understanding should always be understood to be in flux, and this flux, requires us constantly to wrestle with the *meanings* of freedom, rights, voice, fairness, representation, and justice. Critical thinking by reasoning people concerning what may be true or right trumps obedience to eternal truths. Certainly the meaning of rights and of who can be counted as possessing rights has changed through American history—as suffrage has expanded, for example, and those formerly barred from the American community have won inclusion. But the broad concept of rights remained.

Conclusion: Misinterpreting what needs to change

Given our criticisms of the right's analysis, and our view that critical approaches to the American past and to global education aimed at creating a critical democratic patriotism commend themselves, what kinds of education make sense? What sorts of approaches would avoid the weaknesses of current approaches, those pointed out both by the right and by progressives, and would highlight possibilities of critical democratic education?

We argue for education rooted in a social solidarity based on democratic reciprocity and civic deliberation involving all equal humans. We argue for critically knowledgeable and critically patriotic citizens. This requires moral education and is not relativist or "indifferent" but rooted in key democratic principles. We don't see democratic principles as solid and foundational but instead as constructed principles that are to be critically engaged and explored for their fairness and effectiveness by the circumstances each generation faces.

What matters is not the heroes themselves in the American past but the ways that they have tried to bring democratic ideals into political life. This is our challenge; this is moving beyond patriotic inculcation to critical commitment. This is education aimed at helping to create critically deliberative and active citizens who work for a more just and humane national community and world.

We support history and social studies approaches that begin with the fundamental principles of human equality, as written in America's basic documents, and that move from there, not to hero worship and simplification, but to living conflicts to achieve and realize those principles. Such principles focus on Lincoln and Roosevelt, but also on Frederick Douglass, Jane

Addams, and W. E. B. Dubois, and beyond these individuals on many others who have struggled to participate and achieve an inclusive citizenship and stronger nation. Critical approaches that broaden our perspectives beyond national boundaries, and that reframe American history in a global framework, would also enlarge and enhance the picture and offer opportunities to explore what is truly distinctive in America, and also what Americans share with others in the global effort to achieve free and productive lives.

We are intrigued by the agenda to globalize the teaching of American history, to respacialize the narrative and both tell and relate American history in a larger context. Thomas Bender (2002) has written about how in our self-perceptions as Americans we tend to remove the U.S. from the international—America is "here," the international is "there." Areas studies approaches fortify this distinction. In his view, we must move to "understand every dimension of American life as entangled in [and having consequences for] other histories. Other histories are implicated in American history, and the United States is implicated in other histories" (p. 6).

Practical challenges to effecting this in schools are many—the need, for one, of students to be familiar with basic historical concepts, facts and timelines, global geography, and more, the adequate training of teachers, for another. It is also a reality that there will be insular patriots who say "America first." The widespread legitimacy given by state standards and curriculum structures to the expanding horizon framework of social studies education that places the study of the global into a single year, usually 6th or 7th grade, as students explore, first, family, community, state, and nation—in that order—is another problem. Nonetheless, we find inviting the effort not merely to approach our own national history critically but to approach the very notion of the nation as the natural unit critically. It might be helpful to students to imagine an American historical narrative that situates the United States more fully in its larger transnational and intercultural global context.

In this reimagined American historical narrative or social studies, all is not laudatory in the American past—the past is complicated—and students should be assisted to reflect on what went wrong as well as right after the Civil War, what was problematic about American empire in the Philippines, and what were the consequences of immigration restriction in the 1920s for human beings elsewhere in the 1930s and 1940s, as well as on what American involvement in World War II meant for the defeat of fascism and end of colonialism. It should be a historical narrative that treats the nation not as more static and unified than it is but as always in the making, always developing, and as existing in a larger context.

We think the task may also entail less knowledge reproduction or transmission of content, and involve students more in experiences where they perform knowledge: utilizing understanding of principles to develop arguments and, by debate and exchange, obtaining useful experiences in democratic deliberation. Why might Americans divide and debate over the Philippines, involvement in war in Europe, or later over Vietnam or Iraq? Why might Americans, an immigrant nation, debate immigration? Or civil rights? Or intervention? Or the welfare state?

This returns us to the American progressives, whom Jonathan Hansen (2003) described as "cosmopolitan patriots," who, while dedicated Americans committed to making a new America at home, also were other-regarding about immigrants and about humans beyond our boundaries elsewhere in the world. They offer us examples of how to be critical in approach to national history and yet embracing of the basic democratic project at the core of the nation. They offer examples of how to be cosmopolitan in orientation to humans elsewhere in the world yet practical in terms of participation in national politics and policy. In their thought and activities, we can find clues to where to go from here in developing education for critical democratic patriotism. Going to the right, we believe, is going wrong.

Chapter 7

Left back: Punditry or history?

> ... the problem with being a public intellectual is that as time goes on, one may become more and more public and less and less intellectual. ... less reflective, less inclined to question one's own judgments, less likely to embed a conviction in its appropriate context with all the nuance intact. ... A public intellectual is not a paid publicist, not a spinner, not in the pocket of a narrowly defined purpose.
>
> (Elshtain, 2001, p. 28)

As a history of progressive education in the United States, Diane Ravitch's *Left back: A century of failed school reforms* (2000) is a study in rhetoric, oversimplification, and misrepresentation. Beginning with an indiscriminate definition of progressive education, the author proceeds to set up straw men and false dichotomies in an attack on the progressive education movement. Ravitch leaves largely undefined the presumed "academic" ideal she promotes as superior for U.S. schools so that it cannot be meaningfully examined. Finally she chooses to ignore how universalizing secondary education affected the challenge of designing curriculum for all adolescent members of society rather than the 1 in 20 who attended high school in 1900. There is a "narrowly defined purpose" at work in *Left back*, and it is not commensurate with the goals of a public intellectual:

> there's no sense that there are truths and ideas to be pursued. There are only truths and ideas to be used and crafted and made into their most useful and appropriate form. Everyone is thought to be after something, everyone is thought to have some particular goal in mind, independent of the goal that he or she happens to articulate.
>
> (Carter, 2001, p. 29)

Defining progressive education

The self-stated and would-be non-ideological aim in *Left back* is "to trace the origins of America's permanent debate about school standards, curricula, and methods" (2000, p. 15). Its de facto objectives, however, appear to be to diminish John Dewey as a contributor to the advancement of U.S. education and to discredit the term progressive as used in the descriptor "progressive education". The author's technique includes casting Dewey as an extremist, rather than allowing him to inhabit his preferred centrist position amidst dichotomies. The process of achieving these objectives begins with Ravitch's definition of progressive education. In brief, she ascribes "four significant ideas" to the movement:

- education might become a science ... measured with precision ... the basis of the mental testing movement
- the methods and ends of education could be derived from the innate needs and nature of the child ... the basis of the child-centered movement
- the methods and ends of education could be determined by assessing the needs of society and then fitting children for their role in society ... the basis of the social efficiency movement
- the methods and ends of education could be changed in ways that would reform society ... the basis of the social reconstruction movement. (p. 60)

Compare Ravitch's analysis with that of her mentor, Lawrence Cremin, who summarized the meaning of progressivism in U.S. education in his classic *The transformation of the school* (1961, pp. viii–ix) in this way:

- broadening the programme and function of the school to include direct concern for health, vocation, and the quality of family and community life
- applying in the classroom the pedagogical principles derived from new scientific research in psychology and the social sciences
- tailoring instruction more and more to the different kinds and classes of children who were being brought within the purview of the school
- the radical faith that culture could be democratized without being vulgarized, the faith that everyone could share not only in the benefits of the new sciences but in the pursuit of the arts as well.

Redefining social efficiency and science in progressivism

A comparison of these two summaries sets the stage for understanding *Left back*. The most dramatic difference between the descriptions is the prominence of the social efficiency movement in Ravitch's analysis and its absence from Cremin's treatment. Ravitch gives lengthy attention to David Snedden as an admirer of Herbert Spencer and a leading exponent of the social efficiency strand of progressive education (2000, pp. 81–82). John Franklin Bobbitt is also identified with the implementation of efficiency (p. 102). By casting social efficiency as an element of the movement, both men and a number of their curricularist peers (such as W. W. Charters) are set up as exemplars of progressive. In contrast, Cremin never alludes to Snedden or social efficiency in his definitive history of progressive education. Ravitch sets up an easily criticized version of progressive education by lumping efficiency-minded social Darwinists together with socially minded progressives. The former take the social environment as predetermined, whereas the latter are committed to improving society. The consensus view among scholars is, however, that progressives such as Dewey, James, and Mead opposed Spencerian notions while in their own ways actively adapted the evolutionary focus of Darwin to social reform. To collapse the two perspectives is unjustified in the absence of convincing argument and evidence. Ravitch offers neither.

In a related divergence from Ravitch, Cremin considers the "scientism" of educational psychologist E. L. Thorndike, and that of curricularists Bobbitt and Charters, to be indicators of progressive impulses in their early careers – a movement from which they deviated after World War I (Cremin, 1961, p. 369). Of Bobbitt, Cremin writes, "His results may well have sparkled with precision, but in the process he had given up the progressive quest for the better life through education" (p. 200). Cremin appreciates the difficulty of defining progressive education and speaks to this point. As a consequence his treatment is careful and nuanced so as to maintain appropriate historical perspective and acuity.

If we contrast the treatment of the scientific strand of progressive education in the two histories, other difficulties arise. To Ravitch, Edward L. Thorndike is the paramount example of a scientific progressive educator on account of his work in experimental psychology, particularly in transfer of training and intelligence testing. Cremin, on the other hand, struggles with the place of scientism in progressive education because "many of its proponents ... ended as conservatives after World War I" (1961, p. 369). When asserting, as noted above, that Bobbitt "had given up the progressive quest for the better life through education," Cremin cites him as follows: "The school is not an agency of social reform. Its responsibility is to help the growing individual continuously and consistently to hold to the type of living which is the best practical one for him" (p. 200).

Again, in his prudent way, Cremin appears to suggest that educators who should be called progressive either demonstrated to some degree all of the four characteristics he lists or, at a minimum, did not repudiate any of them. Specifying what he calls the "spiritual nub of progressive education" is this citation of the message of Jane Addams: "the good must be extended to all of society before it can be held secure by any one person or any one class ... unless all men and all classes contribute to a good, we cannot even be sure that it is worth having" (1961, p. ix).

Contrast the manner in which Ravitch introduces science to the list of progressive descriptors with that of Cremin. In *Left back*, making education into a science is a progressive aspiration, while Cremin more modestly asserts that progressives sought to apply science in pedagogical situations. Dewey dealt with this discrimination as far back as *The child and the curriculum* in writing: "Every study or subject thus has two aspects: one for the scientist as a scientist; the other for the teacher as a teacher. These two aspects are in no sense opposed or conflicting. But neither are they immediately identical" (Dewey, 1902/1956, p. 22). Late in his career, in *Experience and education*, Dewey reflected once more on this theme:

> I am aware that the emphasis I have placed upon scientific method may be misleading, for it may result only in calling up the special technique of laboratory research as that is conducted by specialists. But the meaning of the emphasis placed upon scientific method has little to do with specialized techniques.
>
> (Dewey, 1938/1963, p. 88)

Also lost in Ravitch's treatment of science and progressive education are at least two mainstreams of scientific thinking: the perspective characterized by the observation and management of phenomena by an elite (e.g., the positivist, behaviorist attitude of Watson and Skinner) as opposed to a participative, reformist social scientific view (e.g., the activist, egalitarian tradition of Dewey, Freire, etc.).

Combined, the proponents of mental (or cognitive) measurement and the advocates of social efficiency are used by Ravitch to attack the progressives in a particularly galling manner: Progressive educators are accused of limiting opportunity to the marginalized or less privileged and consigning them to an inferior societal fate. No consequence could have been further from the conscious intent of these pragmatists who evaluated ideas in terms of their outcomes. Given Addams's sentiments, the fourth element of Cremin's definition, and the democratic socialism espoused by Dewey among others, this is a most serious allegation and it is at the center of *Left back*. For example, Ravitch writes: "in the new way of thinking, equal opportunity meant that a banker's children would get a very different education from a coal miner's children, and all would be fitted to occupy the status of their parents" (2000, p. 90), and, "[Bobbitt] could see only the status quo, and his recommendations were intended to preserve that status quo by limiting opportunities for a liberal education to a very small number of boys and girls" (p. 106).

Specifically regarding the place of social efficiency in curriculum history, an alternative analysis to that of Ravitch is provided, for example, by curriculum historian William Schubert, who writes,

In the debate between social behaviorists (with their adherence to measurement, precision, efficiency, and mechanical technique) and experientialists
(with their child-centered, progressive, democratic, problem-solving orientation), we find a monumental difference in perspective that plagues the curriculum field to this day and centers on two opposing notions of science.

(1986, p. 77)

A concurring, eyewitness voice is that of Paul Klohr, who taught curriculum theory until 1981 at the Ohio State University. This academic work was
a culmination of a progressivist career that began at Ohio State in 1939 with
graduate studies in education and evolved into the directorship of the
Laboratory School, an eight-year study school, all through the McCarthy
years. Klohr calls attention to the varying meanings of the term "social efficiency" and its rise as a cyclically recurring competitor to progressive
thought, rather than as an adjunct of that movement:

The 1920s was a decade of battle between two incompatible ideas that
sought to control U.S. school curriculum. The first round was won, in some
measure, by the social efficiency advocates. Task and activity analysis were
the primary methods of curriculum construction. Business reform had used
this approach. Bobbitt and Charters are representative of this theory ...

In the writing of the National Society for the Study of Education's *26th
Yearbook* [Rugg, 1927], advocates of social efficiency and progressive education failed to reconcile their differences. Prior to 1929, the social efficiency
perspective gained strength, parallel to great business sector expansion. After
the crash, Bobbitt and Charters' so-called "scientific methods" offered little
in a time of great social crisis. The sixth printing of Charters' *Curriculum
Construction* (1929) did not strike a responsive chord. Dewey's [1931/1985]
Inglis lecture, *The Way Out of Educational Confusion,* underlined more
clearly the mood of the country and helped to strengthen progressive views
of curriculum theory and practice.

Other theorists such as L. Thomas Hopkins (1937) in *Integration, Its
Meaning and Application* began to focus on such themes as curriculum correlation and integration – forerunners of core programs, block scheduling,
interdisciplinary studies, etc. In many respects, 1932 marked a significant
move forward for the progressives. George Counts (1932) wrote his famous
Dare the School Build a New Social Order. This statement brought to the
forefront the split between the child-centered and the social wings of the
progressives.

This internal debate hindered the work of the Progressive Education
Association (PEA), although Dewey and Bode, among others, worked hard
to find a middle ground. Clearly the influence of the social efficiency
approach to curriculum development faded well into the background.

The PEA's sponsorship of the Eight Year Study did much to further progressive views. Although much of its role in U.S. educational reform of the secondary school curriculum was lost when the Study ended at the outset of World War II, it stands as a major force in curriculum theory and reform. Among other effects, it brought to prominence a national education spokesman—Ralph Tyler, who had been in charge of the evaluation of the Study [Kridel & Bullough, 2002].

In terms of curriculum history, social efficiency did not play a significant role again until after the 1958 National Defense Act and, of course, thirty years later in the standards and testing movements.

(P. Klohr, personal communication, 2002, pp. 1–2)

In summary, Tanner and Tanner view the issue this way:

The difference between this group [Bobbitt, Charters, Peters, Snedden] who labeled its curriculum theories "scientific," and those who argued that educational decisions should be based on carefully tested hypotheses, open to continuous verification and correction[,] is fundamental. Included in the latter group were Dewey, Bode, and Rugg.

(1975, p. 294)

Progressive v. "academic" visions of the curriculum: Limiting opportunity

Ravitch interprets Cremin's third element – regarding the tailoring of instruction to the needs of all learners so that none would desert the school – as fitting children for their role in society. Perhaps the central complaint of *Left back* is that non-college bound students – particularly the poor – were consigned by the progressives to an inferior curriculum that robbed them of opportunity and created an undemocratic stratification in U.S. society (2000, p. 15).

This analysis can be challenged on several fronts. As has been discussed, the advocates of social efficiency and scientizing education are outside the progressive mainstream, authors of the "intriguing internal contradictions" Cremin (1961, p. 369) identifies. Additionally, however, there are at least two other responses to Ravitch's argument. One response is that the progressives faced the reality of mass secondary education and adapted to it in order to staunch the flow of drop outs. Secondly, they recognized the enlarged, diverse constituency education was now asked to serve and began addressing it. Or, as Alan Ryan puts it in his review of *Left back*:

Is she [Ravitch] not guilty of contrasting the standards of a small number of schools adapted to the requirements of middle-class and well-established families with those appropriate to a vast number of schools catering to 90 percent of a much bigger and more diverse population?

(2001, p. 19)

David Tyack (2000), reviewing *Left back* for *The American Prospect*, concurs and, in another objection to Ravitch's analysis, goes on to list numerous organizations unrelated to the progressives that used their influence to move the curriculum away from the traditional. These include the National Association of Manufacturers, the Women's Christian Temperance Union, the American Legion, the Daughters of the American Revolution, the automobile industry, and public health officials. This critique, in turn, leads us back to a key, summative statement of Ryan's: "it sometimes seems that everything wrong with American public schools is to be laid at the door of progressive education. This is something that no rational person could believe" (2001, p. 18). Or, to make the point in the words of Waller, a contemporary of the progressives:

> The list of those who have sought to use the tax-supported schools as channels for their doctrines is almost as long as the list of those who have axes to grind. Prohibitionists, professional reformers, political parties, public utilities, sectarians, moralists, advocates of the open shop, labor unions, socialists, anti-vivisectionists, jingoes, chauvinists, and patrioteers – all have sought to control the curriculum, the composition of the teaching staff, and the method of instruction.
>
> (1932, pp. 16–17)

The final response to this charge of discrimination is to challenge Ravitch's notion of the progressive curriculum. The debate is difficult to engage because the author expends little effort in explaining the concept of the academic curriculum that she holds up as the betrayed ideal. Here is her main definition of the "academic curriculum": "the systematic study of language and literature, science and mathematics, history, the arts, and foreign languages; these studies, commonly described today as a 'liberal education'..." (2000, p. 15).

William Heard Kilpatrick, a favorite target of Ravitch, along with Dewey and other progressive curricularists, is accused of making "a relentless attack on academic subject matter" (2000, p. 220), although Cremin and a careful reading of the progressives themselves have exposed this generalization as a canard. The academic subject matter, which Ravitch espouses, is at the heart of progressive curriculum. Literacy, numeracy, and a historical perspective are competencies no mainstream progressive would neglect. (In order to blur this key progressive commitment, one would have to identify progressive education with those Dewey decries in *Experience and education*.) These objectives, however, are achieved in the progressive approach through occupations, problems, activities, and projects that elicit student interest, demonstrate the usefulness and integration of knowledge, embed concretia in learning, and, as such, break down the artificial boundaries of the disciplines. The schoolroom atmosphere is not to be that of rote, drill, and decontextualized routine. These traits represent the status quo ante progressive education as R. Freeman Butts describes them:

> The teacher lectured or dictated a lesson and the students copied it in their notebooks. The students then learned by heart what was in their notebooks and recited what they learned from their textbooks. .... Students sat at rows of desks fastened to the floor, and could not move or talk except with permission.

> (1985, p. 717)

Embedding learning in authentic inquiry is at the heart of celebrated contemporary school reforms such as Foxfire (Wigginton, 1972), Essential Schools (Sizer, 2004), and the Centre for Advanced Research and Technology (http://www.cart.org/about/index.php). Ravitch places herself in an extremely conservative position when she argues solely for discrete disciplinary organization of the curriculum – taught apart from application. Similarly, her perspective is extreme when she neglects innovations of method, such as service learning, various project approaches, and internships. By her analysis she suggests that a scholastic absorption in the disciplines themselves should be the goal of K–12 education instead of an emphasis on the disciplines as tools that evolve over time and as means of solving human problems. Where was computer science or biotechnology in past curricula? Of course her arguments fit well with the high-stakes testing/standards movement of today's U.S. policy-making. A review of U.S. curriculum standards typically reveals knowledge objectives that resemble laundry lists with an inadequate sense of priority, proportionality, or application. School accountability is by means of the timed, objective standardized test that further abstracts knowledge from its place in the lived experience. Ravitch is providing an historical defense for a return to the traditional school – one to which she would not consign her own children (as she notes in her acknowledgments, they attended a "private progressive school" [2000, p. 533]). It is little wonder, then, that she minimizes her descriptions of the ideal curriculum. In their imprecision and reductiveness, they likely would not stand up to cursory examination. Ryan (2001, p. 20) summarizes this way: "there is an almost wholly implicit defense of a particular kind of school, very often described by contradiction – that is, by indicating what contemporary schools largely are not."

Tyack (2000) makes a different, also cogent, response to Ravitch's blind faith in her preferred curriculum. He points out that hers is another utopian vision of artificial compartmentalization imposed over a set of disciplines that are fluid, rife with internal contradictions, and constantly moving together in new syntheses. Additionally, the essentialist curriculum that Ravitch idealizes should be seen more in the tradition of "liberal arts" than "liberal education." The former has as its hallmark its connection to a classical academic tradition, while the latter is linked to the living goal of liberating consciousness from the bonds of ignorance, prejudice, and habit. Rousseau, in *Émile*, spoke in this vein of freeing the heart from vice and the mind from error.

It is also worth noting that Ravitch documents the reforms at the turn of the 20th century that brought the introduction of science, modern languages, and history (2000, p. 43), yet she seems to suggest that those are the last curricular reforms that should have occurred. In Ravitch's worldview, today's new structures of knowledge, as well as the pedagogy to convey them – including learning styles, differentiated learning, and multiple intelligences – are not on the side of the angels. Her implicit conclusion is that curricular renewal should have ended in 1900 when, coincidentally, the progressives stepped onto the stage.

An ironic biography for Dewey

A recurring theme throughout *Left back* is that John Dewey was complicit in the abuses of progressive education because, although he criticized extremists, his criticisms were not incisive enough:

> [Dewey] refrained from criticizing the psychologists at Stanford, Teachers College, Harvard, Michigan and elsewhere who were then creating and disseminating the ideas and practices he abhorred. He named no names ... Thus Dewey pulled his punches.
>
> (2000, p. 151)

> Over the years, Dewey was far too tolerant of fellow progressives who adored children but abhorred subject matter.
>
> (p. 173)

> Yet Dewey never rebuked his disciple, never dissociated himself from Kilpatrick's view that how children learn is critically important but what they learn is irrelevant.
>
> (p. 182)

> But [Dewey, in *Experience and education*] offered no reproof for public schools that offered different curricula for different youngsters, based on their likely occupation, nor did he chastise public schools that were institutionalizing social conformism and anti-intellectualism.
>
> (p. 308)

Cremin treated the same issues vis-à-vis Dewey with a much different and arguably more objective style. He can be seen as working toward a subtle portrayal of Dewey as opposed to settling for a partisan tone and heated language. Note Cremin's (1961) approach on these same issues, respectively:

> In an article slamming into President [George B.] Cutten [of Colgate University] [Dewey] too pointed out that the tests were a helpful classificatory device, but that their use beyond classification had reprehensible social overtones ... Barring complete imbecility, he continued, even the most limited member of the citizenry had potentialities that could be enhanced by a genuine education for individuality. "Democracy will not be democracy until education makes it its chief concern to release distinctive aptitudes in art, thought, and companionship." Insofar as tests assisted this goal, they could serve the cause of progress; insofar as they tended in the name of science to sink individuals into numerical classes, they were essentially antithetical to democratic social policy.
>
> (pp. 190–191)

> Yet as the twenties progressed, [Dewey] became less the interpreter and synthesizer of the progressive education movement, and increasingly its critic. As early as 1926, for example, he attacked the studied lack of adult guidance in the child-centered schools with sharpness uncommon in his writing. "Such a method," he observed, "is really stupid."
>
> (p. 234)

> [Bode and Kilpatrick] disagreed significantly in those elements within the progressive tradition each sought to emphasize. But they were one with Dewey in the contention that education is a continuing reconstruction of experience, one in the faith that the supreme task of education is the development of a civilization dedicated to the progressive liberation of intelligence, and one in the belief that schools could never accomplish this task without a thorough-going transformation in spirit as well as practice. Certainly these similarities are at least as important as any differences in estimating the wider significance of Bode and Kilpatrick in the progressive education movement.
>
> (p. 224)

> ... however scandalous the charge that Dewey idealized organization men, or indeed, that their abundance can be traced to his influence on American education, the charge is not downed merely by quoting from the master's books. Rather there is need for further systematic study of Dewey's work and the context in which it proceeded, so that the changes he wrought can be distinguished from the changes he explained – or indeed, criticized.
>
> (p. 239)

As demonstrated here, in *Left back* Ravitch takes issue with Dewey for his public positions but in a manner fueled more by ideology than by inquiry. Perhaps the most curious allegation is one derived from Dewey's comments in a lecture published when he was over 70 years of age: "Dewey was naïve about how his ideas could be implemented in the public schools" (2000, p. 59). As a philosopher, Dewey may have been circumspect, he may have been gentle, but by this point in his life it is difficult to imagine he was naïve. The above comparison between the approaches of Ravitch and Cremin raises legitimate questions about the fairness of *Left back* and illustrates why it can be seen as a work of punditry rather than inquiry or history. Cremin wrestles with the ambiguities and imprecision of writing a history of this diverse movement; Ravitch moves headlong and with unwarranted certitude toward controversial, often unfounded, assertions.

Ravitch is the doyenne of a certain segment of educationists in the United States who are respected by policy-makers and the media while being marginalized by the academic establishment. This can offer some account, perhaps, for the absence of questioned assumptions in favor of polemic proclamations in her prose. *Left back* was widely and in general favorably reviewed by the most prestigious of mainstream publications, including *The New York Times Book Review*, *The New Republic*, *The New Yorker*, *The Nation*, and *The New York Review of Books*. (There is a strong negative correlation, however, between reviewer enthusiasm and the writer's credentials as a scholar in education or in any relevant discipline.) Sales figures for the book are more than respectable. In preparing this chapter, however, we repeatedly found that respected educators, knowledgeable about progressive education and qualified to evaluate *Left back*, had neither read nor planned to read the book. In our contact with more than a dozen education scholars, for whatever reason, Ravitch's work did not compel their attention. If the thesis explored here is accurate—that *Left back* is less history than punditry—their position is understandable. This response does limit scholarly debate, however, and allows *Left back* to stand largely unchallenged in the public forum. The phenomenon of education scholars declining to engage a book of this magnitude is symptomatic of the splits that occur in this large profession. One such divide is that of public school leadership and professors of education; another, as in this instance, is between education policy-makers or media spokespersons and mainstream education scholars.

Dewey the dichotomizer?

Ravitch, in a final irony, excoriates Dewey for being caught in the grip of dichotomies. "With the perspective of time, it is striking to recognize that John Dewey was locked in dualisms, the famous 'either-ors' that he so often wrote about" (2000, p. 40). This allegation will come as a surprise to many students of Dewey since his public intention throughout his career was the reconciliation of opposites, as he clearly and explicitly stated in the opening chapters of writings such as *Democracy and education* (1916/1997) and *Experience and education* (1938/1963). Cremin calls him "an avowed enemy of dualism" (1961, p. 123). On the other hand, Ravitch's style of analysis frequently moves toward the creation of straw men and "either–ors," as she seeks to cast progressive education in the least favorable light by unfairly identifying as progressives those who were in fact extremists who sought to position themselves at the political center. The exaggerations and oversimplifications are familiar:

> Perhaps it did not matter that the new schools of pedagogy had a single-minded devotion to utility and a bias against intellect.
>
> (2000, p. 119)

> When [teachers] were no longer expected to teach subject matter, they had little reason to study it, and they studied pedagogy instead.
>
> (p. 244)

> The response to *A Nation at Risk* revealed a major fault line in American education: On one side were those who believed that the schools had little influence on children's ability to learn as compared to children's heredity, families, and social environment. On the other were those who believed that schools had the responsibility to educate *all* children regardless of their social circumstances or home life.
>
> (p. 415)

Cremin commented on this manner of dealing with Dewey when he wrote "the grossest caricatures of his work have come from otherwise intelligent commentators in the United States and abroad. One is led to wonder why" (1961, p. 237). Dewey himself observed as a warning: "Mankind likes to think in terms of extreme opposites ... in terms of *Either–Ors*" (1938/1963, p. 17). *Left back* is less successful at labeling Dewey a dualist than in establishing dualism as its own favored form of analysis. For the reader this is a source of frustration since the primary tension of the book—between progressive and traditional education—is insufficiently joined. The academic curriculum, as discussed above, is defined only by implicit language and rhetoric, and is, therefore, impossible to hold to meaningful standards.

Advocacy versus authority in scholarship

> The insidious anti-intellectualism that riddles this book, and which is manifest in selective reading, oversimplification, and slanting of the historic record, and

in reliance on rhetorical tactics, ultimately undermines Ravitch's glorification of the academic curriculum and denigration of progressive education.

(Wraga, 2001, p. 38)

Inquiry into education and the curriculum is arrested, rather than advanced, by polemics. U.S. journals of opinion and the popular media continually offer heated prose on educational issues that casts little light on the problems that teachers face. Media punditry has politicized and even theologized educational issues to such an unhealthy degree that there is profound cause for concern about the future of public schools in the United States. Even more troubling is that some of those who opine against public education have serious, undeclared conflicts of interest and stand to gain materially from the privatization of our schools. *Left back* fits comfortably into this landscape. It is identifiable as a screed of one political faction against the heroes and values of another. It serves the agenda of a broad, national network of foundations, think tanks, centers, and publications that aggressively propagandize in unison against what they see as the "education establishment" (Shaker & Heilman, 2002a, p. 3).

Almost incidentally, *Left back* is a text about education and, particularly, the curriculum. It is unrelated in genre when contrasted with the painstaking fairness of Cremin's *The transformation of the school* or the balance and self-criticism of John Dewey's works. This break with the conventions of inquiry and scholarship can explain why numerous scholars so easily dismiss *Left back*. From one perspective, such a judgment is not unfair or unreasonable because much is revealed about the book by its cover. The volume proceeds seamlessly from Diane Ravitch's very public politics and offers little deviation from the predictability of punditry. One can hope, however, that a further discussion will ensue: one that extends Cremin's respected history (now out of print) with new scholarship. In the meantime, we have *Left back* to reflect upon and to inform our judgment of the course the public debate on education has taken.

Both the form and the direction of U.S. public education are at stake in this policy discourse. Opposition to the democratic institution of the public school system is gaining momentum from a range of supporters, from sincere reformers to those who see a profit to be made, even at the expense of children. Within the school, public or private, advocates of control and rote vie to shape the curriculum with a new language of high-stakes testing and state standards, with all its punitive overtones. On the other extreme are those who argue for a limitless romanticism, à la Summerhill, for example (although this style of advocacy has been rare since the 1960s). Somewhere in the middle are educators arguing for authentic assessment, the construction of experience, balanced instruction in literacy, and the engagement of learners. The tension of this debate runs deep in U.S. society and is derived from core values that individuals hold about the relative goodness of human nature, the merits of discipline versus interest as motivators, and the connection of schooling to scientific and social renewal. The philosophic tendency toward idealism, realism, or pragmatism is another stratum in the prevailing heuristics. In some essential ways the situation is strikingly similar to what it was when Dewey started the University Laboratory School in Chicago. The conflict mirrors, to consider one parallel, the Apollonian and Dionysian worldviews described by Nietzsche. Though both have the same goals in mind, the view of those who believe that order is the path to enlightenment and progress is contrasted with the view of those who "follow their bliss" and rapture.

> For educators there must be a place for discipline and desire, for nurturance as well as order in designing the common school and its curriculum. Striking a balance between such factors in just the right measure, student by student, in each teacher's classroom every day is both complex and daunting. The 20th century has not been, as alleged in Ravitch's subtitle, "a century of failed school reforms." It has been a remarkable and revolutionary century in the history of schooling and only the second century in which mass, public education has even been attempted. Inevitably the schools have been drawn into U.S. culture wars, racial conflicts, and class struggles and *Left Back* is a document in that history more than it is itself a history. The public schools prevail: high among the people's priorities, expanding and transforming, addressing unprecedented social problems in new ways, and dogged as neighborhood outposts of democratic and humanistic values. A true reform struggle is played out in public classrooms daily and dedicated people are involved. Their spirit is that of progressive education.
>
> (Campbell & Moyers, 1991, p. 117)

Part III

Visions for change

Chapter 8

A renewed vision of good teaching and good schools

In this chapter, as we seek to examine the issues of the qualifications of teachers and the quality of education, we are confronted by questions about our own worldviews and the values implicit therein. For any practitioner, researcher, scholar, or policy-maker in the field of education, this is a journey worth taking as it is at the heart of education. Further, to go down this path is to bring new insights about the nature of human experience and to enrich ourselves intellectually.

By contrast, however, a number of commentators (including some influential politicians) tend to see teaching as primarily the transmission of information. This deep-seated, clichéd view of education is ancient and persistent and has broad "common-sense" appeal. Historically, or in traditional cultures today, memorizing the saga of a clan and being able to repeat such an oral history perfectly are examples of this type of education. Learning the catechism by heart is a medieval but familiar version of this notion of curriculum. By these measures, teaching is a relatively simple pursuit characterized by rote and drill in an environment of discipline. This deeply entrenched characterization is the foundation of a concept of education that is implicit in U.S. culture—a concept that includes desks in rows and a teacher in front of a chalkboard, lecturing. In their book *The teaching gap* (1999), James Hiebert and James Stigler articulate the notion that societies have images of education so fixed that they are highly resistant to change. Among recent manifestations of this view in the United States are the contemporary curriculum standards and high-stakes testing movements. Both policy positions reinforce this static definition of education. Standards and tests are not by their nature so limited, nor need they be, yet what we find in U.S. practice in these areas rarely rises above this level.

This is not to say there is no place in education for the mastery of factual content, and professional societies in education have done a better job than government at creating such guidelines for the curriculum. Ultimately, however, in the creation of curriculum standards such professional influence has been marginalized by politicians and their appointees in favor of "content" disciplinary specialists and special interest groups. The authority and expertise of professionals in education have a difficult time competing politically with the public's common-sense views of the field. For example, in the popular mind, science educators and their societies are deemed less competent than research scientists to set science standards. The resulting documents, as in California's science and social studies standards, document the hazards of this approach. Standards created in this way take the form of extensive laundry lists of data from the field. There is little recognition of the realities of time and reasonable retention, a chronic avoidance of normative and foundational content, and a lack of integrative and transdisciplinary views of learning.

Focusing on the *California history/social science content standards, grades K–12* it is evident that the document does honor to the discipline of history. The standards are a comfort to those who find history to be a synoptic discipline, in the words of Philip Phenix (1964), and a path to liberal education. The term *social studies*, however, was coined to demonstrate the difference between a family of disciplines, their structures and conventions, and the curricular needs of schoolchildren. The California standards serve the discipline, not the educational needs of students or society at large. This neglect of curricular relevance is manifested in an approach to history teaching that does not create an enlarged cadre of informed, motivated citizens, ready to vote and participate widely in the political system. Ironically, such neglect occurs in the schools of a nation that gave power and dignity to the common person in a revolutionary fashion—one that largely removed religion from the public debate so that faith would not divide its citizens. The United States established a new standard for free speech, allowing controversy to be assimilated through open expression instead of violence. But, today, the country has many unmet challenges and a need for engaged, knowledgeable citizens. The nation is racially divided. American's sense of community and common purpose is fragile and imperfect. Voter turnout rates keep trending downward. Oscillating tendencies between isolationism and unilateralism lure the United States into foreign policy quagmires. Unemployment, federal debt, and the lack of universal health care are not assigned appropriate urgency in the halls of government. Inequity in the distribution of wealth surpasses that of the other developed countries, yet there is denial regarding the class divisions that increasingly characterize society. Social studies curriculum standards need to address such social realities, restore trust in the democratic process, and encourage participation in that process. Laundry lists of data are valuable only insofar as they contribute to achieving such larger goals. Standards that focus on rote trivia at the expense of critical reflection on issues and process in U.S. political and public life undermine the democratic project. Standards that do not integrate the disciplines, showing, for example, the need for sound science in creating environmental policy, similarly detract from the citizenry's ability to adapt to changing times and participate in wise decision-making.

The tendency toward political micromanagement of the curriculum by non-educators is compounded when advocates for testing, textbooks, and standards also have personal or corporate profits at stake. Reforms that educators might favor, such as reducing class size, increasing teacher compensation, or buying teacher time for curriculum development, methodological renewal, and so on bring no education dollars to corporations that are, in turn, campaign donors. The advocacy by for-profit entities for particular school reforms is characteristically traceable to corporate economic interests, as would be expected in the marketplace. Their powerful lobbyists support policies that feed the corporate profit/political contribution cycle. The 1960s-era language labs and microcomputer labs, as well as expensive reading programs in recent days, are other manifestations of profit-driven education reforms that have commanded more than a fair share of education funding due to the push of lobbying interests.

Alternate visions

Tensions over education and the curriculum have deep roots in society and are much more than simple disagreements about what children and youth will study in school. The ongoing curricular debate is one more expression of competing value orientations that vie for dominance in contemporary, postmodern society. The standards and testing movement as conceived by the No Child Left Behind Act itself advocates the view that the purpose of education is the transmission of facts and skills that prepare the next generation to maintain and extend the economic success of the United States. Arguments for school reform—such as those in *A nation at risk*—are framed only in terms of economic competitiveness. By contrast, progressive educators and organizations set a high value on the transformative and humanistic goals of education. This typically includes questioning of established mores and ways of knowing, and a view of students that emphasizes self-realization and holistic development. Economic productivity, social conscience, and good citizenship are seen as flowing organically from such a focus. In this view an individual's economic and civic participation occurs in a context of choice and reflection—not automatically or as an obligation. Individuals grow into citizenship with an attitude of reform and renewal toward their institutions. Such an attitude underlies, for example, the expansion of civil rights.

In the tradition of John Dewey and his peers, progressive education is derived from the philosophical perspective of American pragmatism, that is, a view that sought to consolidate both the significance of ideas and the achievements of modern science and technology for larger purposes. Progressives acknowledged the value of material success but saw this in a context of values that were not exclusively material. Quality of life issues, such as social justice and the long-term sustainability of economic models, were also a consideration. Standard of living is merely one dimension of quality of life. So just as the progressive movement in politics reined in piratical capitalism—such as low standards in food and drug processing or monopolistic corporate practices—in education the progressives opposed the notion of schools as machines for sorting winners and losers in the economic system. Schools became places of agency for social reform and for broadening the franchise of success. Educators attempted to compensate for limitations in home background or aptitude in order to elevate students universally.

Progressives are blamed by revisionists, such as Diane Ravitch (2000), for an invidious propagation of social efficiency and social Darwinist schemes in education. Lawrence Cremin is one of a number of historians, however, who see the progressive use of testing, Carnegie units, junior high schools, tracking, and so forth, as different from the manner in which such "modern" techniques have been abused by others in contemporary education. As stated earlier, standards and tests are not by their nature illegitimate in education. They can, however, be easily misdesigned and overemphasized.

In economic terms, for today's progressives, educated individuals seek not only to participate in wealth generation, but also to raise questions about quality of life issues and to introduce the merits of aesthetic, social justice, and environmental arguments in making judgments about the ways in which business and industry operate. Respected voices for such perspectives include philosophers Richard Rorty, John Rawls, Charles Taylor, and Martha Nussbaum and educators such as Jonathan Kozol, Joel Spring, Nel Noddings, Elliot Eisner, and Michael Apple. Teachers, other educators, and their organizations have become leading societal advocates for this alternative point of view regarding education. Unsurprisingly, the propagation of alternatives has contributed to an adversarial relationship between those who advocate the mainstream, narrowly economic view of U.S. values and those who are seen as the "education establishment," whose values challenge the unbridled pursuit of profit. Teachers' unions in particular have been demonized by right-wing and some mainstream commentators.

The common-sense view characterizes progressive educators as romantic extremists who are child-centered at the expense of standards, discipline, and economic realism. An alternative interpretation is that socially progressive educators take seriously the democratic vision of U.S. society, in which a serious and sustained effort is made to provide equal opportunity for all. Equally important, progressives support material achievement but see it, first, in a context of sustainability, both socially and environmentally. Secondly, they recognize that standard of living involves not only material acquisition but also quality of life issues such as social tranquility, clean air and water, and the opportunity for the development of personality and family relations. Progressives also have an eye for the role of creativity in economic success. Transformative ideas, such as the microcomputer and Internet, which are of great economic value, seem more likely to arise from open educative settings, rather than from those characterized by rote, drill, and orthodoxy.

Graduate education in the United States has earned global respect because of an ability to blend an appreciation for the value of traditional learning with openness to creativity and transformation. This same spirit is widely valued by teachers at primary and secondary levels. Great universities and graduate programs have not emerged in a vacuum or in opposition to the larger values of U.S. education. On the contrary, they are part of a continuum that begins early in the lives of students when they are "asked" and not only "told"; when the unknown is as important as the known; when judgments of quality compete with those of quantity; and when the horizon is extended indefinitely, across all members of society and humanity, as well as into the future, indefinitely.

The common good, a public trust

Perhaps a society's success inevitably breeds a kind of complacency and overconfidence. One consequence of this tendency is a loss of cultural memory regarding the values and institutions that led to great achievement, accompanied by a disregard for those same institutions and values. Mass public education grew up in the United States in a deliberate fashion out of the need for informed citizens in a secular democracy and as a way to assimilate a constant flow of diverse immigrants from the world's many traditions. The franchise of the schools expanded as modern society displaced other methods of building community and raising children. The schools also became a vehicle for caring for those with special needs and as a way to compensate for society's intransigence regarding racial prejudice.

As the United States became more ethnically diverse and (for much of its history) more secular, the schools grew to be protected zones where society attempted to model its better inclinations—that is, schools were places where the myth of American democracy could be felt more deeply than in the marketplace or in more segregated institutions such as churches, unions, and neighborhoods. In their humanistic and imperfect way, the schools have contributed to this struggle, have helped to "Americanize" generations of immigrants, and have opened opportunity to countless individuals. Elementary and secondary education has been at the foundation of a college and university system that has set the highest global standards.

The schools were a public trust, a non-partisan institution established for the common good. Although human visions such as these are always imperfectly realized, the vision certainly did exist widely enough that a zone of protection surrounded the schools and insulated them from the harsher aspects of politics and the marketplace. Gradually, this vision of the schools has been eroded, in part by complacency, in part by a desire to reform the institution after the model of "free enterprise" which would exploit a "market" that has been insulated from full participation by the corporate world. The characteristically market-economy view that any endeavor of government can be more successfully undertaken by the private, for-profit model has gained ascendance in many quarters, and the schools have very much been caught up in the momentum of this movement. The common-sense logic is that, since the free market of capitalism has come to dominate the world generally, it provides a model for all institutions in society, including those in health, education, utilities, and so on.

A competing hypothesis is that it is the balance and integration of profit and non-profit institutions that has led to the United States' economic success and that to impose the rules of the marketplace on institutions such as schools is to undermine a successful system. Just as government domination of the economy countervailed this balance and failed in Soviet communism— or Enron, in a converse manner, upset such a balance in disservice to California— free market domination of education can be expected to fail in the United States. There are early intimations of why the profit model is problematic in schools. The massive economic failure of Edison Schools, for example, as documented by *The New York Times* and other popular media, articulates clearly the limitations of business intervention in school administration. School budgets were not able to sustain the overhead (including executive salaries) to which corporations are accustomed, and the economies Edison felt could be brought to a human service endeavor, such as school administration, were illusory. Spending more per student than its public counterparts, Edison at best was able to maintain pace with them while losing to date $400 million and 95% of its market value. Edison's backers seemed confident that highly paid, bright (business) executives could redesign schools quickly and effectively. Instead, what seems evident is that Edison had little in the way of transformative ideas to bring to bear and, instead of finding a profit by professional business management and the elimination of waste, their executives found the schools to be underfunded. The conventional business assumption that school personnel are not highly qualified because they work for unimpressive salaries fails to account for the non-material compensation human service professionals derive from their work and the value of their vocational zeal. Contrary to corporate ideology, the competence of persons is not necessarily reflected in the size of their paychecks. Other motivations exist and there is more than money at stake.

Interestingly, the emerging debate about childhood obesity and the place of unhealthy food and soft drinks in schools is also informative with respect to privatization of the schools. Public school can be a place where good health practices are modeled and discussed, or it can be defined as a place where many young people gather with money to spend where habits of consumption are shaped. The school as a marketplace of consumption has allowed soft drink companies, among others, increasingly to enter into arrangements with schools so that corporate profits provide discretionary funds for the institution (Molnar, 2005). As childhood obesity begins to compete with smoking as a societal hazard, some are now questioning both the functional and the ethical implications of this policy. Unlike the food court at the local mall, the school cafeteria has been a zone of protection for children. With the legitimate financial need that comes with cuts to school budgets, however, the notion of nutritional habits as part of a school's mission has been displaced by the desire to bring in corporate dollars. Gradually, children are losing one of the few powerful environments in which they can build better eating habits. Yet, with a health crisis looming, particularly for the poorest of children, policies may change.

Again and again the issue arises of whether or not society is better served by the introduction of the profit motive and the characteristics of the marketplace into the school. Might it be possible that some institutions or functions of government are not suited to privatization and the attitude of *caveat emptor*? Might the success of the U.S. economy and political system be derived from its balance and integration of profit and non-profit or governmental organizations?

Stages and ages of education

If we are to evaluate teaching and teachers, we must consider the complexity and competing demands of the field. Alfred North Whitehead, in *The aims of education* (1929), provides a comprehensive framework for the educative process in three stages: the Stage of Precision, the Stage of Romance, and the Stage of Generalization. In Whitehead's Stage of Precision students are steeped in the fundamentals of a field and take command of the data and technique vital to a course of learning. From engineering and accounting to the fine and performing arts, each discipline has its craft knowledge, whether characterized by theory, data, or technique. Lost in a simplified and popularized view of education, however, are Whitehead's other two stages, yet they are at least of equal significance and, in combination with the Stage of Precision, they comprise the whole of learning.

A reflection on the many contemporary settings in which kindergarten has been co-opted into a kind of "Grade Zero" offers an illustration of a focus on precision, at the expense of other stages and approaches to learning. So-called efficiency experts and others in media and politics have asserted during the past two decades that kindergarten could be revised and made in their view more efficient by setting aside the traditional goals of Friedrich Froebel and other early childhood educators. The established norms of freedom and flexibility in kindergarten could be replaced with a more structured, content-oriented curriculum in order to take advantage of untapped opportunity for instruction in precision at Grade Zero.

But for Whitehead, the Stage of Precision is preceded by the Stage of Romance, and it is in such a spirit that kindergarten was conceived. Prior to the discipline of drill and rote, Froebel and his peers asserted there is a need for establishing motivation in the learner—a strong intrinsic desire to learn. An intrinsic desire to learn must be profound enough to sustain a learner through long periods of very disciplined work to master content and technique. Early childhood education sets the stage for more traditional schooling, and it is particularly important for children who have not otherwise found the motivation to learn through their home experiences. Similarly, though some may arrive at school with a disposition to learn, this inclination can be lost if school experiences do not support motivation.

There is sufficient evidence of struggle in youth and adults to illustrate that passing through the developmental stages of life and learning does not happen automatically. Yet, there is a tendency in the popular mind to flog children through school as if they were a herd of cattle, expected to reach adulthood successfully, just as steers reach the railhead. This view grossly underestimates both the intelligence and the perversity of human nature. A better analogy may be that children, youth, and adults more resemble those animals that can never be domesticated and die in captivity or become hopelessly languid or enraged. A humane and productive relationship between established society and its successive generations is characterized by persuasion and insight, not by domination and the use of brute force.

Erik Erikson was one of the preeminent stage theorists who explained (in *Childhood and society* [1950/1963] that the passage to maturity is not a regular and constant path. Development is a series of distinct integrative realizations that transcend their predecessors. To put it another way, the accomplishments of one "age" are surrendered in order to meet the challenges of the next. The independent, ego-oriented personality, for example, is displaced by the bond with a partner. That binary union, in turn, is followed later in life by the introduction of children and the experience of the nuclear family, which typically is succeeded by the "empty nest." All this is compatible with Whitehead's dynamics, as mastering precision entails a loss of romantic freedom and ecstasy, while, eventually, the Stage of Generalization will likewise demand a "letting go" of the strictures of precision. The Stage of Generalization includes creative activity, improvisation, and transcendence of previous patterns and models.

Evaluating experience

Kindergarten and other manifestations of the Stage of Romance have been little valued in the recent era of U.S. school reform. Universal Head Start, for example, remains a distant dream, while punitive high-stakes testing for all at multiple grade levels is very much a reality. There are competing assumptions about the nature of children and youth that underlie this course of events, specifically whether punishment and negative reinforcement should be dominant in directing students in school or whether nurturing environments and appeals to their better instincts prevail in motivating young people. A school environment is not likely to reflect only one or the other of these visions, but without question the No Child Left Behind Act puts its emphasis on the punitive. Given the long-established and well-known consequences of failure in school and dropping out, it is difficult to imagine that more discipline and punishment is likely to offer a cure. Preliminary reports indicate that dropout rates are now increasing in an unprecedented manner as a result of high school exit examinations. The Houston "miracle" has now been revealed as the best documented case in point of high-stakes testing promoting school "pushouts" (McNeil, 2000).

Ultimately, to evaluate quality in teaching and learning, one must take into account the long narrative of life and how individuals contribute to society and derive satisfaction in their own lives. Whitehead speaks to this criterion in his Stage of Generalization. Motivated by romantic visions and equipped with precise tools, the learner eventually becomes a creator by generalizing in his or her preferred field of expertise. The learning process is not complete until the bearers of culture are empowered to reconstruct it according to their own inspired standards. This consummate type of educative experience tends to go beyond the realm of tests and standards, since by its nature it involves transcending established norms. Generalizing or creating is as effective a motivator of youth as the enthusiasm bred by romance. Since apprentices admire the accomplishments and style of masters and intuit that there is satisfaction, indeed pleasure, in such levels of performance, they have ready models to drive their aspirations.

If our system of evaluation does not account for the passage of learners through Whitehead's stages of romance and precision into generalization, we are judging performance through very narrow parameters. The consequence is that worth is assigned only to those who master routine, but who have no glimmer of creativity and innovation. This is one of the great dangers of examination systems because, in the pursuit of speed, low cost, and assumed reliability, such systems may foster performativity rather than performance. That is to say, such techniques reward the masters of test-taking rather than the future masters of arts, sciences, and the professions. "You teach what you test," goes the old educational proverb. In light of current circumstances, perhaps an apt response is, "Be careful what you test for ..."

This is not to say that evaluation, or even testing, has no place in the educational enterprise. First it is useful to employ a broad concept of evaluation, one that includes performance assessment as well as testing or standardized testing. Some varieties of achievement lend themselves to evaluation by quantitative and positivistic tools while others do not. The appraisal tool needs to be fitted to the task at hand rather than imposed on the situation simply because it is a cheap or easy technique or because it confers an aura of accuracy, however misbegotten. The monochromatic, common-sense view of evaluation is that it is best done via testing, particularly objective testing. Once again, however, conventional and popularized views are not necessarily accurate and often have a reactionary flavor.

Although too little used, there are techniques that can assess a child's readiness for formal schooling, that is, entry to kindergarten. Similar judgments can be made later about whether an attitude of eagerness to learn informed by the goals of the Stage of Romance has been established. Just as there is a need for more flexible entry to school in terms of age, so too is there a need for flexibility to exit from kindergarten to the grades. Children, parents, and educators seem captive to calendar age in determining these matters, although we know better, including the characteristic variances in readiness by gender. Some children need more or less than a year of days or half-days to adopt a positive attitude toward schooling. One can justify such student-centeredness on efficiency grounds as readily as on humane ones. The rigid calendar and narrow cognitive approach has left too many students behind, like babies born too soon and unable to sustain life independently.

A third axis

The previous sections suggest that, as we evaluate education, we should account for two axes of performance. One axis is that of quality versus quantity, or narrative versus numerical. Second is the axis of the transformational staircase of stage and age development in which criteria for success change in a fundamental way. Finally, a third axis is reflected in theories of psychological type, such as those of C. G. Jung and the Myers–Briggs Type Indicator (MBTI) of Kathryn Briggs and Isabel Briggs Myers (Myers & McCaulley, 1998). Type thinking is also evident in Howard Gardner's theory of multiple intelligences (1993). MBTI, reflecting Jung's *Psychological types* (1976), categorizes personality in 16 characteristic patterns and illustrates a set of varying styles, values, and modes of interaction among learners or other groups. This indicator, like Jung's underlying theory, has served as a breakthrough for systematically sorting through a standardized instrument and then acknowledging that individual differences must be afforded respect and recognition. With millions of data sets available for research, highly convincing correlations have been arrived at, and among these are the characteristic personality types for whom standardized testing is most compatible. Conversely, there are personality types that correlate with underachievement on such testing and high dropout rates. Entry into certain professions, including teaching, is yet another area of correlation. There are interactive patterns such as the dominance in elementary education of personalities who perform poorly on standardized tests while being favorably disposed toward performance assessment. Evaluation processes are not type-neutral. In the grading of a single course, or in more global appraisals of school achievement, multiple measures are necessary to balance the inherent bias of each type of evaluation tool.

Gardner brings a similar perspective through a different rubric, that of eight "multiple intelligences": linguistic, logical-mathematical, visual-spatial, bodily-kinesthetic, musical, interpersonal, intrapersonal, and naturalist. These intelligences or preferences suggest differing teaching modalities: respectively, words, numbers or logic, pictures, physical experience, music, social experience, self-reflection, and experience in the natural world. Teaching methods are similarly diverse, ranging from cooperative learning to journaling and role-playing to creation in the arts. If they are to be comprehensive and effective, curriculum standards and testing techniques must likewise reflect the range of intelligences. To focus exclusively on the linguistic and logical-mathematical is to perpetuate an unfair hierarchy and deprive individuals and society of the full value of our diverse talent pool. Clearly in society the range of abilities is valued and rewarded. If an artificial and narrow grid is imposed on life in schools, this influential institution is turned against society's larger purpose of gaining full inclusion of the talents and abilities of its citizens. The simplistic and narrow philosophy that undergirds most standards and testing regimes is a prime example of counterproductive educational policy.

Kieran Egan, in *The educated mind* (1997) and elsewhere, applies an awareness of different forms of knowledge and a sensitivity to the concomitant scope of assessment needed to assess that knowledge. Egan's ideas, particularly his application of Vygotsky's concept of tools to delivering the curriculum, alerts us to the varied and multifaceted approach that is integral to a successful curriculum.

Again it is clear how common-sense initiatives by non-educators, to the detriment of all concerned, intervene in the practice of a complex and subtle field to defeat the best insights of professionals devoted to the practice of teaching. In the governance of medicine and other professions, society labors to establish a line between lay political control and the ethical zone of licensed specialists. In education, in the absence of a creed as lucid as the Hippocratic oath, there is little acceptance that such a line should be drawn. On the contrary, there is widespread consensus that educators have no special knowledge or principles such as "do no harm." In an environment of a latent distrust, teachers are increasingly forced to deliver curriculum and testing that contravenes their professional knowledge and ethical sensibilities. There are parallels in medicine when, for example, physicians are forbidden by government to inform their patients of a full range of treatment options. Compare this with teachers who in California have been, at risk to their tenure, obliged to administer standardized tests in English to young children who have little or no knowledge of the language. There is no stage-awareness in such an imposition on primary children. Similarly in Massachusetts, the state recognizes children's reactions to high-stakes tests by packaging the tests with latex gloves and zip-lock bags so that the instruments can be returned after students become sick on them. Examples such as these illustrate some of the lines that educators would not cross if they were free to uphold the standards of ethics and practice of their own profession. They, too, would aspire to "do no harm."

Bankrupt reforms

The most recent federal bureaucratic intervention into education, which began with *A nation at risk* in 1983 and has been abetted by most state legislatures, may be winding down at the same time as it spins off its last few dubious initiatives. Currently emerging is the American Board for Certification of Teaching Excellence's major effort to provide teaching certification to those who have a baccalaureate degree, satisfy a background check, and pass standardized, objective paper and pencil tests. (So much for mentoring, moral inculcation, and professional consciousness.) Former Secretary of Education Rod Paige dedicated more than $35 million to this effort to provide "highly qualified teachers" for all American children. This is the same Rod Paige, of course, whose reputation is based on the quantitative data of the "Houston Education Miracle," a test-driven program of reform that is now known to have been based on false and manipulated data and is, therefore, devoid of credibility. The revelations about Houston, as well as the underfunding and unpopular impact of the No Child Left Behind Act, may be ushering out this era of bureaucratic education "reform." Simplistic, punitive, and top-down education policy is meeting another frustrating denouement. Just as Edison Schools illustrated the bankruptcy of its design through accumulating $400 million in debt and colossal stock market losses, the *Nation at risk*/NCLB family of initiatives repeatedly created a record of unmet expectations, cost overruns, and backtracking government officials. All this is documented in the research of educators such as David Berliner (2005), Gerald Bracey, Susan Ohanian, Linda McNeil, Angela Valenzuela, Alex Molnar, and Jeannie Oakes, among others.

Our public schools remain in the front lines of society's efforts to renew itself through successive generations, and every day several million teachers engage those children and youth to the best of their abilities in what are often highly unfavorable circumstances. This is complicated by a political and media environment that oversimplifies the nature of education, strips it from its community context, and scapegoats its practitioners. Despite attempts to control schools from Washington and statehouses, they remain profound reflections of the communities they serve. Schools are circumscribed in their impact by a complex web of factors affecting the lives of children in each neighborhood. The effect on schooling of community health factors and poverty in general is still stubbornly unrecognized and the interprofessional nature of rearing and educating youth remains hidden from popular understanding. Magical thinking prevails, as evidenced in the notion that testing and laundry lists of curriculum standards can overturn the impact of hunger, poor health and prenatal care, banal early childhood experience, and a myriad of other problems associated with poverty.

The process of education, wrongly associated with factory and production metaphors, is one of humanity's most subtle and profound endeavors. A wise and just society must find means to effectively draw the line between political control and professional practice in education if that society is to prosper in both material and spiritual terms. This popular transformation is not simple, linear, or definitive. It involves an acceptance of the idea that education and the growth of personality it fosters are continually emergent. John Dewey's enigmatic statement is as good a summary as we are likely to see: "We have laid it down that the educative process is a continuous process of growth, having as its aim at every stage an added capacity of growth" (1916/1997, p. 54).

A guiding metaphor

The greatest of sages of history leave us not only with a legacy of clarity and insight, but also with enigma. As their reflections on life reach the limits of expression, we are often left with claims that transcend language and logic. Such ideas may appear "mystical," "tautological," or "vague." They are attempts to stretch the language and concepts of the day to create an understanding of an emerging world. Although such writing may attract the scorn or ridicule of some of their contemporaries, it may, too, carry a very different meaning to those who come later. Signature concepts often become the authors' principal legacy and the cause of their lasting recognition. "Every event in the visible world is the effect of an image," states the *I Ching*. The writing that reaches across time creates those images.

From ancient times, Plato's Theory of Forms can be seen in this light, foreshadowing Gestalt and certain other schools of psychology that have a structural bent. The Beatitudes of the Sermon on the Mount enunciate spiritual values and a way of life that remain beyond the grasp of all but a few Christians two millennia after they were spoken. Buddha's Four Noble Truths also fit this description of a life practice few can adopt or explain, but which constellates an enduring ideal. In the 19th century the Romantic poets and Walt Whitman described and celebrated sublime states and heightened consciousness. In the 20th century C. G. Jung coined terms such as "archetype" and "synchronicity" in an attempt to link science to the mysteries of the human mind. At the same time John Dewey extended the traditions of the Transcendentalists and American pragmatists by putting forward his concept of "growth."

In its many formulations Dewey's statements about "growth" are typically marked by their circularity. Growth is described as the aim of life and defined as that which leads to continuous growth. Truly educative experience is that which leads to further education and growing. Education has as its aim an added capacity for growth. Although the concept of growth is pivotal to Dewey, he nonetheless repeatedly portrays it in such puzzling ways. Stylistically, this is not the Dewey to which we are accustomed. Typically he is a paragon of logic and conventional scientific thought, a consummate rationalist. In the treatment of growth, his central metaphor, he steps out of character with statements that resemble Zen koans more than they do syllogisms. Perhaps in this instance Dewey sought to touch on something that lies beyond the reach of his normal philosopher's tools.

On one level, in his circular and paradoxical idea of growth, Dewey is alerting us to the significance of change. He is employing a familiar natural metaphor to redirect thinking on education toward process rather than product. Dewey subverts traditional thinking about education and its emphasis on "acquiring knowledge" by presenting a central aim that is content-less, open-ended, ineffable, emerging. Today's lesson can only be evaluated in terms of what happens to the student tomorrow, not what the student "knows" today. A course of study, a degree, or a program has value in terms of whether graduates go forward into life, striving for further development as a result of their education.

And when those tomorrows arrive, when we look back and try to determine, through our current achievements, to what extent the education we have received has been of merit, our answer will be determined by yet another tomorrow's events. The process has no end, not even in death, since our influence can survive us, as has Dewey's. All our evaluation is formative, of the day, and not summative, finished and final. Even the best of ideas typically becomes obsolete and can impose a burden on future society because it is valued for its past effects rather than for its current impact. The cost of stasis gives emphasis to the need for a constructive attitude toward change and growth.

> The old order changeth, yielding place to new,
> And God fulfills himself in many ways,
> Lest one good custom should corrupt the world.
>
> (Tennyson, *Idylls of the King*)

Dewey's concept of growth also presents insight on how to think about and accommodate chance. Although in the Western tradition elaborate plans are constructed and they are in turn executed by the use of technology and the exercise of will, there is no escape from the effects of chance. An act of nature, an airplane crash, or a virus can appear without warning and topple any well-laid plans. If the world is a fully predictable place, that code has not yet been broken. Jung offered the maligned concept of synchronicity as an expansion of our understanding. In his later writings he postulated this acausal connecting principle to provide an explanation for what is otherwise labeled chance or coincidence. In the absence of such explanations much of what we experience still has the air of randomness and even chaos. Dewey's formulation of growth does not demystify chance. Instead it provides a method of coping with phenomena that are beyond control or predictability. Dewey's "growth" offers us a means of responding to the unforeseen. This guiding principle allows for encounters with the great reversals of life and emergence with our psyches, if not our families or fortune, intact. Dewey's concept of growth can be found in the great stories of survival and triumph.

> Everything, even life, is eventually taken away from you. You cannot feel, cannot touch its expression. You can only reach its reflection. If you try to grasp happiness itself your fingers only meet a surface of glass, because happiness has no existence of its own.
>
> (Douglas Sirk)

Dewey's idea of growth, however, is more than a way of rationalizing fate and coping with the unforeseen. Ultimately he has by his formulation not only opened the possibility of transformation, but also put an emphasis on it. "Growth" in this sense is the consummate open-ended aspiration. No static state of perfection, bliss, competence, or control is postulated as a goal. Instead Dewey invites those who would be educated to join in an evolving, unending process of living. Implicit in this address to life is perseverance, since by definition the process is ongoing and ends for the individual only with the end of consciousness.

A good school

How would Dewey's metaphor of growth manifest in a contemporary school? The 15 guiding values described below envision such a school in its varied roles and qualities. Among these are community relations, the physical environment, student–teacher–parent communication, curriculum, evaluation, and mentorship:

1. A good school is clear about its mission, vision, and goals, which arise from awareness of democratic values as well as from a collective soul-searching with the relevant constituencies of the school. They reflect traditional wisdom and an awareness of society as it is emerging. Such

statements attend to the central values of society and its highest ideals. They reflect the rightful autonomy of the professional educators who practice in the school. A good school has ideals, wears its heart on its sleeve, and is a force for individual and community advancement.

2. A good school has both polices and curriculum that reflect the democratic values of human equality, justice, and human rights, along with a faith in democratic dialogue and decision-making. The moral strength to persevere, to withstand danger or difficulty, and to influence any situation or the policies of any organization in order to realize democratic principles is fostered—even if it means questioning school leaders. A good school will encourage emotional and intellectual openness to new ideas and experiences and will also hone the capacity for critical dialogue and judgment. A good school will expose students to diverse ideas and life choices. In such a school students and teachers will have the ability to work with others in structured ways toward common goals for the common good.

3. A good school arises out of a caring, supportive community. Schools grow organically from the neighborhoods they serve; they are not exotic transplants. In other words, they are "bottom-up" rather than "top-down" institutions, reflecting a healthy community and contributing to that good health. Although schools are a highly visible manifestation of their communities, they are not autonomous or independent of their social context. Good schools are dependent on the social capital in their communities.

4. A good school organizes itself to engage in dialogue with its community, realizing that external communication is too important to leave to chance. A good school is proactive in fostering input from the widening circles of parents, students, and citizens who have an interest in it. Comprehensive flow of information depends on both formal and informal communication structures and both social and political dialogue. As in all relationships, trust is vital to the higher levels of communication.

5. Education at its best appeals to our higher callings, and good schools reflect states of aspiration, intellect, community, healthfulness, and freedom. A good school also engenders feelings of safety and security. Good schools promote the rise of socially conscious individuals who strike the balance between self-expression and concern for others and the environment. Such schools thrive on diversity and see diversity as a cultural and intellectual enrichment for all.

6. A good school is sensitive to its architecture. The physical presence of a school can be a constant ally in the quest for quality education. The condition and aesthetics of the school are a statement to all who come there about the school's image of itself and the depth of its relationship with its neighborhood. Images speak as loudly as words so that the design, landscape,

and maintenance quality of a school effectively embody its mission. History and tradition also have bearing in schools; architecture can convey messages of stability and continuity.

7. Within a good school the lines of communication among faculty, students, staff, and administration are open and focused on a common vision. Although our economic system employs adversarial means to address many work-related issues, we are also able to rise above this dynamic when the call is there to do so. The climate of the school should reflect the mission of education, not the necessary, day-to-day tensions of the workplace. The school is a human service institution arising from several of society's finest and most generous motives, and in a good school all members of the school community interact in ways sympathetic to this calling.

8. A good school advocates for children and youth. It operates *in loco parentis*, presuming the best about the parental bond. Students are seen in a professional light, not an economic or material one. They are to be nurtured and protected, including when this is at a cost to the adults around them. The school exists for them because the community is best served through the creation of liberally educated, healthy young adults. Such persons will be most able to construct a future society that is successful in psychological and material terms. By elevating the individual in an enlightened way, we serve the common good as well. Truly educated individuals are profoundly conscious of their social responsibilities.

9. A good school reflects the values and ideas of its students—they are its essence—but teachers play a special role as guides and experts. This band of educators is assembled to manifest the school's curriculum, broadly conceived. The school arises in the community from a dialogue among concerned parties. As the interactions unfold, however, the teachers must ultimately convey the content and climate of the school. Only they have direct, intensive access to the students. Only they cross the generational divide between adult and child. Teachers are the translators of culture. Their messages must be infused with insight and inspiration in order to compete with corrupting messages from banal media and disillusioned adults. In order to serve these goals, teachers must have their own time together to focus on curriculum development in the context of the school and to give adult witness to one another's practice.

10. The curriculum of a good school is honest and authentic. It presents multiple sides of issues and places them in widening contexts. The curriculum is negotiated with attention to the curiosities and passions of students, as well as with attention to their cognitive processes of learning styles and cultural ways of being. The scale of the curriculum is realistic in terms of the student time and energy available to study. The curriculum spans the needs of learners: social, cognitive, affective, and somatic.

It is attentive to the self-realizing goals of a liberal education and the goal of realizing a more democratic society, as well as the directly functional objectives of earning a living and of addressing practical life problems. Those who design the curriculum are critically aware that curriculum is a specialized embodiment of knowledge, derived from the vast corpus of scholarship for the purpose of educating the young.

11. Instruction in a good school is developed in a cycle of recurrent feedback from learners. As a profound medium of communication, the quality of instruction is determined by its effectiveness in bringing about changes in behavior and attitudes. Instruction is not adequately defined as "telling" or "teacher talk" except on those occasions when direct techniques happen to be appropriate to a given segment of a lesson. In the great majority of occasions a range of other strategies are called for. Learning is an active pursuit and effective instruction engages students with the focus of their full attention. Excellence in method works to turn the group setting of schools to advantage, since individual tutoring is a rarity in schools. Just as curriculum is something more complex than simply "content" or disciplinary knowledge, instruction is more than telling or talking.

12. In a good school testing is an aid to learning and is not punitive in character. Standardized testing, particularly, is justified as one resource to aid learning and should not be mistaken for being a comprehensive verdict on learning or school quality. Today, the abuse of standardized testing has become one of the central threats to good schools. The use of high stakes tests to evaluate students and teachers has encouraged the abandonment of comprehensive goals for schools and the lamentable practice of "teaching to the test." This reductionist view of schools militates toward public education being employed to single out a few "winners" who are adept at a narrow range of performance while negatively labeling others with false certainty. Teaching a group of persons together and attending to their individual needs is in itself an act of limitless complexity. Teachers need every opportunity to broaden their effectiveness and successfully reach each student in an educative manner every day. Spurious accountability measures that set aside professional wisdom function against the central purposes of a good school.

13. Evaluation is vital to creating and maintaining a good school, and it is understood to involve a range of data gathering and a substantial element of professional peer input. As with any creative endeavor, teaching is practiced with a wide range of technique. Good schools are similarly diverse in the ways in which they deliver success in various community contexts. Although literacy and numeracy are foundational among school goals, salutary social and health practices are also vital. The evaluation of a good school is comprehensive of the school's goals. Evaluation techniques achieve validity by cross-referencing various

measures of achievement. Evaluation is among the subtlest of intellectual undertakings, just as public mass education is one of our most ambitious pursuits. The false certitude of reductionist measures is misleading and destructive of good schools.

14. A good school is a civilizing force to all around it. It is a purveyor of the arts, aesthetics in general, humanism, egalitarianism, respect for individuals and diversity, the triumph of reason over force, and democracy. Humanism includes qualities such as empathy, compassion, appreciation of individuality and the desirability of freedom, and the sanctity of human relationships. Humanism also implies a commitment to liberal education, that is, an education that frees the individual from narrow egotism and encourages an attitude of openness and inquiry in contemplating experience. Liberally educated individuals can appreciate the meaning of ideas and behaviors that are alien to them and derive value from these experiences without fear or prejudice.

15. A good school gives intimations of a better society, populated with persons who have aspired to the highest human purposes. Good schools are central in creating a new social order of greater justice, decency, and health. The alleviation of suffering, an appreciation of nature, and the continuing, vital search for new knowledge all characterize the better society good schools will foster.

Chapter 9

Rediscovering and reclaiming public education in a democratic society

Much of this book has challenged the pro-corporate neoliberal agenda for education. Such a critique implicitly assumes another vision and rationale for education. In these closing chapters (8 and 9), we make our response explicit. Most Western nations are democracies, and democracy is a functioning political system created with reference to constitutional requirements and to a broad set of ideals. As a result, all U.S. public schools explicitly teach about the operations of democratic institutions and about core democratic principles. Yet, in the public's view, American education seems to have lost its civic purpose and its sense of mission and commitment to social responsibility. Public democratic values are different from corporate values or private values; and understanding and promoting these values is both a practical matter and an ethical and even a spiritual endeavor. As Berman (1997) quotes the artist and former president of the Czech Republic, Vaclav Havel, "Democracy requires citizens who feel responsible for something more than their own well-feathered little corner; citizens who want to participate in society's affairs, who insist on it; citizens with backbones; citizens who hold their ideas of democracy at the deepest level" (what Pericles meant when he termed inactive citizens "useless") (p. 36). Ketcham suggests that "the 'certain kind of citizen' required for good democratic government is morally grounded in personal character and in concern for the public good, which leads to virtuous, public-spirited conduct at all levels of social discourse, including family, local affairs, national responsibility, and worldwide concern for peace and justice."

This is not a new idea. Thomas Jefferson in 1776 explained that the key purpose of universal *public* education was that all "would be qualified to understand their rights, to maintain them, and to exercise with intelligence their parts in self-government." Public democratic education is inevitably moral education with visions of the good and the right. It is education in which dispositions and capacities to work for the public good are key, and, since it takes place in power-laden contexts, it is also critical and political education. Such education must be understood as lived, personal, and transforming as well as ethical; it must be more than education about information and technical competence. Public democratic education is actually all of these. Public education is paid for by the public to serve not private but public interests. Private aims may be met as well, but something is ruinously wrong when the public mission is dimly understood and not a learned reality for our students and citizenry.

Possibilities for public education in a democratic society

Clearly, democratic education is a moral, spiritual, and critical endeavor rooted in a particular view of humanity as equal, rational, and cooperative, and a citizenry that asserts responsibility for all people, for all species, and for the environment. Democracy espouses faith in our ethical capacities and in democratic dialogue, decision-making, and lived practice. As Dewey (1916/1997) is so often quoted,

> A democracy is more than a form of government; it is primarily a mode of associated living, of conjoint communicated experience. The extension in space of the number of individuals who participate in an interest so that each has to refer his own action to that of others, and to consider the action of others to give point and direction to his own, is equivalent to breaking down barriers of class, race, and national territory which kept men from perceiving the full import of their activity.
>
> (p. 87)

What does such a vision require today? Now, perhaps more than ever, public education needs to prepare students to be active, pragmatic, lifelong learners rather than mere repositories of information. Although students will continue to master disciplinary knowledge and skills, the pace and nature of information change suggest that how one learns and the dispositions one holds are paramount. The Business-Higher Education Forum, in its recent report *Building a nation of learners* (2003), describes the widening "skills gap" between existing education and "the skills actually needed in today's jobs and those of tomorrow." They affirm an earlier report identifying nine key attributes necessary for today's workplace: leadership, teamwork, problem solving, time management, self-management, adaptability, analytical thinking, global consciousness, and strong communication skills. The report describes exemplary programs, including a curriculum to develop global consciousness at Fairleigh Dickinson University and one delivering interactive learning at the University of Illinois. This sort of vision is also valued elsewhere in higher education. For example, the Boyer Commission on Educating Undergraduates in the Research University (1998) calls for educating individuals "equipped with a spirit of inquiry and a zest for problem solving; one possessed of the skill in communication that is the hallmark of clear thinking . . ." (p. 13).

The sort of learning which the global workplace requires is not incompatible with the learning necessary for satisfying family life, for functioning effectively as a citizen, and for fostering a healthy and just society. Such learning emphasizes critical thinking, strong analytical skills, personal responsibility, self-knowledge, the ability to work with a wide range of people in a range of contexts, the development of a sense of efficacy, flexibility in response to changing situations, and, finally, genuine creativity. This sort of public education develops people who are able to look at any given situation and, in dialogue with others, pragmatically and creatively make use of arts and sciences to identify challenges and solve the resulting problems. Such abilities are needed to solve massive problems such as poverty and global warming, or, more specifically, to create new software, design a public health campaign, or improve family life. Though such visions are not highlighted in more recent national educational policy, they were in the recent past. For example, in 1992 the National Education Goals Panel recommended outcomes, such as critical thinking, problem solving, effective communication, and responsible citizenship. These values and dispositions are not effectively engaged in K–12 education. It is this education for public and democratic life that we wish to reclaim.

Much has been written about what a public education in and for democracy should be. Table 9.1 is neither exhaustive nor authoritative, as we believe these ideas are meant to be continuously explored. Yet it serves as reminder of the principles we think should be at the forefront of debate about public education.

What is the democratic ideal to Dewey?

For Dewey, democracy "is more than a form of government; it is primarily a mode of associated living, of conjoint communicated experience." In other words, it involves the individual having to "refer his own action to that of others, and to consider the action of others to give point and direction to his own (which, in the process, breaks down) those barriers of class, race, and national territory which kept men from perceiving the full import of their activity" (Dewey, 1916/1997). Such separation also causes rigidity and the institutionalization of life, permitting "static and selfish ideals with a group," and a "coterie" of beliefs and assumptions are entrenched. In this regard, Dewey argues that two aspects of the democratic ideal have to be pursued: more shared common interests and the recognition of mutual

Table 9.1 Qualities of an education that support or undermine the public good in a democracy

	Supporting qualities	Undermining qualities
Aims	In an integrated manner, schools serve civic aims as well as private, economic ones.	The main purpose of schools is to meet personal, economic goals and the country's need for economic development.
Orientation to power	Education develops learners who question power, current practices, and authorities with reference to core democratic principles and disciplinary knowledge.	Education develops obedient learners schooled in technical skills but unlikely to challenge authority and unschooled in the theory and practice of free thought in a democracy.
Orientation to knowledge	Education develops critical learners who question ideas, policies, rhetoric and the foundations of knowledge, asking who benefits politically, culturally, materially from this? How does this tell and persuade? What are the relationships among arguments, media, and disciplines?	Education develops acritical learners who learn concepts and understand ideas and polices but do not tend to question their rhetoric and foundations.
Social orientation	Education that develops social, relational, and interpersonal capacities.	Education that focuses on individual academic achieve-ment and skills.
Orientation to diversity	Schools that express and explore diversity in multiple ways, providing an environment in which students consider and contest a wide range of ideas, cultures, and forms of expression.	Schools that tend to toward homogeneity, retreat from encounters across difference, minimize the meaningful exploration of diversity by class, ethnicity, and religion, and promote narrow specialization according to professional, cultural, and religious visions.
Measure of success	Education that develops full human beings as unique imaginative, ethical, social, and spiritual entities who solve complex problems in real world situations.	Education that develops employable students who reproduce a testable canon of knowledge and information.
Orientation to change	Schools that continuously rethink and reenact the goals, forms, and curriculum of schooling in response to a changing society.	Schools that remain largely unchanged across decades and preserve traditional content knowledge and disciplinary boundaries.

interests, and freer interaction among different social groups following the social intercourse. Dewey envisioned communities of inquiry as communities that internally reflect "numerous and varied interests" and "full and free interplay with other forms of association" (1916/1997, p. 83). This conception is in opposition to our usual school communities in which interests and memberships are excessively individualistic, and it is in opposition to the increasing practice of private interest schooling.

Throughout the preceding chapters, we have outlined the challenges of this moment in U.S. education history, the methods through which these challenges are posed, and the motivations that underlie them. In *The public and its problems*, Dewey (1954/1991) criticizes the popular view that democracy springs up from a single root toward a finite end. For him, it is not a "movement [that] originated in a single clear-cut idea, and has proceeded by a single unbroken impetus to unfold itself to a predestined end, whether triumphantly glorious or fatally catastrophic" (p. 83). In Dewey's spirit our purpose is, rather, to describe the problems challenging educators and to put forward a revitalized vision for public democratic education which rises above the current debate as it has been constructed to date. It is in such a Hegelian manner that we think conflicts of this type are reconciled. There is no question regarding the importance of this project.

As we have suggested, mainstream modernist curricula often assume a pose of ethical neutrality, issues are presented as neutral information, and key questions of compassion and non-violence, of inclusivity and difference, of environmentalism, sustainability, and global stewardship, as well as of power and positionality, are left unexplored or are skirted. The citizens Vaclav Havel and Berman (1997) describe above are not value-neutral and nor should our schools be. But democratic education aimed at influencing a moral sensibility has been thwarted by the policy debates that confound and confuse the nature of private religious ethics and public democratic ethics and also by the epistemological context of the curriculum. Mainstream modernist curricula place emphasis on empiricism and positivism over multiple methods of knowing, on certainty and truth over contestation, on real knowledge instead of positioned and contextualized knowledge, and on developing reason to the exclusion of promoting imagination. Yet there can be a different epistemological and ethical expression of democratic public education—revitalization—when spiritual, critical, Deweyian pragmatist and postmodern perspectives are considered. Contrary to the democratic spirit, in general, curriculum currently reflects the disciplining, sorting, and narrow departmentalization of knowledge, and the removal of identity, meaning, passion, ethics, and imagination from education.

The possibility of democratic education would be enhanced by reflection on the modernist and disciplinary nature of curricula. For example, character education and fundamentalist approaches to education in which there are catechisms of easy rights and wrongs need to be rethought. At its most holistic, democratic public education suggests a positioning beyond rationality alone—not only education offering knowledge, but education offering meaning, identity, and community as well. Understanding our selves and our society, particularly in an increasingly global era, where localities are linked in complex global ties, requires interdisciplinarity, spirituality, and criticality, so that key Western, modernist, and market ways of understanding can be refined and improved.

Corporate faith and individual freedom

One of the longstanding debates about public education in the United States has to do with the role of religion and morality in the curriculum and more broadly about the relationship between spirituality and democracy. After decades of struggle to remove explicit Protestant teaching from school practices and curricula, public education had largely retreated from religion and, correspondingly, from spirituality. While we also support the separation of church and state, we believe that it is a mistake for progressive-minded educators to abandon issues of spirituality in education and to leave this basic human need as the exclusive claim of the right, similar to the way that the right seems to claim patriotism as its preserve alone. Developmental theorists who write about spiritual development frequently integrate it with the other important aspects of personal development. Typically psychologists connect spiritual development with cognitive and moral development, for example in the work of Maslow, Piaget, and Kohlberg. Furthermore, this theme arises when writers describe the compassionate, imaginative connections to others that a democratic community and a global citizenry require.

Theorists often employ terms that can best be described as spiritual. For many, civic goodness and spiritual good are entwined. As Tisdell (2007) points out, spirituality was important in the personal and collective passion of the civil rights movement. Further, Horton and Freire (1990) were clear about the influence of spirituality on their own educational work. Foundational questions in which teachers and students engage are reflections of existential human struggles for meaning and connection as well as our attempts to confront everyday challenges. They are spiritual questions but need not be religious or faith-based. The spiritual self is integrated with, but distinct from, the intellectual self and the ethical self; similarly, spiritual development is not the same as intellectual development or moral development. It might seem at first glance an improper topic for public education, but we argue that spirituality is distinctive and also centrally important for education in a democracy.

The word spirit comes from the Latin *spiritus*, meaning "soul, courage, vigor, breath," and has developed in English to mean "animating or vital principle in man and animals" (Online Etymology Dictionary, 2001; http://www.etymonline.com). Notice that the concept of spirit originally referred to the breath, respiration, which was the invisible, intangible part of a person that gives life, what Wordnet defines as the "vital principle or animating force within living things." "Spirit" evolved to refer to the invisible soul that would survive and depart at death. Later in the development of the English language the concept of spirit returned to the body to suggest the invisible "fundamental emotional and activating principle determining one's character." Silver (2006) argues "the spiritual and religious have been closely linked and are, to some, synonymous. But they are not synonymous" (p. 62). He explains,

> Spirit was the finest part of ourselves in the most literal sense of the word: the lightest thinness most ethereal part of the self. But it also began to be thought of as the finest part of ourselves in the more common sense of the term: the highest and most valuable part of the self ... we are artists, scholars, poets because we are inspired beings.
>
> (p. 63)

This concept *includes* the notion of the spiritual as the most Godlike aspect of the self, but it does not *require* a theistic metaphysics. Spirituality is described by Wright (2000) as "the developing relationship of the individual, within community and tradition, to that which is—or is perceived to be—of ultimate concern, ultimate value and ultimate truth" (p. 102), and by Schultze (2002) as "a transcendentally framed and morally directed way of life that faithfully aims to rebind the broken cosmos from generation to generation" (p. 75). Some, for example Schaper (2000), worry that spirituality suggests an unhealthy self-absorption compared with organized religion, which directs one to an obvious community. But most often, as these writers suggest, the concept of spirituality is connected to broad human purposes antithetical to self-absorption.

This is a spirituality rooted in axiology, the branch of philosophy concerned with ethics, aesthetics, and politics rather than metaphysics. Spirituality in this broad sense relies on transcendent expressions of the good and integrates experiences in a way that simultaneously evokes emotion, provides meaning, frames morality, hones aesthetics, creates human connections, and provides the impetus and story line for one's life myth as well as stories about collective histories. While spirituality is inevitably a contested concept, most definitions include these elements, which are clearly important for democratic citizenship and a good society. Further, such a notion of spirituality is meaningful while remaining inclusive of social justice, feminist, indigenous, Eastern, and secular agnostic spiritualities, among others. Allowing for real diversity within the concept of spirituality is also crucial if we are to address the cultural ethnocentrism that has tended to locate discussion about spirituality in education narrowly within Christian versus secular humanist conversations.

Attending to this spiritual reality both in the curriculum and in the professional personae of teachers represents some of the ways a democratic institution should reflect and serve its larger community. One of the more prominent voices calling for a spiritual perspective in education is Palmer Parker (1999), who explains that he wants to "shake off the narrow notion that spiritual questions ... must include the word God. He points out that, as "I explore ways to evoke the spiritual in education, I want neither to violate separation of church and state nor to encourage those who would impose their religious belief on others" (p. 6). And yet this terrain can easily turn rocky. One notable example of this is in the theistic "Intelligent Design" point of view that state and local school boards insert into the science curriculum of secondary schools, aligning themselves with a fundamentalist Christian movement thriving today in the United States. Schools cannot be exempt from the deeply felt convictions which give meaning to the lives of millions. One interpretation of this movement of the religious right is that it is a response to the disappointment many feel with the outcomes of the Enlightenment by attempting to roll it back in favor of the perspective of the Age of Faith. This reaction stems from an impulse that is neither malevolent nor irrational. It is a predictable and very human set of concerns amidst uncertainty and chaos and in response to the ongoing spiritual crisis of modern society. Unfortunately, the response to the concerns is intellectually corrupting, substituting fantasy and fictive certainty for scientific thought.

Corporate faith and individual freedom

There is some cause for alarm. This movement of culturally conservative people of faith has been effectively conjoined in recent years with a political coalition whose other members are committed to a specific libertarian view of political economy. This coalition of religious and market fundamentalists, as described in chapter 4, has since 1980 grown to become a pivotal force in American politics. On the market fundamentalist side, there is a particular commitment among the "faithful" to values such as those expressed most notably by Milton Friedman. This economic and political movement is better understood not by considering the motives and experience of individuals, but by analyzing the role of that legally constructed "person," the corporation. Corporations are the "leading individuals" projecting this perspective. In corporations, the most important operating principle and obligation is making profits for the shareholders. This can put them in opposition to the gentler, broader aims of the public. Just as religions or other mass movements have shaped history through fomenting collective action, certain of today's corporations have seized political life. Their alliance with the religious right is a manifestation of this expansion of influence. "Increasingly, corporations dictate the decisions of their supposed overseers in government and control domains of society once firmly embedded within the public sphere" (Bakan, 2004, p. 5).

This isn't the only corporate reality. There are, of course, many corporations not allied with the religious right, and many corporations with progressive agendas and policies (including, at least on some levels, Patagonia, the Body Shop, Ben & Jerry's, and UPS). Those corporations who pursue power and profit in an antisocial manner, however, also threaten progressive public education.

The unfolding story of democracy today is, in part, a record of the struggle between the high liberal sentiment of modernism and the new collectivist faith promoted by the recently aligned religious and market-oriented right. The failure of hypermodernity to satisfy the needs of people for meaning and spirituality is creating two definable movements. One can be understood as the "integral vision" of thinkers such as Jung, Wilber, and others that constructs a qualitatively different and postmodern idea of human consciousness and aspiration. The other is the retreat into faith, which is usually manifested as an acceptance of assertions based on tradition, familiarity, and authority. As an example of the integral vision, postmodern spirituality is attractive to many of those influenced by liberal education because it represents an expansion of the role and concept of the individual, including characteristics such as autonomy and freedom. By contrast, the return to faith is marked not only by the expected problem of collectivism, but also by the introduction of a new vehicle of control. This vehicle of control is corporate mass media, as shaped by the interests and techniques of public relations and advertising.

Whereas in the past institutions such as church, political parties, and the state have had dramatic success in mobilizing mass movements (at times in the interest and at times to the detriment of their individual participants), in the past 100 years there has been a shift in such movements as they have gained access to the tools of truly mass communication that is not dependent on the print literacy of citizens. At first governments themselves exercised these tools for political gain. The ultimate influence now, however, is *on* government in the United States, where those who fund the quest for power increasingly have become the holders of that power. Out of an exponentially increasing need to raise money to effectively communicate their message through the costly vehicles of mass media, political parties have more and more adapted their values to align with those of their major donors. Those donors, in terms of gross dollars, are predominantly corporate and advocate for global, financial aims. As an autocrat would have in the past, the corporate collectives of today pursue consolidation of power and wealth. Whether individuals as voters in democracies will recognize their personal interests as distinct from the commercial messages sent to them remains to be seen. This book is one of many "wake-up calls" that has been sent out in recent decades during the right's consolidation of power.

As we have detailed, particularly in chapters 3, 4, and 5, media matter. Advertising matters. Repetition, association, engaging imagery, and other techniques of communication cut deeply into human consciousness and have been perfected during the television era. With the population subject to thousands of advertising messages daily, it is only through a kind of heroic discipline that meaningful independence of mind and individuality are maintained. This critical awareness has always been at the forefront of liberal education, but how many people have the advantage of such a degree of high quality, extended education? How many people have the resources and will to construct individually their own system of symbols and meaning— one that attends to their own best instincts and interests and their own personal truths rather than those of the market? Market-driven messages are carefully and skillfully packaged and, if successful, conceal their motive as a kind of paid-for propaganda for corporate and consumer culture and for a narrow, vocational orientation that emphasizes "fitting in" with the marketplace. As an illustration of this, note the *New York Times* editorial labeling as a "sham" Philip Morris' $100 million youth anti-smoking campaign: "[ads] aimed at parents were actually harmful to young people ... The greater the teenagers' potential exposure to the ads, the stronger their intention to smoke" (November 27, 2006, p. A24). Elsewhere other messages are well intentioned but confused, self-contradictory, and sentimental. All are presented with conviction and apparent authority. On the other hand, the informed talk of scholars, intellectuals, and professionals is far less accessible than the talk that dominates in mainstream media. Pundits, politicians, and "men in the street" propound glaring errors of fact or definition into the public space unchallenged by authorities in science, history, theology, and philosophy. Paid-for right-wing commentators (compare Armstrong Williams's advocacy of NCLB) and fervent preachers fill radio with their messages while alternate voices are left to public broadcasting and Internet blogs, or are entirely absent from the public commons.

This confusion of message is apparent in the words of evangelists such as Rick Warren, the author of *The purpose-driven life* (2002), a volume now well past 20 million copies in sales. In his preaching Warren combines a truly admirable commitment to social justice and aid to Africa with an inarticulate, flat-earth condemnation of homosexuality. When pressed by Larry King of CNN to explain his objections, Warren could offer only that same-sex attraction is not "natural" and that one need only look at the male and female bodies to know what is appropriate in sexuality: "When you look at a female body and you look at a male body it seems that naturally certain parts go together ... I would just say I think to me the issue is, is it natural? Is it the natural thing?" (CNN, 2005). Warren's combination of laudable goals with his simplistic intolerance typifies the confusion we find among values in the contemporary United States. There is poignancy as well as irony in a massive movement such as an evangelical Christianity that targets some of the oppressed for support (African victims of AIDS) while consigning others to prejudice and persecution (American homosexuals).

Perhaps the good news is that today's collectivist moving force, the international corporations, in the interest of expanding market operations, ultimately look beyond race, religion, and nation-states. In that sense they are potentially harbingers of human unity. This could help explain why, when Islamic fundamentalists view the West, they see a "godless" face. They recognize the current dominance of the corporate, global, supra-religious view. On the other hand, Christian fundamentalists are led to believe that the interests of the corporate world are compatible with their own values and that they have nothing to fear from an alliance with the titans of globalization. That fiction is at the heart of the religious–market fundamentalist coalition and explains why political leaders who sit astride this union carve a careful path between corporate interests and Christian ones in policy decisions such as stem-cell research, cloning, and the morning-after pill. Corporations need a rational political universe and unfettered science; the faithful act as though they need neither.

The bad news implicit in corporatism rests in the implications it has for some fundamental human values. Corporations in a free market political economy are profit-making machines turned loose in the political realm. There is no question of the corporate value system: they are inherently materialistic and they are created and operate to maximize profits for shareholders. With ultimate irony they will, however, assume a mantle of spiritual values in order to promote their bottom lines. Such dissembling is another example of the desperately complicated world of messages surrounding people. In the language of advertising, people are reduced to target markets and bought and sold as such. This is done with a "no holds barred" manipulation of our senses and sensibilities. Does British Petroleum really advocate conservation? (Their current slogan is "Beyond Petroleum.") Does Philip Morris ultimately oppose excessive drinking and underage smoking? (David Davies, senior vice-president, states: "Miller Brewing Company, another of our sister companies, is one of the leaders in the beer industry in promoting efforts to curtail underage drinking ... we voluntarily label our cigarette packs with an 'Underage sale prohibited' notice—even in markets with no current minimum age restrictions" (Davies, 2001).) Is Benetton committed to diversity and ecology? ("The 2004 Benetton communication campaign is dedicated to primates [gorilla, chimpanzees, orang-utans and bonobos] ... Luciano Benetton's belief that 'communication should never be commissioned from outside the company, but conceived within its heart'" [United Colors of Benetton, 2005]). Does Coca-Cola really care whether third world children go to school? ("All over the world, we are involved in innovative programs that give hard-working knowledge-hungry students books, supplies, places to study and scholarships" [Coca-Cola, 2005]). The propaganda cycle has gone so far that, in the interest of co-opting spiritual values, corporations advocate for positions that would undo the corporations themselves. In the short term this works. In the long term, if they actually sell their messages, it could result in healthy changes for society. Or, in the long term, such a degree of cynicism may result in further alienation and confusion for people as they become lost in a very sophisticated world of doublespeak. Mission accomplished.

Inevitably the language and packaging of propaganda has entered the education debate and affected the profession of teaching and the curriculum of schools. Corporations and the corporate-influenced federal government campaign for reforms that lead to the privatization and commercialization of schools. These partners on the right reduce altruism to sloganeering and imply that politicians, test and textbook publishers, and for-profit tutoring firms care more about schoolchildren than professional educators do. The right alleges that educators are guilty of the soft bigotry of low expectations and of leaving children behind. The great propaganda and advertising machines that have sold sugar, nicotine, alcohol, and materialism so well have set their sights on education, all under the banner of advocacy. A central aim of this book has been to look beyond the corporate façade of advocacy to uncover what are the thinly veiled interests of the corporate elite and their political partners on the right. What is at stake are the foundations of the profession of teaching, the continuing existence of which as an independent, credible profession has been called into question. The market fundamentalists in their drive toward universal privatization have obscured the concept of a "public good." They have eroded the idea that any public institutions should be held apart from the profit and loss dynamic in order to serve non-material aims of society. They have demeaned those in the education profession as a workforce that should be replaced by persons with little or no specialized preparation beyond the successful completion of a standardized test. School superintendencies, they advocate, are best filled by retired military officers and corporate executives on leave. The market fundamentalists reject the concept that public schools should create a public ethos for society, and they reduce the purpose of public education to career preparation of a rote and mundane kind, fully evaluated by performance on standardized tests. As Bredo writes:

> One of the political problems in the United States at present seems to be that the center cannot hold. ... The result is neglect of the public interest and cynicism about the very concept. Much the same seems to be true of education.

Pressures to centralize and rationalize control, like performance-based accountability, seem to come primarily from a set of political factions bent on reducing taxes for public services and imposing a business-oriented, bottom-line mindset. These are opposed by those on the left, including teachers' unions, concerned with maintaining salaries and enhancing funding equity. ... In short, education seems torn between various factions, each of which tends to adopt a dichotomous, either/or way of framing the issues.

(2005, pp. 238–239)

This barren and one-dimensional notion of government and schooling as divorced from the public interest threatens to become the dominant rationale for public education in the United States today. The success of this peculiar view is testament to the powerful propaganda of the right wing in U.S. politics and media. We are living through an era that may be characterized as the triumph of public relations. The manufactured reality of spin-doctors has made easy work of convincing just enough voters that public health, progressive taxes, unions, secure pensions, secular government, and progressive schools all act against their interests. There seems to be no limit on what can be sold currently in American politics. The road to prosperity is through unprecedented debt; the road to peace is through ongoing war. "We're through the looking glass. White is black. And black is white" (JFK Script, 2006).

There are several great repositories of liberal thought in U.S. society. One is the liberal religious community characterized by the Unitarian Church and many of the other progressive Christian and Jewish faithful. Throughout U.S. history leaders from these denominations have paved the way and taken great risks on behalf of the expansion of justice and human freedom. Civil rights of all types, together with the peace and anti-poverty movements, are their lasting legacies. They have fought for these goals in the face of their conservative religious peers. In retrospect, and from a great distance, religious conservatives try to claim victories for "religion" such as the abolition of slavery, but there were people of faith on both sides of such issues, dramatically demonstrating the difference between liberal and conservative confessions and the ambiguity of the Christian legacy in American society. Liberal Southern Baptists such as Jimmy Carter and Al Gore are today pushed to the fringe of their religion. Similarly we saw religious communities split to the core over civil rights in the 1950s and 1960s as they are over gay rights in the Anglican Church today.

The arts community is another voice for human freedom and tolerance. The manifestations of liberal thought among rock stars, film directors, playwrights, and other artists are legion. Collectively their work represents the "counter-propaganda" of the left and plants the seeds of heightened awareness in the usual fare of mass media consumers. The fatal flaw of corporations, alleged Michael Moore in his film *The corporation* (2003), is that, in the interest of profit, they will allow their products, like films, to be used against their larger interests. As media continue to be absorbed into a few multinational corporations, one can only wonder whether or when this loop-hole will be closed. The independent voices of so many print and electronic entities have already been silenced and replaced by "fair and balanced" cor-porate voices. In this sense we are in a race between the imagery of liberation being co-opted, manipulated, and adopted to serve a corporate agenda versus that same imagery of liberation being employed for altruistic purposes and the propagation of heightened consciousness or a postmodern spirituality.

Educators themselves are another key repository of liberal sentiment, with a major institutional infrastructure through which to communicate their messages. This has made the co-optation of schools and the curriculum of particular urgency to cultural conservatives and neoliberals alike. As we have discussed elsewhere, education as construed in the progressive tradition is inherently subversive of materialism and totalitarianism. The cult of the individual, so fundamental to North American public education, alongside the Enlightenment emphasis on independent reflection and inquiry, creates a countermovement in modernity to collectivism, faith, and materialism. Mass public education in our Western democracies has brought society to the verge of remaking itself in a postmodern way, that is, in a manner that tran-scends the dichotomies of modern life with a spirituality that works across traditional lines that divide communities. At the same historical moment, however, the forces of reaction have found powerful allies in faith and mate-rialism and have created the struggle that we characterize as advocacy versus authority in education.

Rethinking "progress" on its own terms

In the United States polling data indicate that Americans are moving toward a cluster of values labeled by pollster Michael Adams in *Fire and ice* (2003, p. 176) "survival and individuality." These values include sexism, fatalism, confidence in big business, personal escape, civic apathy, multiculturalism, buying on impulse, more power for business, anomie, and aimlessness. Adams's most predictive item for sorting values is "The father of the family must be master in his own home." In the United States this value rose from 42% in 1992, to 44% in 1996, to 49% in 2000 (p. 50). Such data give us an idea of which values are held by a majority of persons, in what direction values are trending, and how political and other advertising messages can be shaped to tune in on these dispositions. The dominance of the right in U.S. politics today is due to an effective exploitation of this mainstream point of view. More disconcerting is that there is a feedback effect through which successful exploitation of these voters may begin to drive the process of value formation rather than merely feed off existing points of view. Also worth remembering, Adams tells us in *American backlash*, is that "the values of American voters strikingly diverge from the values of Americans who don't vote and that this divergence is increasing" (2005, pp. 66–67). Despite the fact that the non-voters number approximately half of eligible (not registered) voters, political power remains largely in the hands of voters.

There are, of course, points of view that are generally regarded as unacceptable and fringe and in some cases extremist and dangerous. In this category we might place those of polygamists, white supremacy groups, Holocaust deniers, and their ilk. Fundamentalist preachers such as Jerry Falwell and Pat Robertson have flirted with this status when ascribing 9/11 to the sexual sins of New York or calling for the assassination of foreign leaders. There are limits for what is perceived as common decency and rationality, even though in recent decades the evolution of political discourse has led to questions about whether extremism is becoming the norm.

On a more hopeful note we find Nobel Peace Prize winners and others in political life and the humanities who inform and inspire us. Adams associates this set of values with idealism, autonomy, and well-being. Some specific attributes include global ecological awareness, new social responsibility, control of destiny, fulfillment through work, adaptability to complexity, flexible gender identity, personal creativity, and so on (2005, pp. 193, 175). Positioning oneself "out in front" can be an insecure and dangerous place for those in public life, many of whom are only appreciated long after their work has been done. As a politician it is safer to stay on familiar ground, echoing mainstream sentiments and abjuring true leadership, leaving society to be guided by chance, cultural selection, or divine providence, depending on one's point of view.

Changes in human behavior and attitude are occurring as we speak of them. Norms and consensus are evolving and in flux. Generalizations are difficult, since society is governed by a shaky coalition and comprised of a number of quite different constituencies whose values are often contradictory. In such an environment we have chosen to focus on the advocates of the right and their initiatives in education, particularly in the past decade. Nevertheless we are aware of the larger contexts in which we work where there are multiple points of view within each theoretical camp. In order to illustrate this complexity, let us look further into the data of *Fire and ice*, Adams's comparative study of U.S. and Canadian values (2003).

Canada is allegedly the most "Americanized" country in the world, and yet it is increasingly at variance with the United States in its value orientation. The alternative direction of Canadian society invites speculation on possible futures for the United States should cultural and political trends change. Senator Barack Obama's distinctive politics may prefigure this type of change. A striking example of value difference occurred in the debate over gay marriage when former Prime Minister Paul Martin sponsored recognition of this institution in the face of evenly divided polling results. Resisting calls for a free vote on the issue and instead daring to lead public opinion and his Liberal Party, Martin said, "We are a nation of minorities. And in a nation of minorities, it is important that you don't cherry-pick rights. A right is a right and that is what this vote tonight is all about" (Panetta, 2005).

Regarding the "litmus test" question about whether "the father of the family must be master in his own home," Canadian support dropped from 26% in 1992, to 20% in 1996, to 18% in 2000 (Adams, 2003, p. 51). Every Canadian region rejects this assertion to a greater degree than every American region. That is to say, oil-province Alberta, the "Texas of Canada," is more liberal on this issue than New England, the U.S. region polling most strongly on the left (p. 87). From a more general perspective, in Adams's terms, the "trajectory of social change" in the United States trended toward exclusion and intensity during those years, while in Canada the trend is toward idealism and autonomy. The 2006 Conservative Party minority victory in Canada should not be read as a countertrend, since it appears to be a disciplining of the Liberal Party for a financial scandal in office and not a shift in values. In fact the Tories were at pains to soften their views on social issues (not pressing for an end to gay marriage, for example) and began espousing green views for the first time.

These data are presented to indicate that a minor shift in public opinion in the United States will open the door for very different politics. The myth of inevitability that the right has created around itself hangs on a few percentage points in voting in key states. The direction of American politics and education policy in the post-Reagan era is neither inevitable nor irreversible. Other developed democracies, most notably America's closest neighbor, Canada, are pursuing other paths. To illustrate, the October 2005 teachers' strike in British Columbia, led by the British Columbia Teachers Federation (BCTF), closed schools for two weeks and maintained massive popular support, as an educated and liberal citizenry trusted the claims of teachers regarding learning conditions and rejected those of the neoliberal, technocratic provincial government. This successful strike was yet another example of the capacity of the public to support teachers and schools and to show appreciation for the place of public education and a strong teaching profession in a free, democratic society. The BCTF had successfully led progressive change in the province. The politicians who were outflanked have responded by changing their positions to align with public sentiment. The story of this landmark labor action was almost fully ignored by media in the United States. U.S. teachers' unions have gradually begun to take notice of the strike and the work of then BCTF president, Jinny Sims.

The BCTF is an organization worthy of study by educators and others interested in progressive politics and the reassertion of liberal values in society. Although characterized by some as "far to the left" and a battleground between "Leninists and Trotskyites," the BCTF has sustained a position of respect among the citizens of British Columbia and continues to be a force in provincial politics. It succeeds in these areas in part by being unafraid to stake out clear positions regarding social justice with an international perspective. The teachers of British Columbia put their dues where their values are and spend millions of dollars on initiatives for world peace, women's rights, and similar causes. The 2005 strike demonstrated how these commitments have struck a chord with the public. Many in media, politics, and the business community were thereby frustrated in their unsuccessful efforts to stereotype and demean the teachers' resistance to diminished teaching and learning conditions in the public schools. General estimates and polls suggested that public opinion ran two to one in favor of the job action and the teachers' stance. No amount of blustering by pundits and politicos could shift the tide, and the teachers (at least for the moment) rewrote the common sense of contemporary education policy in British Columbia.

One of the current mysteries of North American sociology and political science is why Canada deviates as it does from the U.S. model. With so much in common and with such a high degree of U.S. media, economic, and cultural influence, how is it that Canada hews to a truly liberal path of development while the United States has slid rightward for many years? This phenomenon of Canadian difference brings to the fore the question of whether for U.S. citizens there is something to be learned from their neighbor's evolution. Of course people in the States are discouraged from looking to Canada for ideas and models by politicians and media voices that stereotype Canada as a land of high taxes and poor medical care. This type of disinformation has encouraged a dismissive attitude toward the Canadian model and feeds on chauvinism and the idea that the world's only superpower should be followed, not led, in matters of political development. The propaganda efforts to discredit the successes of Canadian democracy are a case in point of U.S. media dependence and corruption. (One astonishing underreported datum is that the murder rate with guns in the United States is 14.5 times the Canadian per capita rate [Coalition for Gun Control, 2005]. In 1998, 151 gun homicides occurred in Canada, while 11,789 were recorded in the USA [Illinois Council against Handgun Violence, 2005]. Per capita gun ownership in the two countries is similar.)

Nevertheless, Canada continues to build a society with a larger middle class, better safety nets, livable cities, and higher citizen satisfaction with government. The social fabric seems stronger, as does the understanding of civic and public responsibility, although nationalism is certainly not an explanation for these phenomena in this notoriously decentralized nation. Education in particular is a jealously guarded "provincial responsibility," with its control kept in the provinces and local communities. (However, contra to the "savage inequalities" of the United States, and in the

Commonwealth tradition, all students in the province are funded equally, according to learning needs rather than municipal boundaries.) This and other factors have allowed teaching to continue as a respected and powerful profession in Canada. In turn, the influence of educators, singly and through their organizations, may be one of the factors that keeps Canada on a liberal pathway. To renew our earlier analysis, it is also true that the arts enjoy strong taxpayer support, magnifying artists' voices in society through film and other media. The sensibilities of the liberal religious confessions are overtly subdued, since Canada is increasingly secular. (Ipsos-Reid polling indicates that only 59% of British Columbians and 57% of Quebecois believe in God [Bauer, 2005].) It may be that the influence of progressive Christianity has been assimilated by the society, which is no longer dependent on its institutional voice. The message of the social gospel seems alive and well in the caring attitude of Canadians, who vote to maintain their progressive tax structure in order that effective public health, public schools and social safety nets continue and expand. In any event, Canada gives a glimpse of the light of a new, more hopeful and humanistic day—a day in which society's values transcend the debate defined by faith and materialism.

Reclaiming spirituality for democratic education

In contemporary society, the language associated with spirituality and the evolution of consciousness is largely bankrupt. Confusion reigns as terms such as spirit, religion, soul, faith, and hope all are popularly used in confounding and careless ways. This loss of meaning and judgment is illustrated by the platitude "Killing for Christ," which expresses a consummate irony that the faithful believe that God is on their side—both sides, in fact—in every war. The language of spirituality, including the definition of the word itself, is contradictory and ill-defined in a way that defeats efforts by educators and others to put society on a progressive path of non-violence and compassion toward all others. We seem unable to differentiate religion from spirituality, creating the appearance that the non-religious are materialists and cannot therefore be spiritual. The retrograde response of the religious right, derived from the Age of Faith, is fierce and exclusionary, that is, only born-again followers of Christ are fully human and worthy of heavenly reward. The modernist response is the cult of ego-maximization. As Kovel (1999) describes, "Thus the meaningful life is held to be the life in which one profits and succeeds the most" (p. 92). "No one is actually told not to have a soul," he continues. "By soulless conditions is simply meant that those ways of being which are conducive to soul are not rewarded with worldly success" (p. 93).

But, as we have delineated above, spirituality is a broader concept and one of which religion can be understood forming as a part, rather than the two being synonymous. When religion aspires to our highest values it is indeed spiritual. These values have a universal, not an exclusionary, character. "Ethics requires us to go beyond 'I' and 'you' to the universal law, the universalizable judgment, the standpoint of the impartial spectator or ideal observer" (Singer, 2000, p. 15). Spirituality is a quest for meaning that can be universalized, and this claim has strong implications for creeds that diminish the humanity of non-believers. They may be called religions but, by this definition, they are not spiritual. At the risk of belaboring the obvious, here is one more tragic example of what passes as religion:

> Militants broke into the home of a headmaster of a school in central Afghanistan that educates girls and beheaded him while forcing his family to watch ...

> The insurgents claim that educating girls is against Islam and they even oppose government-funded schools for boys because the schools teach subjects besides religion.

> (Khan, 2006, p. A-9)

Lest we begin to feel spiritually superior, Nussbaum's characterization of Christian-influenced, contemporary U.S. society is a wake-up call:

> It is clear, for example, that the general public culture of the United States teaches many things that militate against benevolence: that the poor cause their poverty, that a "real man" is self-sufficient and not needy, and many other pernicious fictions that abound in our popular culture.

> (2006, p. 413)

Others continue to define this "benevolence" outside of a religious context. For example, Tisdell (2007), in her treatment of the interplay between spirituality and diversity, discusses with considerable insight the relationship between religion and spirituality and the respective definitions of each: "spirituality tends to focus on finding meaning in life, or meaning-making, and personal experiences. Religions are *organized* communities of faith that, in addition to a concern with nurturing a sense of spirituality in their members, have far many more aspects involved in them" (p. 5). Religious practice and doctrine may or may not demonstrate spirituality in this sense, although according to common definition there may be a naïve consensus that all religions are inherently spiritual.

Similarly, a materialist point of view that manages the concrete things of this world not for ego-maximization or greed, but for a greater ethical purpose, enters the spiritual realm. From his reading of Marx, for example, Kovel concludes "that the founder of modern communism—a doctrine widely denounced for its hostility to religion and spirit—was in fact a spiritually motivated man (though certainly not a religious one)" (1999, p. 94). In a

Deweyan sense, the dichotomy between religion and materialism can, therefore, be seen as false, as it is derived from wrong-headed definitions of both
points of view. A deeper reading of religion and materialism leads to reconciliation of the apparent opposites as transitional stages in pursuit of a non-
material and non-theistic spirituality. Marx concurs with Matthew in Kovel's
citation: "Truly I say to you, as you did it to one of the least of these my
brethren, you did it to me," (Matt. 25:40 [Douay-Rheimo Bible]).

Similarly problematic is the manner in which faith is defined in popular
discourse. When seen as trust in a truly spiritual higher power and trust in a
worthy religion, faith can clearly contribute to spirituality. This presumes
the caveats described above regarding the definition of spirituality. When
extrapolated into a general attitude of committing belief despite a lack of evidence, however, faith can be ruinous, delusory. Faith *in this sense* is the
poster child of irrationality and an attack on the entire Enlightenment project. When extended into politics or the politics of curriculum construction
for schools, faith of this type ends the possibility of communication and
compromise and leads inevitably to conflict. Irreconcilable political disagreements such as those over Creationism/Intelligent Design in the curriculum,
the rights of homosexuals, and legalized abortion are the result of this attitude of certainty. In the past, faith (so defined) justified racism, slavery,
sexism, and genocide as easily as it lifted humanity toward worthy ideals.
Similar to other forms of unchecked subjectivity, belief absent reason and
dialogue can be a most dangerous and cruel attitude.

It should be added that ideals such as the sanctity of life, whether manifested in resistance to war, abortion, or the death penalty, may well be
admirable and spiritual. The politics and other practical means through
which we reach those ideals, however, are of equal significance and require
a commitment to communication and compromise that tends to be eschewed
by zealots. Conversion rather than coercion is the preferred path and education is a central vehicle for this process. These tensions and dichotomies lend
themselves to graphing (see figure 9.1). On the x-axis we can plot the range
of attitude between "faith," in the sense of "belief without evidence," and
"reason," the mechanism of modern science and Socratic doubt. On the
y-axis we can array values from those of a purely "material" or positivist
point of view to, at the other extreme, acknowledgement only of the realm
of "spirit" or psyche. Fundamentalists' orientations, we hypothesize, align
with a commitment to materialism and faith (of the latter type described
above). The market fundamentalists target wealth and acquisition, while the
religious fundamentalists seek control over other people. Pentecostals and
mystics tend also toward faith, but for the purpose of spiritual, experiential
rewards. Evangelicals, too, focus on faith, but define a more balanced position that admits of some tolerance for others, and a mix of worldly success
and attention to the soul or spirit.

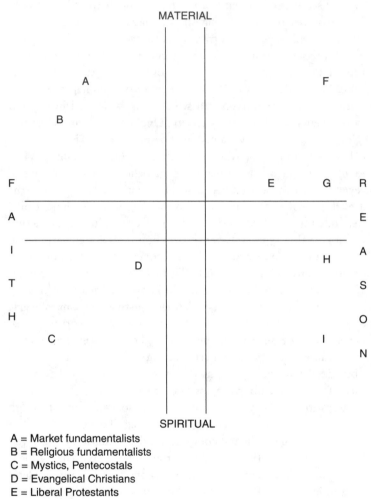

A = Market fundamentalists
B = Religious fundamentalists
C = Mystics, Pentecostals
D = Evangelical Christians
E = Liberal Protestants
F = Globalist corporations
G = Marx
H = Dewey
I = Jung

Figure 9.1

On the rationalist side of the analysis we find liberal Protestants and some Jewish segments who subordinate unquestioning and traditional faith in order to adapt to new visions of human rights and ecological awareness. The globalist corporations apotheosize a rational attitude combined with a cold-blooded material value system. Marx, as described above, is hyper-rational, but employs material means toward spiritual ends. Through an economic restructuring he aspired toward general, heightened dignity for humanity. Dewey aspires to similar outcomes, but with more overt recognition of the primacy of the psychological and philosophical as means to these ends. Jung also considered himself a scientist and rationalist, but valued even more extensively the spiritual dimension of human affairs and opened the discussion to as yet unverified influences such as instinct, archetype, and synchronicity. In this sense he was visionary and foreshadowed some of the genomic and neuroscientific analyses of today. We offer this heuristic as another way of clarifying definitions and reducing confusion around the terminology of meaning, faith, and spirit.

In this confusion over the vocabulary of spirituality, "hope" is often lost. In this sense hope is a future-oriented, less assured version of the trusting faith described above. Hope is confidence in the future without certainty and without the need for a creed or higher power. It is an attitude, a disposition, rather than a conviction. Hope permits unprecedented possibility, unconstrained by past injuries and dogmas. Hope assumes gradual transformation through the creation of possibilities rather than the reestablishment or revisitation of a past utopia. Hope is therefore aligned with the Deweyan notion of process or ongoing renewal and with our idea of human progress and benevolence.

This hoped-for future recognizes egoistic individualism as a stage of consciousness that may be transcended by an inclusive and authentic individualism oriented to what can be called the Self. Self-realized spirituality is oriented to a search for universal principles and Natural Law. These principles would include ones such as compassion and non-violence, inclusivity, environmentalism, and sustainability. Relativism would not obscure commitment to such agreed-upon values. A balance between *mythos* and *logos* would characterize the conduct of human affairs. The journey to this future of hope will, it seems, continue to pass tragically through the horrors of violence and suffering. The path to a non-violent future still leads through times of "just war" and the inequitable distribution of the world's resources. Our task as educators at this time in history is first to help define the goals that local and global society should have and to work through the confusion that currently reigns. Nussbaum speaks of "pernicious sentiments in the public culture of the United States ... undermined over time by criticism and replacement of the conceptions and beliefs that inform them" (2006, p. 413). Without a better understanding of the psychology of development and a definition of spirituality and the conditions conducive to it, we find ourselves caught in frustrating contradiction and irreconcilable conflict. With such understanding and purpose, we can change the course of events.

Spirituality can be understood as the realization of meaning for humans individually and collectively in their society. Correspondingly, education is the conscious and deliberate pursuit of that aim. "Spirituality is always present though often unacknowledged in the learning environment" (Tisdell, 2007, p. 3). We as educators have a particular responsibility to establish a vision worthy of emulation and to offer insights derived from that vision to our students. The complicated and volatile times we live in are ominous as well as motivating, but the fundamental challenge for educators has remained the same since ancient times: the transmission and reconstruction of culture. For this reason, it is predictable that the great debate over values has come eventually to settle in education, since it is perhaps the most normative of public endeavors. Deregulation and privatization of utilities and other services do not threaten the soul of contemporary society, while surrendering education to religions or markets does, and does so in a manner devastating to the most vulnerable of our children. As Dewey knew, education is the application of philosophy to the social order. Teachers, it follows, are conscious bearers of society's values as embodied in their relationship with students and the curriculum itself. Given this responsibility, educators can be guided by creeds or markets or they can look toward a higher synthesis in human affairs, resist pointless argument and conflict, and have the courage to declare the possibility of a world largely undreamed of in the minds of our contemporaries. We have the privilege of carrying forth our message in society's seminal institution, the public schools. Will we have the vision as well as the conviction to fulfill the ultimate mission of our profession?

Possibilities for public education in a democratic society

We have first to acknowledge deeply that education in a democracy is necessarily a public education. Democracy suggests a value system that honors both our human needs and our collective responsibility for creating communities and societies that respect human rights. Public education, in a similar manner to the democracies in which these institutions are located, has clear values. As Vaclav Havel suggests, a public education requires educating students to have civic courage. A society framed in the public interest requires a commitment to all citizens. Revitalizing democracy and education requires rethinking private–public spheres, crossing the ever shifting public and private divide, and revisioning education as a rich hybrid of public and private that allows for development in both arenas.

Yet this education should never be didactic. Democratic education needs to be exploratory education that departs from essentialism and reframes spiritual and cultural matters as dynamic processes amidst changing social, linguistic, intellectual, and aesthetic values. It is an integrated, poststructural education that recognizes intermixture, hybridity, and complexity and questions the supposed fixed realities, boundaries, and understandings of an earlier era such as the meaning of progress, of identity, of divisions between art/science/nature, reality/appearance, center/periphery, etc. Democratic capacities include the ability to critically examine and explore knowledge and values from a range of orientations, among them purposes, persuasiveness, and a consideration of who benefits and who pays the costs. Having a sense of human connection, collective responsibility, and a willingness to be civically active are also essential democratic capacities. Democracy requires the ability to care for and listen to others, including those who seem alien to us. These democratic understandings should always be understood to be in flux, requiring us constantly to wrestle with the meanings of community, connection, caring, freedom, rights, voice, fairness, representation, and justice. As our discussion of postmodern spirituality highlights, it is a mistake to think of postmodernism in caricature as radical skepticism or a "belief" in an ontological "nothing" or to think of postmodernism as an ethical stance in which anything goes. Instead, postmodernism and poststructuralism offer deconstructive *methods* of exploring and sometimes repositioning meaning, including educational meaning.

Democratic education functions on a manageable scale that acts in the here and now. It is a personal education rooted in the everyday. This personal education fully acknowledges spirituality and focuses on finding meaning in life through personal experiences that connect with public life and visions of the good. While democratic education embodies an ethic of value acknowledging loyalty to all human beings and every person's right to nutrition, health, shelter, and security, as well as autonomy and cultural freedom, it is also an ethical education of practice requiring not just understanding but also action and change. Such action may aim for improvement rather than revolutionary transformation; it may be commonplace rather than exceptional, ordinary rather than extraordinary, and often creative of something better rather than something true or absolute. It is a democratic critical education that explores meaning, power, and positionality and is cautiously aware that all teachings, texts, and media claim, distort, enhance, and open as well as close perspectives. It is also a democratically constructive education that asserts meaning and identity and it is comfortable with power. The vision and action of this education is local and changing rather than preordained and universal, and it is imperfect, incomplete, and formative. The possibility for a more just world rests on an educated public and on educating this public. Modernity and, more recently, technology and globalization have brought forth something new in human history that challenges us to maintain democratic values and institutions while creating a fundamentally new education that is equal to our emerging times.

References

Adams, M. (2003). *Fire and ice: United States, Canada, and the myth of converging values*. Toronto: Penguin.

Adams, M. (2005). *American backlash: The untold story of social change in the U.S.*. Toronto: Viking.

Afflerbach, P. (2002). The road to folly and redemption: Perspectives on the legitimacy of high-stakes testing. *Reading Research Quarterly, 37*, 348–360.

Alcoholics Alcoholics Anonymous (1972). The twelve steps of Alcoholics Anonymous. Retrieved December 6, 2005, from http://www.aa.org/en_ services_for_members.cfm?PageId = 98&SubPage = 117

American Association of Colleges for Teacher Education (2000, August). Education schools nationwide faced with year of challenges. *Briefs*, 1.

American Association of Colleges for Teacher Education (2003). *Press release: American board receives $35 million in federal funding*. Retrieved September 29, 2003, from http://www.edpolicy.org/news/archives/2003/week39.php# article391

American Association of School Administrators (2003). Government relations. Retrieved February 25, 2003, from http://www.aasa.org/government_ relations/esea/Chief_SEA.pdf

American Civic Forum (1994). *Civic declaration: A call for a new citizenship. A new citizenship project of the American Civic Forum. An occasional paper of the Kettering Foundation*. Dayton, OH: Kettering Foundation.

American Educational Research Association, American Psychological Association, & National Council for Measurement in Education, Joint Committee on Educational and Psychological Testing (1999). *Standards for educational and psychological testing 1999*. Washington, DC: American Educational Research Association.

American Educational Research Association, American Psychological Association, & National Council for Measurement in Education, Joint Committee on Educational and Psychological Testing (2000). *High stakes testing in preK–12 education*. Washington, DC: American Educational Research Association.

American Federation of Teachers (2000). *Building a profession: Strengthening teacher preparation and induction: Report of the K–16 teacher education task force*. Washington, DC: Author.

Amrein, A. L., & Berliner, D. C. (2002). High-stakes testing, uncertainty, and student learning. *Education Policy and Analysis Archives, 10*(18). Retrieved March 28, 2002, from http://epaa.asu.edu/epaa/v10n18/

Anagnostopoulos, D. (2003). Testing and student engagement in urban classrooms: A multi-layered perspective. *Research in Teaching English*, *38*(2), 177–212.

Anagnostopoulos, D. (2005). Testing, tests and classroom texts. *Journal of Curriculum Studies*, *37*(1), 35–63.

Anderson, G. L. & Irvine, P. (1993). Informing critical literacy with ethnography. In C. Lankshear & P. L. McLaren (Eds.), *Critical literacy: Politics, praxis, and the postmodern* (pp. 81–104). Albany: State University of New York Press.

Anderson, S., Cavanagh, J., Klinger, S., & Stanton, L. (2005). *Executive excess 2005: Defense contractors get more bucks for the bang*. Washington, DC: Institute for Policy Studies and United for a Fair Economy.

Appiah, K. A. (2005). *The ethics of identity*. Princeton, NJ: Princeton University Press.

Apple, M. (2001). *Educating the "right" way: Markets, standards, God and inequality*. New York: Routledge.

Armstrong, K. (2001). *The battle for God*. New York: Ballantine Books.

Aronowitz, S., & Giroux, H. (1993). *Education still under siege*. Westport, CT: Bergin & Garvey.

Askew, B. J., Kay, E., Frasier, D. F., Mobasher, M., Anderson, N., & Rodriguez, Y. (2002). Making a case for prevention in education. *Literacy Teaching and Learning: An International Journal of Reading and Writing*, *6*(2), 43–73.

Ayling, R. (1997). *The downsizing of America*. Commack, NY: Nova Science.

Bagdikian, B. (2000). *The media monopoly* (6th ed.). Boston: Beacon Press.

Bahmueller, C. F. (1997). A framework for teaching democratic citizenship: An international project. *International Journal of Social Education*, *12*, 101–112.

Bakan, J. (2004). *Corporation: The pathological pursuit of profit and power*. Toronto: Penguin Canada.

Barber, B. (1996a). Foundationalism and democracy. In S. Benhabib (Ed.), *Democracy and difference* (pp. 348–359). Princeton, NJ: Princeton University Press.

Barber, B. (1996b). Constitutional faith. In M. Nussbaum (Ed.), *For love of country: Debating the limits of patriotism* (pp. 30–37). Boston: Beacon Press.

Barber, B. R. (2002, January 21). Beyond Jihad vs. Mcworld: On terrorism and the new democratic realism. *The Nation*, p. 17.

Barr, R., Barth, J. L., & Shermis, S. S. (1977). *Defining the social studies*. Arlington, VA: National Council for the Social Studies.

Bauer, G. (2005). *God other mysteries. Soul or spirit, angel or afterlife: Here's what Canadians believe, and why*. Retrieved December 15, 2005, from http://www.readersdigest.ca/mag/2003/11/god.html

Bauman, Z. (1999). *In search of politics*. Stanford, CA: Stanford University Press.

Begley, S. (2007). *Train your mind, change your brain*. New York: Ballantine Books.

Bender, T. (Ed.) (2002). *Rethinking American history in a global age*. Berkeley: University of California Press.

Berger, P. (Ed.). (1999). *The desecularization of the world: Resurgent religions and world politics*. Grand Rapids, MI: Eerdmans.

Berlak, H. (2000). Cultural politics, the science of assessment and democratic renewal of public education. In A. Filer (Ed.), *Assessment: Social practice and social product* (pp. 189–207). New York: RoutledgeFalmer.

Berlak, H. (2005). From local control to government and corporate takeover: The No Child Left Behind Act and the "Reading First" program. In H. Shapiro &

D. E. Purpel (Eds.), *Critical social issues in American education: Democracy and meaning in a globalizing world* (pp. 267–286). Mahwah, NJ: Erlbaum.

Berliner, D. (2005, August 2). *Our impoverished view of educational reform.* Retrieved September 9, 2005, from http://www.tcrecord.org

Berliner, D., & Biddle, B. (1995). *The manufactured crisis: Myth, fraud, and the attack on America's public schools.* Reading, MA: Addison Wesley.

Berman, P. (1997, May 11). The philosopher-king is mortal. *New York Times Magazine,* p. 37.

Best, S., & Keller, D. (1997). *The postmodern turn.* New York: Guilford Press.

Best, S., & Keller, D. (2001). *The postmodern adventure: Science, technology, and cultural studies at the third millennium.* London: Routledge.

Blueprint (2001). *A blueprint for new beginnings: A responsible budget for America's priorities.* Retrieved May 29, 2002, from http://www.whitehouse.gov/news/usbudget/blueprint/bud34.html.

Boyd, J. (Ed.). (1950). *The papers of Thomas Jefferson.* Princeton, NJ: Princeton University Press.

Boyer Commission on Educating Undergraduates in the Research University (1998). *Reinventing undergraduate education: A blueprint for America's research universities.* Retrieved January 22, 2008, from http://naples.cc.stonybrook.edu/Pres/boyer.nsf/

Bracey, G. (1997). *Setting the record straight.* Alexandria, VA: Association for Supervision and Curriculum Development.

Bracey, G. (2001). The 11th Bracey report on the condition of public education. *Phi Delta Kappan, 83,* 157–169.

Bredo, E. (2005). Addressing the social foundations "accountability" dilemma. *Educational Studies, 38,* 230–241.

Brock, D. (2002). *Blinded by the right: The conscience of an ex-conservative.* New York: Crown.

Burack, J. (2003). The student, the world, and the global education ideology. In J. Leming, L. Ellington, & K. Porter-Magee (Eds.), *Where did social studies go wrong?* (pp. 40–69). Retrieved from http://www.edexcellence.net/institute/publication/publication.cfm?id=317

Bush, G. W. (1999a). *Excerpts from speech on education.* Retrieved January 22, 2008, from http://query.nytimes.com/gst/fullpage.html?res=9B04E7DA133BF930A35752 C1A96F958260

Bush, G. W. (1999b). *Texas Governor George W. Bush in Gorham, NH.* Retrieved January 22, 2008, from http://www.greatnorthwoods.org/19991102 bushgorham/

Bush, G. W. (2002). *Radio address, March 2, 2002.* Retrieved May 14, 2002, from http://edworkforce.house.gov/issues/107th/education/nclb/bushradioaddress.htm

Bush, G. W. (2003). *Remarks by the president on the first anniversary of the No Child Left Behind Act.* Retrieved March 14, 2003, from http://www.whitehouse.gov/news/releases/2003/01/20030108-4.html

Business-Higher Education Forum (2003). *Building a nation of learners.* Retrieved January 22, 2008, from http://www.bhef.com/publications/2003_build_nation.pdf

Butts, R. (1985). Progressive education. *The World Book Encyclopedia: Vol. 15.* Chicago: World Book.

Byrd, R. (2001). *Learning the lessons of American history.* Retrieved April 12, 2003, from http://www.narhist.ewu.edu/Pathways/byrd.html

California Commission on Teacher Credentialing (1999). *Annual report on the reading instruction competence assessment (RICA) June 1998–June 1999 (preliminary version).* Sacramento, CA: Author.

Camilli, G., Vargas, S., & Yurecko, M. (2003, May 8). Teaching children to read: The fragile link between science and federal education policy. *Education Policy Analysis Archives, 11*(15). Retrieved May 16, 2003, from http://epaa.asu.edu/ epaa/v11n15/

Campbell, J., & Moyers, B. (1991). *The power of myth.* New York: Anchor Doubleday.

Carlson, D. (1993). The politics of educational policy: Urban school reform in unsettling times. *Educational Policy, 7,* 149–166.

Carnegie Corporation of New York (1986). *A nation prepared: Teachers for the 21st century.* New York: Author.

Carnoy, M., Loeb, S., & Smith, T. (2001, April). *Do higher state test scores in Texas make for better high school outcomes?* Paper presented at the annual meeting of the American Educational Research Association, New Orleans.

Carson, C. C., Huelskamp, R. M., & Woodall, T. D. (1993). Perspectives on education. *American Journal of Educational Research, 86,* 259–310.

Carter, S., et al. (2001, February 12). The future of the public intellectual: A forum. *The Nation, 272,* 25–35.

Catholic Campaign for Human Development (2007). *January is "poverty in America awareness month".* Retrieved July 23, 2007, from http://www. nccbuscc.org/cchd/povertyusa/press.shtml

Charters, W. W. (1929). *Curriculum construction.* New York: Macmillan. (Original work published 1923)

Children's Defense Fund (2003). *Truly comprehensive bill.* Retrieved April 20, 2003, from http://www.childrensdefense.org/release030212.php

Clotfelter, C. T., & Ladd, H. F. (1996). Recognizing and rewarding success in public schools. In H. F. Ladd (Ed.), *Holding schools accountable: Performance-based reform in education* (pp.23–63). Washington, DC: Brookings Institution.

CNN, Larry King Live (2005, Dec. 2). *Interview with Rick Warren.* Retrieved December 14, 2005, from http://transcripts.cnn.com/TRANSCRIPTS/0512/02/lkl.01.html

Coalition for Gun Control (2005). *Canada–US comparison.* Retrieved December 14, 2005, from http://www.guncontrol.ca/Content/Cda-US.htm

Coca-Cola (2005). *Education.* Retrieved December 14, 2005, from http://www2.coca-cola.com/citizenship/education.html

Cochran, M. (1999). *Normative theory in international relations.* Cambridge, England: Cambridge University Press.

Cohen, P. (1995). Looking for excellent teaching: Performance assessment of teachers gains ground. *Association for Supervision and Curriculum Development Education Update, 37*(3), 1–8.

College Board (1977). *On further examination.* New York: Author.

Cookson, P., Molnar, A., & Embree, K. (2001). *Let the buyer beware: An analysis of the social science value and methodological quality of educational studies published by the Mackinac Center for Public Policy (1990–2001).*

Retrieved January 2, 2002, from www.asu.edu/educ/epsl/Reports/epru/ EPRU%202001-102/epru-1109- 102.htm

The corporatized university (1997). *Multinational Monitor, 18*(11). Retrieved May 28, 2002, from http://multinationalmonitor.org/hyper/mm1197.02.html

Cornwell, G. H., & Stoddard, E. W. (2003). Peripheral visions: Towards a geoethics of citizenship. *Liberal Education, 89.*

Corwin, T. (2003, March). *The No Child Left Behind Act: How are we now and where are we going?* Paper presented at the annual meeting of the Association of Supervision and Curriculum Development, San Francisco.

Council for Basic Education. (2004). *Academic atrophy: The condition of the liberal arts in America's public schools.* Retrieved from http://www.ecs.org/html/ Document.asp?chouseid=5058

Counts, G. (1932). *Dare the school build a new social order?* New York: John Day.

Crawford, J. (2002). Obituary: The bilingual ad act, 1969–2002. *Rethinking Schools, 16*(4), 5.

Cremin, L.A. (1961). *The transformation of the school: Progressivism in American education 1876–1957.* New York: Vintage Books.

Cronbach, L. (1975). The two disciplines of scientific psychology. *American Psychologist, 12,* 671–684.

Cunningham, J. (2001). The National Reading Panel report. *Reading Research Quarterly, 36,* 326–335.

Curti, M. (1959). *The social ideas of American educators.* Patterson, NJ: Littlefield, Adams. (Original work published 1935)

Danner, M. (2005). The secret way to war. *The New York Review of Books, 52*(10), 70–74.

Darling-Hammond, L. (2001). *The research and rhetoric on teacher certification: A response to "teacher certification reconsidered".* Retrieved May 31, 2002, from www.nctaf.org/publications/abell_response.pdf

Davies, D. (2001). *Living the brand with your stakeholders.* Retrieved December 15, 2005, from: http://www.philipmorrisinternational.com/PMINTL/pages/ eng/press/speec hes/DDavies_200111.asp

Delandshere, G., & Petrosky, A. (2004). Political rationales and ideological stances of the standards-based reform of teacher education in the US. *Teaching and Teacher Education, 20*(1), 1–15.

Dewey, J. (1929). My pedagogic creed. *Journal of the National Education Association, 18,* 291–295.

Dewey, J. (1956). *The child and the curriculum.* Chicago: University of Chicago Press. (Original work published 1902)

Dewey, J. (1985). *The way out of educational confusion.* Cambridge, MA: Harvard University Press. (Original work published 1931)

Dewey, J. (1987). *Experience and education.* New York: Collier Books. (Original work published 1938)

Dewey, J. (1991). *The public and its problems.* Chicago: Swallow Press. (Original work published 1954)

Dewey, J. (1997). *Democracy and education: An introduction to the philosophy of education.* New York: Free Press. (Original work published 1916)

Dilthey, W. (1989). *Introduction to the human sciences: Selected works,* Vol. 1 (M. Neville, Trans.). Princeton, NJ: Princeton University Press.

Dotson, A. C., & Wisont, K. (2001). *The character education handbook: Establishing a character program in your school.* n.p.: Character Press.

Downey, J. D. (1999). From Americanization to multiculturalism: Political symbols and struggles for cultural diversity in twentieth-century American race relations. *Sociological Perspectives, 42*, 249–278.

Drew, L. (2000). Call to arms. *Teacher Magazine, 11*(7), 21–31.

Education for Democracy Initiative (2003). Education for democracy. *American Educator, 27*(3), 6–23.

Egan, K. (1997). *The educated mind*. Chicago: University of Chicago Press.

Eisner, E. (1967). Educational objectives – Help or hindrance? In D. Flinders & S. Thorton (Eds.), *The curriculum studies reader* (pp.69–75). New York: Routledge.

Elder, C. D., & Cobb, R. W. (1983). *The political use of symbols*. New York: Longman.

Elshtain, J. B., et al. (2001, February 12). The future of the public intellectual: A forum. *The Nation, 272*, 25–35.

Erikson, E. (1963). *Childhood and society*. New York: Norton. (Original work published 1950)

Evans, R, W. (2004). *The social studies wars*. New York: Teachers College Press.

Feyerabend, P. (1999). *The conquest of abundance: A tale of abstraction versus the richness of being*. Chicago: University of Chicago Press.

Finn, C. E. (2002). The limits of peer review. *Education Week, 21*(34), 30–34.

Flippo, R., and Riccards, M. (2000). Initial teacher certification testing in Massachusetts. *Phi Delta Kappan, 82*, 34–37.

Foner, E. (2002). *Who owns history? Rethinking the past in a changing world*. New York: Hill & Wang.

Foucault, M. (1977). *Discipline and punish: The birth of the prison*. New York: Vintage Books.

Friedman, B. (1989). *Day of reckoning: The consequences of American economic policy*. New York: Vintage Books.

Fuentes, A. (2005). Failing students, rising profits. *The Nation, 281*(8), 18–24.

Garan, E. (2001a). Beyond the smoke and mirrors: A critique of the National Reading Panel Report on phonics. *Phi Delta Kappan, 82*, 500–506.

Garan, E. (2001b). Backtalk. *Phi Delta Kappan, 82*, 801.

Garan, E. (2001c). More smoking guns: A response to Linnea Aehri and Steven Stahl. *Phi Delta Kappan, 83*, 21–27.

Garan, E. (2001d). What does the report of the National Reading Panel really tell us about teaching phonics? *Language Arts, 79*(1), 61–70.

Garan, E. (2002). *Resisting reading mandates: How to triumph with the truth*. Portsmouth, NH: Heinemann.

Gardner, H. (1993). *Frames of mind: The theory of multiple intelligences*. New York: Basic Books.

Gardner, H. (2002). The quality and qualities of educational research. *Education Week, 22*(1), 49–72.

Gingrich, N. (1995a). *To renew America*. New York: HarperCollins.

Gingrich, N. (1995b). *Renewing American civilization, class 2: The historic lessons of American civilization*. Retrieved 5 March 2008 from http://terrenceberres.com/ginren02.html

Giroux, H. (2004). *The terror of neoliberalism*. Boulder, CO: Paradigm.

Gitlin, T. (2002, November 30). Straight from the sixties. *American Prospect*. Retrieved January 22, 2008, from http://www.prospect.org/cs/articles?article=straight_from_the_sixties

Goleman, D. (1995). *Emotional intelligence.* New York: Bantam Books.

Goode, E. (2000, August 8). How culture molds habits of thought. *The New York Times,* p. D-1.

Goodnough, A. (2000, August 23). Proving fit to teach, by a half measure. *The New York Times,* p. A-18.

Gore, A. (2007). *The assault on reason.* New York: Penguin Press.

Gowri, A. (2000). A market approach to research integrity. *Proceedings of the first ORI Research Conference on Research Integrity, USA, 1,* 315–319.

Gray, K. (1996). The baccalaureate game: Is it right for all teens? *Phi Delta Kappan, 77,* 528–535.

Gray, K. (2004). Is high school career and technical education obsolete? *Phi Delta Kappan, 86,* 128–135.

Green, B. (1988). Subject-specific literacy and school learning: A focus on writing. *Australian Journal of Education, 32,* 156–179.

Green, B. (1997a, July). *Literacy, information and the learning society.* Keynote address at the Joint Conference of the Australian Association for the Teaching of English, the Australian Literacy Educators' Association, and the Australian School Library Association, Northern Territory, Australia.

Green, B. (1997b, May). *Literacies and school learning in new times.* Keynote address at the "Literacies in practice: progress and possibilities" conference, Adelaide, South Australia.

Greene, J. P. (1993). *The intellectual construction of America: American exceptionalism 1492–1800.* Chapel Hill: University of North Carolina Press.

Guba, E., & Clark, D. (1975). The configurational perspective: A new view of educational knowledge and production. *Educational Researcher, 4*(4), 6–9.

Guillaume, A. M., & Yopp, H. K. (1995). Professional portfolios for student teachers. *Teacher Education Quarterly, 22*(1), 93.

Gutmann, A. (1987). *Democratic education.* Princeton, NJ: Princeton University Press.

Halvorsen, A. (2006). *How history at the elementary level lost its way: Perspectives from the American Historical Association, 1884 to 1921.* Unpublished manuscript.

Hansen, D. (2005, August 4). Teachers can bring politics to class court. *The Vancouver Sun,* p. A-1. Retrieved from http://proxy.lib.sfu.ca/login?url=http://proquest.umi.com/pqdweb?did=878295671&sid=Fmt=3&clientID=3667&RQT=309&Vname=PQD

Hansen, J. M. (2003). *The lost promise of patriotism: debating American identity 1890–1920.* Chicago: University of Chicago Press.

Henriques, D. (2002, May 25). A learning curve for Whistler venture. *The New York Times,* p. C1.

Herman, E. (1997). The illiberal media. *Zmagazine.* Retrieved May 22, 2002, from www.zmag.org/zmag/articles/jan97herman.htm

Hickok, E. (2002, March 26). *Speech before the Renaissance Group annual meeting.* Washington, DC: Renaissance Group.

Hiebert, J., & Stigler, J. (1999). *The teaching gap: Best ideas from the world's teachers for improving education in the classroom.* New York: Simon & Schuster.

Hillocks, G., Jr. (2002). *The testing trap: How state writing assessments control learning.* New York: Teachers College Press.

Hopkins, L. T. (Ed.) (1937). *Integration, its meaning and application*. New York: Appleton-Century.

Horton, N., & Freire, P. (1990). *We make the road by walking: Conversations on education and social change*. Philadelphia: Temple University Press.

Howe, K. (2002, April 10). Free market free-for-all. *Education Week, 21*(30), 32–35.

Howell, W., & Peterson, P. (2002). *The education gap: Vouchers and urban schools*. Washington, DC: Brookings Institution.

Humphrey, N. (2006). *Seeing red*. Cambridge, MA: Belknap Press.

Hursh, D., & Martina, C. A. (2003). Noeliberalism and schooling in the U.S.: How state and federal government education policies perpetuate inequality. *Journal for Critical Education Policy Studies, 1*(2). Retrieved March 22, 2004, from http://jceps.com/?pageID=article&articleID=12

Illinois Council against Handgun Violence (2005). *General gun violence statistics*. Retrieved December 14, 2005, from http://www.ichv.org/Statistics.htm

Interstate New Teacher Assessment and Support Consortium (1995). *INTASC core standards*. Washington, DC: Council of Chief State School Officers.

Issues—Education (2001). Retrieved May 14, 2003, from http://www.georgewbush.com/issues/index.html.

Jary, D., & Jary, J. (1991). *Collins dictionary of sociology*. Glasgow: HarperCollins.

JFK Script. (2006). *Drew's Script-o-rama*. Retrieved January 5, 2006, from http://www.script-o-rama.com/movie_scripts/j/jfk-script-transcript-oliver-stone.html

Johnson, H. M. (1936). Pseudo-mathematics in the social sciences. *American Journal of Psychology, 48*, 342–351.

Jones, K., & Whitford, B. L. (2000). The next generation of school accountability. In B.L. Whitford & K. Jones (Eds.), *Accountability, assessment, and teachers' commitment: Lessons from Kentucky's reform efforts* (pp. 233– 246). Albany: State University of New York Press.

Jung, C. G. (1976). *Psychological types*. Princeton, NJ: Princeton University Press.

Kammen, M. (1993). The problem of American exceptionalism. *American Quarterly, 45*(1), 1–43.

Kennickell, A. B. (2003). *A rolling tide: Changes in the distribution of wealth in the U.S. 1989–2001*. Washington, DC: Federal Reserve Board.

Ketcham, R. (2005). Citizenship and good democratic government. *eJournal USA*. Retrieved November 20, 2006, from http://usinfo.state.gov/journals/itdhr/1205/ijde/ketcham.htm

Kevill, S. (2003, February 20). *The BBC's plans for digital democracy*. Retrieved March 27 2007, from http://www.opendemocracy.net/media- edemocracy/article_995.jsp

Khan, N. (2006, January 5). Girls' teacher beheaded by Taliban while family watches. *The Vancouver Sun*, p. A-9.

King, J. (2004). *Paige calls NEA "terrorist organization"*. Retrieved from http://edition.cun.com/2004/EDUCATION/02/23/paige.terrorist.nea/

Klages, M. (1997). *Postmodernism*. Retrieved April 3, 2003, from http://www.colorado.edu/ English/ENGL2012Klages/ pomo.html

Kohn, A. (2002). *The case against standardized testing: Raising the scores, ruining the schools*. New York: Heinemann.

Kovel, J. (1999). *History and spirit*. Warner, NH: Glad Day Books.

Krashen, S. (2001). A critical analysis of the N.R.P. report on fluency. *Phi Delta Kappan, 83*, 119–122.

Kridel, C., & Bullough, R. (2002). Conceptions and misperceptions of the eight year study. *Journal of Curriculum and Supervision, 18*(1), 63–82.

Kridel, C., & Bullough, R.V., Jr. (2007). *Stories of the eight-year study*. Albany: State University of New York Press.

Krugman, P. (2004). *The great unraveling: Losing our way in the new century*. New York: Norton.

Labaree, D. (1997). Public goods, private goods: The American struggle over educational goals. *American Educational Research Journal, 34*, 39–81.

Lemann, N. (1999). *The big test: The secret history of the American meritocracy*. New York: Farrar, Straus & Giroux.

Leming, J., Ellington, L., & Porter-Magee, K. (2003). *Where did social studies go wrong?* Retrieved from http://www.edexcellence.net/institute/publication/publication.cfm?id=317

Levine, A. (2005). *Educating school leaders*. New York: Education Schools Project.

Levister, C. (2006). D's and F's for "No Child Left Behind". *Black Voice News*. Retrieved from http://news.newamericamedia.org/news/view_article.html?article_id= d3f92560b6b9fd5649c79ee89cf4cc34

Levitas, D. (2002). *The terrorist next door: The militia movement and the radical right*. New York: Thomas Dunne Books/St. Martin's Press.

Lind, M. (1995, June). To have and to have not: Notes on the progress of the American class war. *Harper's Magazine, 290*(1741), 35–47.

Lipman, P. (2004). *High stakes education: Inequality, globalization, and urban school reform*. New York: RoutledgeFalmer.

Lyotard, J. F. (1984). *The postmodern condition: A report on knowledge* (G. Bennington & B. Massumi, Trans.). Manchester, England: Manchester University Press. (Original work published 1979)

Madaus, G. F. (1988). The influence of testing on the curriculum. In L. N. Tanner (Ed.), *Critical issues in curriculum: Eighty-seventh yearbook of the National Society for the Study of Education* (pp. 83–121). Chicago: University of Chicago Press.

Madison, A. (1989). *The world economy in the twentieth century*. Washington, DC: OECD.

Mallery, J. C., Hurwitz, R., & Duffy, G. (1987). Hermeneutics: From textual explication to computer understanding? In S. C. Shapiro (Ed.), *The encyclopedia of artificial intelligence*. New York: Wiley.

Mann, H. (1842). *Fifth annual report of Horace Mann as Secretary of Massachusetts State Board of Education*. Boston: Dutton & Wentworth.

Mann, H. (1848). *Twelfth annual report of Horace Mann as Secretary of Massachusetts State Board of Education*. Boston: Dutton & Wentworth.

Mansbridge, J. (1990a). *Beyond adversary democracy*. Chicago: University of Chicago Press.

Mansbridge, J. (1990b). *Beyond self-interest*. Chicago: University of Chicago Press.

Manzo, K. K. (2004, September 8). Select group ushers in reading policy. *Education Week, 24*(2), 1.

Marshall, T. H. (1950). *Citizenship and social class and other essays*. Cambridge, England: Cambridge University Press.

Maslow, A. (1998). *Toward a psychology of being*. Hoboken, NJ: Wiley.

Mathison, S., & Freeman, M. (2003). Constraining elementary teachers' work: Dilemmas and paradoxes created by state mandated testing. *Educational Policy Analysis Archives, 11*(34). Retrieved September 29, 2003, from http://epaa.asu.edu/epaa/v11n34

Maxwell, L. (2002, May 2). Assembly halts Autry bid. *The Fresno Bee*, p. A-1.

McDowell, K. C. (2000). Teacher competency tests: Disparate impact, disparate treatment, and judicial scrutiny. *The State Education Standard, 1*(1), 45–47.

McNeil, L. (2000). *Contradictions of school reform: Educational costs of standardized testing*. New York: Routledge.

McNeil, L., & Valenzuela, A. (2001). The harmful impact of the TAAS system of testing in Texas: Beneath the accountability rhetoric. In G. Orfield & M. L. Kornhaber (Eds.), *Raising standards or raising barriers? Inequality and high-stakes testing in public education*. New York: Century Foundation Press.

Melnick, S., & Pullin, D. (2000). Can you take dictation? Prescribing teacher quality through testing. *Journal of Teacher Education, 51*, 262–275.

Melville, H. (1970). White-jacket, or, The world in a man-of-war (H. Hayford, H. Parker, & G. T. Tanselle, Eds.). Evanston, IL: Northwestern University Press. (original work published 1850)

Messick, S. (1989). Validity. In R. L. Linn (Ed.), *Educational measurement* (3rd ed.). New York: Macmillan.

Metcalf, S. (2002, January 8). Reading between the lines. *The Nation, 274*(3), 18–22.

Mirel, J. (2003). *Defending democracy. Terrorists, despots, and democracy: What our children need to know*. Washington, DC: Fordham Foundation.

Mishel, L., Bernstein, J., & Schmitt, J. (1997). *The state of working America, 1996– 97*. Armonk, NY: M.E. Sharpe.

Molnar, A. (2005). *School commercialization*. New York: Routledge.

Moritz, A. F. (2000). New freedom. In *The end of the age*. Toronto: Watershed Books.

Moyers, B. (2001, November 19). Which America will we be now? *The Nation*, 11–13.

Myers, I. B., & McCaulley, M. (1998). *Manual: A guide to the development and use of the Myers–Briggs Type Indicator*. Palo Alto: Consulting Psychologists Press.

Namier, L. (1955). *Personalities and powers*. New York: Macmillan.

National Center for Fair & Open Testing (2003). *What's wrong with standardized tests?* Retrieved February 8, 2002, from http://www.fairtest.org/facts/whatwron.htm

National Commission on Civic Renewal (1998). *A nation of spectators: How civic disengagement weakens America and what we can do about it*. College Park: University of Maryland Press.

National Commission on Excellence in Education (1983). *A nation at risk: The imperative for educational reform*. Washington, DC: Author.

National Council for Educational Statistics (2002). *Safety in numbers: Collecting and using crime, violence, and discipline incident data to make a difference in schools*. Washington, DC: U.S. Department of Education.

National Council for the Social Studies (1994). *Expectations of excellence: Curriculum standards for social studies.* Washington, DC: Author.

National Council for the Social Studies (n.d.). *Curriculum standards for social studies: Executive summary.* Retrieved from http://www.socialstudies.org/standards/execsummary/

National Council on Teacher Quality (2001). *NCTQ—Press release, 22 February 2001.* Retrieved May 22, 2002, from http://www.nctq.org/press/ets3.html

National Council on Teacher Quality (2002). *National council on teacher quality.* Retrieved May 23, 2002, from http://nctq.org/issues/nbpts.html

National Data Evaluation Center (2002). *Reading recovery and Descubriendo la lectura national report 2000–2001.* Columbus: Ohio State University Press.

National Education Association (2002). *Accountability and testing.* Retrieved July 14, 2002, from http://www.nea.org/accountability/

National Education Association (2004, January 14). *Schools need more flexibility and funding to meet promise of "No Child Left Behind" law, NEA bipartisan poll shows.* Retrieved January 22, 2008, from http://www.nea.org/newsreleases/2004/nr040114.html

National Education Knowledge Industry Association (2002). *2002 OERI reauthorization recommendations.* Washington, DC: Author. Retrieved May 22, 2002, from http://www.nekia.org/pdg/NEKIA-OERI-RECOMMENDATIONS.PDF

National Institute of Child Health and Human Development (1999a). *Report of the National Reading Panel: Teaching children to read. … Reports of the subgroups.* Washington DC: National Reading Panel.

National Institute of Child Health and Human Development (1999b). *Report of the National Reading Panel: Teaching children to read. Summary.* Washington DC: National Reading Panel.

National Institute of Child Health and Human Development (2000, April 13). *Press release: National Reading Panel reports combination of teaching phonics, word sounds, giving feedback on oral reading most effective way to teach reading.* Retrieved January 23, 2003, from http://www.nichd.nih.gov/new/releases/ nrp.cfm

National Science Foundation (2002). Federal survey shows defense funding of industry is largest share of federal R&D in FY 2000. *Data Brief.* Washington, DC: National Science Foundation. Retrieved May 22, 2002, from http://www.nsf.gov/sbe/srs/databrf/sdb00309.htm

Nichols, J. (2001). The beat. *The Nation, 272*(18), 8.

Nichols, S. L., & Berliner, D. C. (2007). *Collateral damage: How high-stakes testing corrupts America's schools.* Cambridge, MA: Harvard Education Press.

Noddings, N. (1993). *Educating for intelligent belief or unbelief.* New York: Teachers College Press.

Novick, P. (1988). *That noble dream.* Cambridge, England: Cambridge University Press.

Nussbaum, M. (2006). *Frontiers of justice: Disability, nationality, species membership.* Harvard, MA: Harvard University Press.

Office of Superintendent of Public Instruction (n.d.). *Title I/Learning assistance program.* Retrieved January 22, 2008, from http://www.k12.wa.us/TitleI/default.aspx

Oldfield, A. (1990). *Citizenship and community: Civic republicanism and the modern world.* London: Routledge.

Olson, L. (2002, May 29). Board acts to bring NAEP in line with ESEA. *Education Week, 21*(38), 24.

Owen, D. (1985). *None of the above: Behind the myth of scholastic aptitude.* New York: Houghton Mifflin.

Paige, R. (2001, June 21). *Remarks as prepared for delivery by U.S. Secretary of Education, Southeastern Character Education Conference.* Retrieved from http://www.ed.gov/news/speeches/2001/06/010622.html

Paige, R. (2003). *Remarks of the honorable Rod Paige U.S. Secretary of Education National Association of State Boards of Education.* Retrieved April 3, 2003, from http://www.ed.gov/Speeches/03-2003/03142003.html

Palmer, P. J. (1999). Evoking the spirit in public education. *Educational Leadership, 6,* 6–12.

Panetta, A. (2005, June 28). *Canadian Press.* Retrieved December 12, 2005, from http://www.canada.com/national/story.html?id=e0905a7a-c1c9-47ad-8e1e-f35ccd7b6a6f

Paone, J. (2002). When big pharma courts academia. *The Scientist, 16*(3), 48.

Pearl, J. (2007). "A mighty heart" needs moral clarity. *The New Republic.* Retrieved July 3, 2007, from http://www.tnr.com/doc.mhtml?i=w070702&s=pearl070307

Perez-Pena, R. (2001, May 8). Opponents of new Regents exam take protest to Capitol. *The New York Times,* p. B-5.

Perks, M. (2003, March 20). *Social software – get real.* Retrieved March 27, 2007, from http://www.spiked-online.com/Articles/00000006DCF1.htm

Phenix, P. (1964). *Realms of meaning: A philosophy of the curriculum for general education.* New York: McGraw-Hill.

Phipps, S., & Adler, S. (2003). Where's the history? *Social Education, 67*(5), 296–298.

Pinnell, G. S. (1989). Reading Recovery: Helping at-risk children learn to read. *The Elementary School Journal, 90,* 161–183.

Pinnell, G. S., Lyons, C. A., DeFord, D. E., Bryk, A., & Seltzer, M. (1993). Comparing instructional models for the literacy education of high risk first graders. *Reading Research Quarterly, 29*(1), 8–39.

Pinsky, R. (1996). Eros against esperanto. In J. Cohen (Ed.), *For love of country: Debating the limits of patriotism* (pp. 85–90). Boston: Beacon Press.

Poetter, T. (1998). International assessment of student achievement. *Clearing House, 71,* 196–198.

Prados, J. (1996). *The presidents' secret wars: CIA and Pentagon covert operations from World War II through the Persian Gulf.* Chicago: I. R. Dee.

Press, E., & Washburn, J. (2000). The kept university. *Atlantic Monthly, 285*(3), 39–54.

Putnam, R. (1995). Bowling alone: America's declining social capital. *Journal of Democracy, 6*(1), 65–78.

Putnam, R. (1997). *Bowling alone: America's declining social capital.* New York: Simon & Schuster.

Putnam, R. (2000). *Bowling alone: The collapse and revival of American community.* New York: Simon & Schuster.

Rabinow, P., & Sullivan, W. (Eds.) (1979). *Interpretive social science: A look.* Berkeley: University of California Press.

Randall, E. V., Cooper, B. S., & Hite, S. J. (1999). *Accuracy or advocacy? The politics of educational research.* Thousand Oaks, CA: Corwin Press.

Ravitch, D. (2000). Left back: *A century of failed school reform*. New York: Simon & Schuster.

Reading Recovery Council of North America (2002). *What evidence says about Reading Recovery*. Columbus, OH: Author.

Reeves, D. (2002). Galileo's dilemma. *Education Week, 21*(34).

Reich, R. (2004). *Reason: Why liberals will win the battle for America*. New York: Vintage.

Reichenbach, H. (1951). *The rise of scientific philosophy*. Berkeley: University of California Press.

Robbins, B. (1999). *Magic tales: Child as other, child as dream*. Retrieved December 6, 2005, from http://mythosandlogos.com/fairytalepaper.html

Robelen, E. (2002). Critics contend tutors must also be "highly qualified". *Education Week 2*(4), 26.

Rorty, R. (1998). *Achieving our country: Leftist thought in twentieth-century America*. Cambridge, MA: Harvard University Press.

Ross, E. W., & Marker, P. M. (2005). If social studies is wrong (I don't want to be right). *Theory and Research in Social Education, 33*(1), 142–151.

Rothstein, R. (2000, September 13). Lessons: How standardized tests can drop the ball. *The New York Times*, p. A-19.

Rothstein, R. (2001, October 10). Lessons: National crises, real and imagined. *The New York Times*, p. A-4.

Rothstein, R. (2004). *Class and schools: using social, economic, and educational reform to close the black–white achievement gap*. New York: Economic Policy Institute.

Rugg, H. O. (Ed.) (1927). *Curriculum making: Past and present. Twenty-sixth yearbook of the National Society for the Study of Education (Part I, II)*. Bloomington, IN: Public School Publishing.

Ryan, A. (2001). Schools: The price of "progress". *The New York Review of Books, 48*(3), 18–21.

Schaper, D. (2000, August 18). Me-first "spirituality" is a sorry substitute for organized religion on campus. *Chronicle of Higher Education: Point of View*, pp. 1–5.

Schieffer, J. (2000). *CACTE comments*. Los Angeles: California Association of Colleges for Teacher Education.

Schmitt, M. C., & Gregory, A. E. (2001, December). *The impact of early interventions: Where are the children now?* Paper presented at the annual meeting of the National Reading Conference, San Antonio, Texas.

Schrag, P. (2001, June 25). Edison's red ink schoolhouse. *The Nation, 272*, 20–24.

Schubert, W. (1985). *Curriculum: Perspective paradigm and possibility*. Upper Saddle River, NJ: Prentice-Hall.

Schultze, Q. J. (2002). *Habits of the high-tech heart*. Grand Rapids, MI: Baker Academic.

Shaker, L. (2006). In Google we trust: Information integrity in the digital age. *First Monday, 11*(4). Retrieved January 24, 2008, from http://www.uic.edu/htbin/cgiwrap/bin/ojs/index.php/fm/article/view/1320/1240

Shaker, P., & Heilman, E. (2002a). Advocacy versus authority—Silencing the education professoriate. *AACTE Policy Perspectives, 3*(1), 1–6.

Shaker, P., & Heilman, E. (2002b). Silencing the education professorate: Advocacy, pseudo-science, and cash corrupt the debate on our public schools. *Policy Perspectives, 14*(1).

Shavelson, R. J., & Towne, L. (Eds.) (2002). *Scientific research in education: Committee on scientific principles for education research, National Research Council.* Washington, DC: National Academy Press.

Shecter, D. (1998, September). *Part 2, chapter 2: Peace journalism and media war: The fight to reform journalism. What are journalists for?* Paper presented at the Conflict and Peace Forums, New York.

Sheehy, G. (1977). *Passages.* New York: Bantam Books.

Silver, M. (2006). *Respecting the wicked child.* Boston: University of Massachusetts Press.

Singer, P. (2000). *Writings on an ethical life.* New York: HarperCollins.

Sizer, T. (2004). *Horace's compromise.* Boston: Houghton Mifflin.

Smith, M. L. (1991). Meanings of test preparation. *American Educational Research Journal, 28*(3), 521–542.

Spring, J. (1997). *Political agendas for education: From the Christian coalition to the Green party.* New York: Lawrence Erlbaum Associates.

Spring, J. (1998a). *American education* (8th ed.). Boston: McGraw-Hill.

Spring, J. (1998b). *Education and the rise of the global economy.* Mahwah, NJ: Lawrence Erlbaum Associates.

Spring, J. (2002). *Conflict of interests.* New York: McGraw-Hill.

Stanley, W. B., & Nelson, J. L. (1994). The foundations of social education in historical context. In R. M. Martusewicz & W. M. Reynolds (Eds.), *Inside/out: Contemporary critical perspectives in education* (pp. 266–284). New York: St. Martin's Press.

Stecher, B. M., & Hamilton, L. S. (2002). Putting theory to the test: Systems of "educational accountability" should be held accountable. *RAND Review, 26*(1). Retrieved March 23, 2004, from http://www.rand.org/publications/randreview/issues/rr.04.02/theory.html

Steffens, H., & Cookson, P. (2002, August 7). Limitations of the market model. *Education Week, 21*(43), 48–51.

Steinberg, J. (2000, August 20). Increase in test scores counters dire forecasts for bilingual ban. *The New York Times,* p. A-1.

Steneck, N. H. (2000). Assessing the integrity of publicly funded research. *Proceedings of the First ORI Research Conference on Research Integrity, USA, 1,* 1–16.

Sternberg, R. J., et al. (2000). *Practical intelligence in everyday life.* Cambridge, England: Cambridge University Press.

Stigler, J. W., & Hiebert, J. (1999). *The teaching gap.* New York: Free Press.

Stone, J. E. (2002). *The value-added gains of NBPTS-certified teachers in Tennessee: A brief report.* Retrieved November 13, 2002, from http://www.education-consumers.com

Tacey, D. (2004). *The spirituality revolution.* Hove, England: Brunner-Routledge.

Tanner, D., & Tanner, L. (1975). *Curriculum development: Theory into practice.* New York: Macmillan.

Taylor, C. (1985). *Philosophy and the human sciences.* Cambridge, England: Cambridge University Press.

Taylor, C. (2004). *Modern social imaginaries.* Durham, NC: Duke University Press.

Tisdell, E. J. (2007). *In the new millennium: The role of spirituality and the cultural imagination in dealing with diversity and equity in the higher education classroom.* Retrieved November 4, 2005, from http://www.tcrecord.org

Tocqueville, A. de (1980). *Democracy in America* (Vols. 1–2, H. Reeves, Trans.). New York: Alfred A. Knopf. (original work published 1835, 1840)

Toppo, G. (2002, April 18). Dean wants state to reject education aid. *Rutland Herald.* Retrieved from http://rutlandherald.nybor.com/News/Story/45527.html

Tyack, D. (2000). School reform is dead (long live school reform). *The American Prospect, 11*(22). Retrieved January 24, 2008, from http://www.prospect.org/cs/articles?article=school_reform_is_dead_long_live_school_reform

United Colors of Benetton. (2005). *About Benetton—Cultural and social activities.* Retrieved December 14, 2005, from http://press.benettongroup.com/ben_en/about/cultural/

U.S. Bureau of Labor Statistics (2007). *Occupational outlook handbook (OOH) 2006–07 edition.* Retrieved March 23, 2007, from http://www.bls.gov/oco

U.S. Department of Education (2002a). *Education department releases guidance update on highly qualified teachers.* Retrieved February 23, 2003, from http://www.ed.gov/news/pressreleases/2002/12/12202002.html

U.S. Department of Education (2002b). *No Child Left Behind. Subpart 1—Reading First SEC. 1201.* Retrieved May 2, 2002, from http://www.ed.gov/legislation/ESEA02/pg4.html#sec1208

U.S. Department of Education (2002c). *The federal role in education.* Retrieved May 28, 2002, from http://www.ed.gov/offices/OUS/fedrole.html

U.S. Department of Education (2002d). *What to know & where to go: Parents' guide to No Child Left Behind.* Retrieved May 23, 2002, from http://www.nochildleftbehind.gov/next/where/

U.S. Department of Education (2002e). *No Child Left Behind: A desktop reference.* Retrieved January 22, 2008, from http://www.ed.gov/admins/lead/account/nclbreference/page_pg65.html

U.S. Department of Education (2002f). *No Child Left Behind: President Bush's education reform plan.* Retrieved January 22, 2008, from http://www.ed.gov/nclb/overview/intro/presidentplan/page_pg6.html

U.S. Department of Education (2003a). *Academic citizen help.* Retrieved February 25, 2003, from http://www.ed.gov/parents/academic/html

U.S. Department of Education (2003b). *Annual plan 2002.* Retrieved January 28, 2003, from http://www.ed.gov/pubs/AnnualPlan2002/Goal_1.pdf

U.S. Department of Education (2003c). *Characteristics of scientifically based research.* Retrieved February 23, 2003, from http://www.ed.gov/offices/OESE/compreform/csrdoverview/tsld011.html

U.S. Department of Education (2003d). *Facts about ... math achievement.* Retrieved January 8, 2003, from http://www.nochildleftbehind.gov/start/facts/math.html

U.S. Department of Education. (2003e). *Facts about science achievement.* Retrieved February 23, 2003, from http://www.nclb/gov/start/facts_pdf/science.pdf

U.S. Department of Education (2003f). *No Child Left Behind: Academic assessments requirements.* Retrieved January 28, 2003, from http://www.ed.gov.legislation/ESEA02/pg1.html

U.S. Department of Education (2003g). *No Child Left Behind Newsletter.* Retrieved February 23, 2003, from http://www.nclb.gov/Newsletter/20030115.html

U.S. Department of Education (2003h). *No Child Left Behind Part 6.* Retrieved February 23, 2003, from http://www.ed.gov/offices/OESE/esea/nclb/part6.html

U.S. Department of Education (2003i). *October 2001 press release (1).* Retrieved February 25, 2003, from http://www.ed.gov/PressReleases/10-2001/100921001a.html

U.S. Department of Education (2003j). *October 2001 press release (2)*. Retrieved February 25, 2003, from http://www.ed.gov/PressReleases/wh- 011030.html

U.S. Department of Education (2003k). *U.S. Department of Education speech*. Retrieved February 25, 2003, from http://www.ed.gov/speeches/03-2003/03142003.html

U.S. Department of Labor (2006). *20 leading occupations of employed women 2006 annual averages (employment in thousands)*. Retrieved January 22, 2008, from http://www.dol.gov/wb/factsheets/20lead2006.htm

Vesey, L. (1979). The autonomy of American history reconsidered. *American Quarterly, 31*, 455–477.

Viadero, D. (2002). Researching the researchers. *Education Week, 21*(23), 26–29.

Waller, W. (1932). *The sociology of teaching*. New York: John Wiley.

Walzer, M. (1996). *What it means to be an American: essays on the American experience*. New York: Marsilio.

Warren, R. (2002). *The purpose-driven life*. Grand Rapids, MI: Zondervan.

Wellman, B. (2001). Physical place and cyberspace: The rise of networked individualism. *International Journal for Urban and Regional Research, 25*, 227–252.

Wells, L. C. (2002). *No child left alone by military recruiters*. Retrieved from http://www.wagingpeace.org/articles/2002/12/06_wells_no-child.htm

Wheaton, S. (2008, January 25). The ad campaign: Obama delivers an anticorporate message. Retrieved 5 March 2008 from http://www.nytimes.com/2008/01/25/us/politics/25oadbox.html

Whitehead, A. N. (1929). *The aims of education*. New York: Macmillan.

Wiese, A. M., & Garcia, E. E. (1998). The Bilingual Education Act: Language minority students and equal educational opportunity. *Bilingual Research Journal, 22*(1), 1–18.

Wigginton, E. (1972). *The Foxfire book*. New York: Anchor Doubleday.

Wilber, K. (2000). *A theory of everything*. Boston: Shambhala.

Wiley, T. G. (1996). *Literacy and language diversity in the United States*. McHenry, IL: Center for Applied Linguistics and Delta Systems.

Willinsky, J. (1998). *Learning to divide the world: Education at empire's end*. Minneapolis: University of Minnesota Press.

Wilson, T. (2004). *Strangers to ourselves*. Cambridge, MA: Belknap Press.

Winerip, M. (2003, May 7). What some much-noted data really showed about vouchers. *The New York Times*, p. A-27.

Wraga, W. (2001) Left out: The villainization of progressive education. *Educational Researcher, 30*(7), 34–39.

Wright, Andrew (2000). *Spirituality and education*. London: RoutledgeFalmer.

Yatvin, J. (2001). Backtalk. *Phi Delta Kappan, 82*, 81.

Yatvin, J. (2002). Babes in the woods: The wanderings of the National Reading Panel. *Phi Delta Kappan, 83*(5), 364–369.

Zehr, M. (2002). ECS review discounts study critical of Teaching Board. *Education Week, 22*(5), 12.

Zehr, M. (2005). Not for publication. *Education Week, 25*(1), 28.

Zinn, H. (1999). *A people's history of the United States*. New York: HarperCollins.

Index